LANGUAGE DEVELOPMENT

COGNITIVE DEVELOPMENT

EARLY COGNITIVE DEVELOPMENT
edited by John Oates

LANGUAGE DEVELOPMENT
edited by Andrew Lock and Eunice Fisher

COGNITIVE DEVELOPMENT IN THE SCHOOL YEARS
edited by Ann Floyd

Language Development

A Reader edited by Andrew Lock and Eunice Fisher
for the Cognitive Development Course
at the Open University

CROOM HELM LONDON
in association with
THE OPEN UNIVERSITY

Selection and editorial material
copyright © The Open University 1984

Croom Helm Ltd, Provident House, Burrell Row,
Beckenham, Kent BR3 1AT
Croom Helm Australia, PO Box 391
Maruka, ACT 2603, Australia

British Library Cataloguing in Publication Data

Language development. – (Cognitive development)
1. Children – Language
I. Lock, Andrew II. Fisher, Eunice, III. Series
401'.9   LB1139.L3

ISBN 0-7099-1932-8

Printed and bound in Great Britain
by Billing & Sons Limited, Worcester.

CONTENTS

Cognitive Development course team

John Oates
Eve Braley-Smith
Ronnie Carr
Lydia Chant
Chris Cuthbertson
Pam Czerniewska
Philippe Duchastel
Eunice Fisher

Ann Floyd
Peter Griffith
Victor Lee
Gill Mason
Ken Richardson (Chairman)
Will Swann
Martin Woodhead

Consultants

Peter Barnes
Margaret Berry
Robert Borger
Alan Blyth
Margaret Brown
Ray Derricott
Wynne Harlen
Godfrey Harrison
Michael Howe

Andrew Lock
Kenneth Lovell
John Newson
Martin Richards
Marjorie Smith
Neil Warren
Gordon Wells
Michael Wood

Dedication

To Liz Bates and Patricia Greenfield as another morsel in a long-distance dialogue.

PREFACE

While we hope that this book of readings will be useful to anyone with an interest in the topic, it has been prepared to accompany the Open University third-level course of the same name. A comparison of it with the collection it replaces (Lee, 1979) reveals quite marked differences. These are due to a change of editors and a change in time. Language development is a very active field of research, and so it is not surprising that the contents of a Reader aimed at reflecting our ideas about the topic should change. The nature of those changes, however, is to a large measure dependent on the purposes and biases of the editors: this would seem the appropriate place to come clean on those.

One of the major transformations over the past two decades of language development research has occurred through the changing relationship between the inputs of its two parent disciplines, linguistics and psychology. The work of linguists initially opened new horizons for psychologists who had previously been strait–jacketed in the theoretical encumbrance of behaviourist dogma. Linguists not only went where psychologists had been afraid to tread, they even seemed to walk on water. Linguistic theories thus both defined the questions and provided the theories that determined how those questions should be pursued. As the emphasis of linguistic theories changed in response to the problems of linguists, so psychologists vied with each other to be the first to publish a paper drawing on the 'new deal': perhaps no other literature in psychology was as peppered with references to papers that were 'in press' or 'manuscript copy' as was language development for a period. It was a blissful relationship.

This relationship began to crack when psychologists had had sufficient time to realise that linguists were after different goals to their own. Linguists wanted to know about language, psychologists wanted to know about children. The former were concerned with language as structure, the latter with language in process. Where linguists made pronouncements about the mind, they did so from a concern with their abstract characterisations of language as a grammatical system, and paid little or no attention to what developing minds actually did. Psychologists gave notice of their disenchantment with this by beginning to formulate their own questions, and proceeding with a degree of independence. It is difficult, though, to throw off one's background, and it has only been recently that psychologists have started to formulate properly the questions that need answering; and even this may prove to be a premature judgement. There thus exists at the time of writing the possibility of a *rapprochement* between the parent disciplines, as each can provide an explicit set of demands for the other to accommodate to through a renewed dialogue. Bates *et al.* (in press (!)) observe that 'they tell us love is better the second time around'. Let us hope so.

This assessment of the current state of play makes an editor's task terribly hard. The 'story so far' may be entirely irrelevant to what comes next; the present position of our 'base-camp' may be inappropriate to the next part of the climb; we have as much chance of predicting the future route as of winning the pools. How, then are we to provide a useful collection that will not be superseded by events before it even appears, let alone be useful for a few years to come? The course we have chosen is to select readings that bear on what we take to be the fundamental questions the discipline faces. At the same time, we have tried to make our selections representative of the nature of recent concerns, but this has been a secondary goal, for on occasion what appears to us to be a fundamental question is one that we have failed to find a suitable contemporary reading to illustrate.

These aims require us to give the reader some preparatory warnings and guidance. A large part of the thrill that researchers get from pursuing a science comes from those fleeting moments of clear vision, frustratingly inarticulable, when they feel they can see to the heart of the matter. To feel that thrill is to make the transition from being a student to a practitioner of a subject; from being a learner to being an inventor. No teacher or guide is able to provide that thrill by saying 'read this', for the heart of the matter always lies intangibly behind the printed (or spoken) word. And this fact is, in many ways, one of the enigmas of studying language and its development. In trying to illuminate the central questions in a more traditional academic context, we have tried to keep what many would regard as a more mystical goal in view. The papers included here should be approached both for the facts they contain as well as the thoughts they provoke. They should be approached both critically and charitably. Good luck.

Reference

Lee V. (ed.) (1979) *Language Development*, Croom Helm, London.

SECTION I: INTRODUCTORY OVERVIEW

The chapter by Branigan and Stokes reviews the findings of that period of research when linguistic theories were playing the dominant role in the study of child language. They make it amply clear how productive this period was. Perhaps the major achievement was to establish a framework in which universal aspects of development could be seen. That all children, everywhere, break into language in broadly the same way is a finding that we take so much for granted today that we tend to forget how recently and with how much effort it was gained. It is a finding that sits at the crux of many questions. The prime one of these concerns the innate component of language development. Surely, the argument goes, if language develops along such similar paths under what must be vastly different environments — one language vs. another, a high-technology, nuclear-family vs. a low-technology, extended-family environment, affluence vs. poverty — surely language development must have an innate component. While it is quite difficult empirically to establish that all these different environments are actually different in the opportunities they present to a language learner, few would deny that there must be some biological component to the process. But what we regard as that component depends very much on our theoretical bias. As can be seen in this chapter, the prevailing motivation from linguistics was to almost equate language with grammar, and a grammar in which word-meaning and sentence-structure were independent of each other. Hence, the innate component was connected with grammar. Infants were regarded as coming into the world with an Innate Language Acquisition Device incorporating distinctly grammatical knowledge: 'virtually everything that occurs in language acquisition depends on *prior* knowledge of the basic aspects of sentence structure. The concept of a sentence may be part of man's innate mental capacity' (McNeill, 1970, p. 2). A Piagetian psychologist, by contrast, would offer a different interpretation. He or she might take another biological example of the construction of a structure, say a honeycomb by a honey-bee. Consider a honey-bee with a perfectly round head that is genetically programmed to bang its head at wax, leaving obviously

1

circular imprints. A hexagonally-structured honeycomb will eventually emerge from this process, since if one packs malleable circles closely together they will naturally distort to hexagons to completely fill the available space. Thus, the fact that all honeycombs are hexagonal has nothing to do with the innate knowledge of the honey-bee. An interaction between some much less closely specified genetic component and the environment it develops in may be responsible. *Ergo*, a child requires sufficient information to interact with his environment, but structure may result from the demands of that interaction, and not from anything exclusively attributable to either the infant (innate) or the environment (learning). This is a question to which we will return in the Course Text.

The chapter by Tamir provides a good review of the changes in emphasis that psychological approaches led to. It is interesting to note that no reference is made to Chomsky at all, and few of those whose work is reviewed would label themselves linguists. There are two points that should be noted about this work. Firstly, the new video-based observational technology that much of it has adopted is a very time-consuming one. It is a decade since such studies began, and as a result we now know something about what we are looking for. Consequently, more clear-cut and generalisable findings are emerging. Few, though, would honestly deny that in the beginning their approach to newly-collected videotapes of mother and child activities was 'Great! . . . but what shall we do with it?' Modes of analysis were often based on intuition and trial-and-error. A large number of these studies was in a pioneering spirit; based on a massive investment of time on a small amount of actual 'data'; and fuelled by brilliant 'guesswork'. Today, it is like the adage applied to the Greeks; we stand on the shoulders of giants. While we can spin elegant and compelling stories about the roots of language development, we are only now getting the data that will (we hope) substantiate them. At present, our enthusiasm should be tempered with caution. A second and related point has been made by Schaffer (1977), and stems from the nature of these early studies: intense investigations of small samples. There is an absence of longitudinal data from large samples. Thus we do not really know whether any of what we have looked at is really related to language development:

Under the circumstances it is not surprising to find a tendency to resort to argument based on analogy — no more. Developmental continuity therefore remains an assumption. At any rate let us be clear that there are at least three senses in which one may talk of continuity: first with regard to the *functions* of communication (the wish to obtain certain objects, to affect the other person's behaviour, and so on); second with regard to the *constituent skills* required for communication (such as intentionality, role alternation, etc.); and third, with regard to the *situation* in which communication occurs. The last can be particularly misleading: vocal turn-taking, for instance . . . may be found in quite early interactions, providing them with the 'mature' appearance of later verbal exchanges, and yet this may be brought about entirely by the mother's skill at inserting her vocalisations at appropriate moments into the child's sequence of vocal activity. The continuity . . . is in this instance inherent in the dyadic situation and does not refer to a constituent skill of the child's. (Schaffer, ibid., pp.14-15)

This is, then, another reason for caution.

There is one important development that Tamir's review omits. It concerns the different models of a child that researchers subscribe to. At the beginning of this period a notion such as intention occupied a very perilous position in academic psychology: perhaps 'in' is an inappropriate word, for it was practically beyond the pale of acceptable theoretical discourse. Intentionality is not a phenomenon that sits easily in a mechanistic psychology. Today we are more used to adopting the concept as a part of our explanatory framework, but a number of workers, Shotter, Newson and Trevarthen in particular, have argued that being used to using it doesn't of itself make it fit more coherently into our theories. Largely drawing on Macmurray (1957, 1961) they have argued that we need to conceive of the child in very different ways from those we have implicitly adopted in the past. Briefly, we should regard the child as a *person* rather than an organism or mechanism; as a social being who has to develop individuality rather than an individual who has to become social. These arguments are more complex than we can do justice to here, but the following passage from Macmurray conveys their essence:

. . . the baby is not an animal organism, but a person, or in traditional terms, a rational being. The reason is that his life, and even his bodily survival, depends upon intentional activity, and therefore upon knowledge. If nobody intends his survival and acts with intention to secure it, he cannot survive. That he cannot act intentionally, that he cannot even think for himself and has no knowledge by which to live is true, and is of first importance. It does not signify, however, that he is merely an animal organism; if it did it would mean that he could live by the satisfaction of organic impulse, by reaction to stimulus, by instinctive adaptation to his natural environment. But this is totally untrue. He cannot live at all by any initiative, whether personal or organic, of his own. He can only live through other people and in dynamic relation with them. In virtue of this fact he is a person, for the personal is constituted by the relation of persons. His rationality is already present, though only germinally, in the fact that he lives and can only live by communication (1961, p. 51) . . . the unit of personal existence is not the individual, but two persons in personal relation . . . we are persons not by individual right, but in virtue of our relation to one another. The personal is constituted by personal relatedness. The unit of the personal is not the 'I', but the 'You and I'. (ibid., p. 61)

This approach has much in common with the changes of perspective that have been accruing in social psychology since about 1970. It is not one subscribed to by all investigators, and is absent from Tamir's review. We deal with it in greater detail in the course text itself.

References

Macmurray, J. (1957) *The Self as Agent*, Faber and Faber, London
Macmurray, J. (1961) *Persons in Relation*, Faber and Faber, London
McNeill, D. (1970) *The Acquisition of Language*, Harper and Row, New York
Schaffer, R. (1977) *Studies in Mother-Infant Interaction*, Academic Press, London

Suggested Further Reading

A short, yet clear and comprehensive, overview of grammatically-oriented approaches to language development may be found in Chapter 1 of P.M. Greenfield and J. Smith, *The Structure of Communication in Early Language Development* (Academic Press, New York, 1976). A longer review is provided by E. Clark (1977) 'First language acquisition' in J. Morton and J. C. Marshall (eds.), *Psycholinguistic Papers, Vol. 1*, Paul Elek, London. Most textbooks in psychology and linguistics generally devote a chapter to this material.

1 INTRODUCTION: A SKETCH OF LANGUAGE DEVELOPMENT

George Branigan and William Stokes

Source: *Journal of Education*, Vol. 158, Part 2, 1976, pp. 4-11.

The current perspective on language development derives from a convergence of developments in several fields of inquiry. From Wundt in the late nineteenth century, through Piaget and Werner, to recent statements by Brown and Bruner, cognitive psychologists have maintained that the child acquires knowledge of his world and, more specifically, his language through active re-creation of that knowledge.

Recent advances in linguistics, following upon the work of the last three centuries, have enriched the characterization of that knowledge of language. Noam Chomsky (1965, 1975) has proposed that to know a language is to know abstract principles (or rules). The acquisition of such a system of abstract knowledge necessarily demands that children actively formulate rules (or hypotheses) and test these against experience. This position presupposes rich innate predispositions towards the re-creation of a human language.

The counter-position, which prevailed until the early 1960s, was based on behaviorist learning theory and a taxonomic (structural) description of language. This view maintains that mechanisms like association, conditioning, reinforcement and passive imitation account for language learning. In light of recent evidence the behaviorist position does not appear strong enough to account for the basically creative nature of language acquisition.

During the past fifteen years, research into child language acquisition has proceeded at a great pace. A wide variety of problems have been considered: (1) the linguistic description of phases of development (McNeil, 1970; Brown, 1970; Menyuk, 1971); (2) the biological and/or cognitive bases of that development (Lenneberg, 1967; Bloom, 1973; Brown, 1973; Slobin, 1973); (3) social influences on development (Cazden, 1965; Snow, 1972); and (4) the nature of the creative processes which make the universal and complex achievment of language acquisition possible (cf., Brown, 1973).

This research provides strong evidence in support of the view that: (1) children approach the task of language acquisition with specific predispositions to perceive and organize speech sounds in a linguistic relevant fashion (Eimas *et al.*, 1971); (2) children integrate linguistic and social experiences to formulate hypotheses regarding the rules of form and use of their language (Bloom, 1973; Clark, 1977); and (3) children test their hypotheses about language against the linguistic data available under the demands of social interaction (Chomsky, 1965; Slobin, 1975).

In the context of this view, it is our intent to provide a brief sketch of

    (i)   the course of normal language development
    (ii) the creative processes underlying language development
    (iii) the social influences on language development.

Normal Language Development

Children learning any language progress through similar periods of development (Brown, 1973; Menyuk, 1971; Slobin, 1973). The following outline lists the major periods of development (usually named for the *form* of the utterances which predominate) and describes (a) the types of linguistic structures children produce; (b) the types of linguistic structures children understand; and (c) the functions which a child's utterances may serve over these development periods. These periods do not represent discrete stages, rather there are subtle and complex transitions between the major periods.

(1) a. *Cooing* — non-cry vocalic sounds.
    b. speech sound discriminations (e.g.,/ba/,/pa/).
    c. expression of needs and manipulation of the environment.
(2) a. *Babbling* — consonant-vowel syllables with intonation patterns.
    b. response to speech sounds, especially intonation patterns.
    c. communication, play, primitive vocal exchanges with parents.
(3) a. *First words* — meaningful one and two syllable approximations of adult words, with systematic refinement of speech sound categories throughout the period.

     b. comprehension of highly simplified speech discrimination of minimal word pairs (e.g., 'bat,' 'pat').

     c. expression of intentions to name, to request.

(4) a. *One word utterances* — meaningful expression of person and object names and some relational words (e.g., 'up,' 'no,' 'more'), first sequences of words appear.

     b. comprehension of simple instructions and questions, participation in simple conversations and naming games.

     c. expression of intentions utilizing words, intonation, gesture, and contextual cues.

(5) a. *Two word utterances* — ordered combinations of words to express semantic relations (e.g., agent, action, object, location, possession, recurrence, negation, absence and identity).

     b. comprehension of progressively more highly differentiated relations expressed in canonical form including questions, requests.

     c. expression of explicit relations, organization of the world in terms of linguistic categories in memory.

(6) a. *Morpheme inclusion* — first sentences and orderly appearance of grammatical markers (e.g., progressive, plural, tense).

     b. comprehension of more complex utterances.

     c. expression of intentions with less reliance on immediate context.

(7) a. *Transformations* — appearance of questions and internal negation in approximation of adult structures, errors of overgeneralization (e.g., 'wented').

     b. confusions in comprehending complex embedded, conjoined, or non-canonical structures.

     c. linguistic means of marking syntactic, semantic, and pragmatic relations.

(8) a. *Complex constructions* — embedded, conjoined, and otherwise transformed structures, observe exceptions and constraints.

(9) a. *Graphic representations* — appearance of concern for alphabet, writing, and reading of names, signs and isolated words in texts.

One outstanding fact about this sequence of development is

that children all over the world, regardless of the language they are learning or the culture they are part of, progress through these major periods in the same order and at approximately the same ages (Slobin, 1973). They begin by learning the elements of the sound system of their language. Children first distinguish the major classes of vowels and consonants and then acquire distinctions among the elements of these classes. At the beginning of the second year, children begin to speak in one word utterances and at approximately the end of the second year, children begin to combine words into two and three word utterances. These utterances express a variety of meanings. For example, 'more juice' represents a request for the recurrence of a substance; 'baby shoe' might express a possessive relation; and 'baby eat cookie' encodes the agent-action-object relations. Some time after words are used in combination, children begin to mark tense, number, possession and progressive aspect by using the appropriate grammatical forms. The above examples might, now, be produced as 'baby's shoe(s)' and 'baby eating cookie(s).' Not only does the marking system continue to develop for some time, but the grammatical markers are acquired in an orderly sequence (Brown, 1973). By age three, most children begin to produce a variety of sentence types which do not exactly match fully grammatical adult forms. Typically, WH-questions appear with a question word added to a sentence, as in, 'What you buyed?' Later, as the auxiliary forms emerge, children may produce forms like, 'What did you buyed?' Finally, they will progress to using the full adult form, 'What did you buy?', where tense is marked on the auxiliary verb only. Negatives, which also require the auxiliary 'DO' form, develop in a similar fashion (Klima and Bellugi-Klima, 1966).

Creative Processes Underlying Language Development

In this section we provide a brief illustration of several processes which underlie language development, i.e., the development of rules of language structure and use. Language behavior can be described at a number of levels — phonology (sound), syntax (structure), semantics (meaning) and pragmatics (use) — in terms of sets of rules which govern behavior. For example, the rules of phonology govern the ways in which speech sounds can combine to create words and rules of syntax govern permissible combinations of words into sentences.

In learning a language, the child must re-create or discover the precise rules of his language. Initially, the child may construct a tentative rule and then, on the basis of the language he hears around him, test whether or not that rule is correct, incorrect or only partially correct. These tentative rules can be considered hypotheses about the form of the language and the process by which the child accepts, rejects or modifies a rule can be described as hypothesis testing.

The development of knowledge at any level can be considered in terms of the general process of *generalization, differentiation, categorization,* and *hierarchical organization.* To illustrate these matters, let us consider the 'errors' in a child's utterance, 'I seed him brooming' (I saw him sweeping or using a broom). The regular past tense rule has been applied to an irregular verb even though the child has probably never heard the verb used that way by adults. That is, we can say that the child has formulated an hypothesis regarding the construction of past tense in English and has applied that rule in new instances (generalization). Children often use correct irregular past tense forms in early development, but they will change these forms when they discover the more highly regular rule. This behavior indicates a rejection of individually learned forms in favor of a general rule — even when inappropriate forms result. In addition, the word 'brooming' (in this example) has been created. The strict categorization of broom as a noun has been violated. Given the large number of pairs like, 'hammer-hammering,' 'comb-combing,' 'brush-brushing,' 'shovel-shoveling,' the child appears to have formulated an hypothesis regarding the use of certain words as both nouns and verbs and generalized that rule to the case of broom. Note also that once the word is categorized as a verb, the appropriate grammatical marker is used even though the child never heard the word used that way before. Later, exceptions to general rules will be learned as such, and new categorizations and hypotheses will result.

Children generate approximations of fully grammatical adult sentences which reveal some of the same processes. A child may produce inappropriate forms in some context 'I know *where is she hiding*' while producing appropriate forms in isolation 'Where is she hiding?' For some sentences, such as 'She is hiding,' a simple embedding (hierarchical organization) is possible — 'I think *she is hiding.*' The child appears to have formulated an hypothesis about combining sentences and has generalized it to an exceptional instance. Again, exceptions will be differentiated and appropriately categorized later.

Furthermore, these processes appear long before children begin putting words together into sentences. Consider, on a *micro*-scale, what is required just to produce a word, for instance, 'cat'. This word represents a differentiated articulation of three sound segments (distinguishing it from 'bat' or 'cut' or 'cap'), in the appropriate sequence (distinguishing it from 'tac') and with specific pitch, volume, and duration. In addition, the word may be employed pragmatically as a statement (That is a *cat*.), a question (Is that a *cat*?) or as a request (I want the *cat*.) by varying the intonation with which it is produced. The development of the relevant differentiations and categorizations can also be characterized as hypothesis formation.

Finally, these processes are very clear in the acquisition of word meanings. Young children often refer to many furry creatures as 'cat' or to cows and horses as 'doggie.' We may describe this activity as indicative of the child's hypotheses regarding word meanings, that is, the child's notions of what are the semantic features of 'cat' or 'doggie' (Clark, 1973). If, at first, such features as 'furry' or 'four-legged' are the *meaning*, then the term may be applied to many creatures or objects. Gradually, the child will have the opportunity to test his hypotheses and revise them, producing finer differentiations and categorizations. He will then make fewer generalized errors and eventually achieve the hierarchical organization for the features which appropriately specify the meanings of these words (e.g., cats, dogs, cows and horses are all types of animals, however, the first two are pets and the second two are farm animals).

Social Influences

Thus far we have discussed hypothesis formation but have not elaborated on how children test hypotheses to arrive at the correct set of grammatical rules. This can be considered best in the context of social influences. Three aspects of social influence on language development can be distinguished: (1) establishing the communicative functions of language; (2) providing models of the form and use of language; and (3) placing demands on children to communicate effectively.

(1) During early infancy the primitive interactions between parent and child establish the communicative functions of vocalizations (Lewis and Freedle, 1972; Bateson, 1969). This accomplishment is fundamental to all later development, for it is in the use of language that language is acquired.

(2) Throughout development adults simplify their speech directed toward children. That is, they provide models of well articulated, short and complete sentences closely approximating the complexity of the child's own speech. In addition, parents play 'word games' which offer access to vocabulary and sentence structure: for example, question routines ('where's your ear?,' 'what's this?,' 'this is a what?' and naming routines 'see the kitty,' 'that's a big kitty,' and 'there are two kitties'). Parents have been found to repeat and expand upon their children's utterances, perhaps ackowledging to the child that he was understood, and also, perhaps, providing models of more adult-like speech. In summary, parents interact with their children in ways which are well suited to provide the child with clear data (information) about the language he is learning. In part, from these interactions, the child may formulate hypotheses and also test those hypotheses against further productions by the parent. For example, children may first hypothesize that sentences like 'He is here' must be expressed in uncontracted form (perhaps for maximum clarity). Later, on the basis of further models, the child will learn that copulas can be contracted and will produce forms like 'He's here.'

(3) Parents do not intentionally provide formal instruction in language. Instead, they use language to communicate, to play and to maintain contact. In doing so, they expose children to the language and, in fact, make demands upon children to communicate effectively and efficiently in return. Parents tend to be accepting of 'errors,' but they occasionally provide corrections and seek clarifications if they fail to understand the child's speech. In responding to corrections and misunderstandings, children may have the opportunity to test their hypotheses regarding the form (structure) and function (use) of the language. It is through use of language to communicate with parents and, perhaps, especially with strangers, that children learn to be brief, clear, informative and appropriate in their use of language in various contexts. It is important to keep in mind, however, that the child's accommoda-

tion to these social influences is spontaneous; it is not the result of formal instruction.

This sketch of development, although necessarily brief, attempts to capture some of the features of normal language acquisition discovered over the past fifteen to twenty years. Essentially, children seem to acquire language spontaneously by re-creating, for themselves, the system of rules which generate the sentences of their language. The 'errors' produced by children are not random mistakes. Rather they are systematic and the products of general processes for discovering how the adult grammar is organized. Major periods and progress across periods is predictable. The types of errors children will make are predictable. Further, the processes which form the basis of the evolving grammatical system are discoverable.

References

Bateson, M. C. (1971) 'The Interpersonal Context of Infant Vocalization', *Research Laboratory of Electronics Quarterly Progress Report*, No. 100
Bloom, L. (1973) *One Word at a Time: The Use of Single Word Utterances Before Syntax*, Mouton, The Hague
Brown, R. (1970) *Psycholinguistics*, New York: Free Press, 1970
Brown, R. (1973) *A First Language: The Early Stages*, Harvard University Press, Cambridge
Cazden, C.B. (1965) 'Environmental Assistance to the Child's Acquisition of Grammar', unpublished doctoral dissertation, Harvard University
Chomsky, N. (1965) *Aspects of the Theory of Syntax*, MIT Press, Cambridge
Chomsky, N. (1975) *Reflections on Language*, Pantheon Books, New York
Clark, E. (1975) 'What's In a Word? On Children's Acquisition of Semantics in his First Language' in T.E. Moore (ed.), *Cognitive Development and the Acquisition of Language*, Academic Press, New York
Clark, E. (1977) 'First Language Acquisition', to appear in J. Morton and J. C. Marshall (eds.), *Psycholinguistic Series*, Paul Elek, London
Eimas, P.; Siqueland, E.; Jusczyk, P. & Vigorito, J. (1971) 'Speech Perception in infants', *Science, 171*, 303-6.
Klima, E. S. and Bellugi-Klima, U. (1966) 'Syntactic Regularities in the Speech of Children' in Lyons, J. and Wales, R. J. (eds.), *Psycholinguistic Papers*, Aldine, Chicago, 183-208
Lenneberg, E. H. (1967) *'Biological Foundations of Language'*, Wiley, New York
Lewis, M. & Freedle, R. (1972) 'Mother-infant Dyad: The Cradle of Meaning', *Educational Testing Service Research Bulletin*, RB-72-22
Menyuk, P. (1971) *'The Acquisition and Development of Language'*, Prentice-Hall, Englewood Cliffs, New Jersey
Slobin, D. (1973) 'Cognitive Prerequisites for the Development of Grammar' in Ferguson, C. A. & Slobin, D. I. (eds.), *Studies in Child Development*, Holt Rinehart & Winston, New York, 175-208

2 LANGUAGE DEVELOPMENT: NEW DIRECTIONS

Lois Tamir

Source: *Human Development*, *22*, 1979, pp. 263-9.

In light of recent theory and research, the field of child *language development* may be more appropriately labeled *communication development*. For the past several years, psychologists have gone beyond an examination of the child's isolated utterance and its syntactic complexity, to study the dialogic context of language development, its social and cognitive precursors, and the functions served by communicative exchanges. Underlying this shift in focus is the premise that linguistic, social, and cognitive domains of functioning are highly interrelated, and that there is considerable functional continuity of communicative behaviors and meaning structures from pre-speech stages to those of linguistic exchanges, which are characterized by the addition and integration of vocabulary and grammar (Bates, 1978; Bloom, 1976; Bruner, 1974/5, 1975; Freedle and Lewis, 1977; Halliday, 1973; Harris, 1975; Lewis and Cherry, 1977; Riegel, 1978; Ryan, 1974). The present review will briefly outline several of the more recent innovations in the field of communication development. These include: (1) 'protoconversations' between caretaker and infant; (2) the structure of 'joint action' between caretaker and infant as precursors to language; (3) the development of intention within the communicative exchange; (4) the prominence of cognitive over syntactic strategies of language behaviors; and (5) longitudinal data which are beginning to emerge within the field.

(1) Technological advances available to researchers of early communication, such as the ability to perform frame-by-frame analysis of video data, have facilitated the discovery of communicative behaviors of the caretaker-child dyad as early as the first weeks of life (e.g., Bateson, 1975; Brazelton *et al.*, 1974; Condon and Sander, 1974; Kaye, 1976, 1977; Stern, 1971; Stern *et al.*, 1975). It is at this point that precursors to language are hypothesized to begin. Specifically, there initially appears to be a biologically regulated cycle of attention and withdrawal of attention to social stimuli (in most cases, the mother) which is

13

different from responses toward objects by the infant (Bateson, 1975; Brazelton *et al.*, 1974; Bruner, 1975; Richards, 1974). Over time, mutual phasing with the caretaker becomes one of the infant's earliest social and cognitive accomplishments, as the infant becomes increasingly capable of behaviors such as imitation and adjustment of timing (Kaye, 1977; Richards, 1974). Within the context of the mutual physical-visual frame, or in other words, the face-to-face alignment of caretaker and infant, social dialogue begins to take place. As early as 6 weeks, mutual smiling games have been observed, and vocalization in turn becomes increasingly common by 3 months of age (Bateson, 1975; Kaye, 1977; Lewis and Freedle, 1973; Snow, 1977a; Stern, 1974; Stern *et al.*, 1975; Watson, 1972). The turn-taking structure of these exchanges and its regulation by gaze behaviors of caretaker and infant is strikingly similar to adult dialogic interaction, and has consequently been termed 'protoconversation' or 'protodialogue'.

(2) A special form of caretaker-child interaction, most explicitly described by Bruner (1974/5, 1975), has been termed 'joint action'. Joint action consists of three components: caretaker, child, and object. Prerequisite to joint action is a mutual focus upon the object, usually achieved by 4 months, when both dyad members have become capable of following the other's line of regard (Bruner, 1974/5; Kaye, 1976). Once mutual focus upon this *topic* is achieved, a behavior or vocalization will serve the purpose of *commenting* upon the object and/or the activity with the object. Bruner suggests that the topic-comment structure of joint action reflects the structure of language use, which involves the mutual perception of some object or action, and the comment upon it.

Corroborative evidence has been accumulating in this direction. For example, Snow (1977a) has found that at about 5–7 months the mother begins to increase her reference to things in the world in her speech to the infant. Similarly, the themes of topic-comment dialogue structure, and topic elaboration in caretaker-child linguistic interaction, have become especially prominent in language development research (e.g. Bates, 1978). Cross (1975, 1977) and Soderberg (1974), for example, stress the facilitating effects of parental elaboration of child-initiated topics in dialogue upon the child's language acquisition. Keenan *et al.* (1976) link the extensive use of interrogatives by adults in dialogue with children, to the attempt to establish mutual topics for subsequent comment within the dialogic exchange. And Bloom *et al.* (1976) show that with increasing linguistic and communicative sophistication, the child becomes capable of incorporating adult initiated topics within his/her own utterances in dialogue.

Additionally, language acquisition researchers have posited the onset of semantics, or referential abilities, within the joint action situation. The earliest act of reference is that of indicating. Within the context of the situational and social conditions which constrain the behaviors of the dyad, both meaning and recognition of the referential nature of language develop (Bruner, 1975; Freedle and Lewis, 1977; Lewis and Freedle, 1973; Shatz, 1977). Hence, reference is initially a social act. It is no wonder that the child, in the process of word acquisition, specifically learns the names of things she/he acts upon (Nelson, 1973).

It is important to note the facilitating effects of the caretaker's interpretation of the infant and young child, which originates in joint action sequences (Bates *et al.* 1975; Bruner, 1974/75, 1975; Ryan, 1974; Snow, 1977a). At first, the caretaker has attempted to distinguish states of satisfaction of the infant. Once mutual exchanges develop, she begins to interpret the infant's intent, although prior to 10 months the infant does not necessarily recognize the signal value of his/her behaviors (Bates *et al.* 1975). Nevertheless, Snow (1977a) asserts that viewing the infant's behaviors as intentional constitutes a prerequisite of communication, and gives meaning to the dyadic exchange.

(3) An interesting and related development within the field of child language is the adoption of *speech act* theory of interpersonal communication and its derivatives (Austin, 1962; Searle, 1965; 1969, 1975). Generally, this theory posits that each utterance within a communicative exchange contains propositional or conceptual content, and a 'force', or intention underlying the utterance. Subsequently, researchers have attempted to trace the development of intention within the child's communicative behaviors (e.g., Bates *et al.* 1975; Dore, 1975; Halliday, 1973; Ryan, 1974). Correspondingly, intentional communicative behaviors have been identified prior to the acquisition of mature language forms (see especially Bates *et al.*, 1975), and again, the early caretaker-child interaction is identified as the origin of intentional exchange. Dore (1976), however, notes the further task of integrating our notions of communicative intent with the development of those linguistic structures used to represent them.

(4) A final shift in focus within child language research concerns

the search for cognitive rather than syntactic structure underlying input to and output from the child within a dialogic context. Early in the 1970s there was a proliferation of research concerning adult linguistic input to children, sometimes termed 'motherese', in order to correlate (especially syntactic) features of adult speech to the child with features of child speech (e.g. Blount, 1972; Broen, 1972; Drach, 1969; Moerk, 1974; Pfuderer, 1969; Snow, 1972). In general, mothers have been found to simplify their linguistic input to children, although their utterances are geared more towards the child's cognitive or semantic level of functioning than syntactic level (e.g., Cross, 1977; Newport *et al.*, 1977; Snow, 1977a). A most recent collection of articles which describe this research is the volume *Talking to Children*, edited by Snow and Ferguson (1977). It appears that the major aim of mother-child dialogue is the construction of conversational meaning within a context of mutual engagement, whereby the function of the utterances exchanged overrides syntactic considerations (e.g., Cross, 1975; 1977; Newport *et al.*, 1977; Soderberg, 1974; Tamir, in press). Once again, therefore, the theme of mutual dialogic engagement appears within the literature. Lack of strong or extensive syntactic correlations between mother and child utterances substantiates conclusions such as that of Snow (1977b), who states that conversation with an interested adult may be more important for the ultimate acquisition of syntactic skills than the particular technique practiced by the interacting adult.

These findings and conclusions are paralleled by research which suggests a lack of syntactic strategies by the very young child in interpreting linguistic input (e.g., Shatz, 1977) and expressing him/herself linguistically (e.g., Braine, 1976). Initially, there is a heavy reliance upon context, both verbal and nonverbal (Bates, 1978; Keenan *et al.*, 1976), and sensorimotor cognitive strategies have been posited to underly the child's earliest utterances (Bates *et al.*, 1975; Brown, 1973). Overall, it becomes apparent that the field has moved far beyond the syntactic analyses of psycholinguists of the 1960s to a more concerted attempt to integrate linguistic, cognitive, and social processes of developmental phenomena.

(5) A major critique of research and theory which analyzes the so-called precursors to mature linguistic development concerns the need for longitudinal data which confirm the impact of early communicative exchanges upon later developmental processes. Evidence which displays continuity of communicative patterns is

beginning to emerge from a variety of longitudinal projects (e.g. Stern, 1971). Short-term longitudinal observations (e.g., of approximately one year's duration) have indicated factors such as maternal sensitivity within communicative exchanges as crucial in the acceleration of the language acquisition process (e.g., Cross, 1975, 1977; Nelson, 1973). More directly, Freedle and Lewis (1977) have found that the structure of vocal communicative exchanges between mother and child at 3 months of age correlates with language acquisition at 2 years of age within their longitudinal sample. The common finding that there are individual differences between, and stable interaction patterns within caretaker-infant dyads (e.g., Lewis and Freedle, 1973; Lewis and Lee-Painter, 1974; Osofsky, 1976) substantiates the need to follow dyadic patterns of interaction throughout the early years of development. This in turn may help to account for the wide range of individual differences displayed by children in both speed and method of language acquisition (e.g., Bloom, 1976; Moerk, 1977; Ryan, 1974). Overall, it appears that the more sensitive and consequently facilitative caretakers are those who most allow the child to influence their own behaviors, and who build upon the capacities that the child displays developmentally.

In sum, the shift in emphasis within language development research to one of a dialogic context, and integration of social and cognitive processes represents an advance in the field and a fuller account of communication development. However, transition points throughout this developmental process remain only vaguely delineated. For example, during early infancy, communication and action are essentially one and the same phenomenon (Bloom, 1976; Dance, 1970). At what point does communication *with* the caretaker become communication *to* the caretaker by the infant? Research on the development of intention should help to clarify this process. Additionally, we still remain relatively unclear as to when the child replaces contextual cognitive strategies of communicative behaviors with more abstract, syntactically governed rule systems (Bates, 1978), if, in fact, this does occur. Maternal language to the child is facilitative, but the details of how and why this is so need to be further analyzed. However, due to the widening of the field of communication development, child language research is now, more than ever, open to the contributions of cognitive and social development psychologists, as well as those of linguists and psycholinguists, so well utilized in the past.

From a wider perspective, the newly introduced concepts such as the mutual focus of interlocutors, communicative intent, and the importance of context within the dialogic exchange are concepts which can be expanded by theorists and researchers who study communicative processes not only in childhood, but throughout the life cycle of the developing individual. For example, with the aid of these conceptual tools now used in language acquisition research we can speculate about the form and function of communication between generations, among individuals who share mutual contexts and topics of concern, and among strangers, who must work to establish this mutuality. In this way developmental psychologists can view communication processes as more continuous through the life span, as the individual participates in increasingly diverse as well as increasingly familiar communicative exchanges over time.

References

Austin, J. L. (1962) *How to Do Things with Words*, Harvard University Press, Cambridge

Bates, E. (1978) 'Functionalism and the Biology of Language', *Pap. Rep. Child Language Dev.*, *15*, K1-K26

Bates, E., Camaoni, L., and Volterra, V. (1975) 'The Acquisition of Performatives Prior to Speech', *Merrill-Palmer Q.*, *21*, 205-26

Bateson, M. C. (1975) 'Mother-infant Exchanges: The Epigenesis of Conversational Interaction', *Ann. NY Acad. Sci.* (*Devl Psycholinguist. Commun. Disorders*). *263* 101-13

Bloom, L. (1976) 'An Integrative Perspective on Language Development', *Pap. Rep. Child Language Dev.*, *12*, 1-22

Bloom, L., Roscissano, L., and Hood, L. (1976) 'Adult-child Discourse: Developmental Interaction between Information Processing and Linguistic Knowledge', *Cognitive Psychol.*, *8*, 521-52

Blount, B. G. (1972) 'Parental Speech and Language Acquisition: Some Luo and Samoan Examples', *Anthrop. Linguist.*, *14*, 119-30

Braine, M. D. S. (1976) 'Children's First Word Combinations', *Monogr. Soc. Res. Child Dev.*, *41*; Serial No. 164

Brazelton,, T. B., Koslowski, B., and Main, M. (1974) 'The Origins of Reciprocity: The Early Mother-infant Interaction', in Lewis and Rosenblum, *The Effect of the Infant on the Caregiver*, Wiley, New York, pp. 49-76

Broen, P. A. (1972) 'The Verbal Environment of the Language-learning Child', *Am. Hearing Ass. Monogr.*, *17*

Brown, R. (1973) *A First Language*, Harvard University Press, Cambridge

Bruner, J. (1974/75) 'From Communication to Language — A Psychological Perspective', *Cognition*, *3*, 255-87

Bruner, J. (1975) 'The Ontogenesis of Speech Acts', *J. Child Language*, *2*, 1-19

Condon, W. S. and Sander, L. W. (1974) 'Neonate Movement is Synchronized with Adult Speech: Interactional Participation and Language Acquisition', *Science*,

183, 99-101

Cross I. (1975) 'Some Relations Between Mothers and Linguistic Level in Accelerated Children', *Pap. Rep. Child Language Dev.*, *10*, 117-35

Cross, I. (1977) 'Mothers' Speech Adjustments: The Contribution of Selected Listener Variables' in Snow and Ferguson, *Talking to Children*, Cambridge University Press, Cambridge, pp. 151-88

Dance, F. E. X. (1970) 'A Helical Model of Communication' in Sereno and Mortenson, *Foundations of Communication Theory*, Harper & Row, New York

Dore, J. (1975) 'Holophrases, Speech Acts, and Language Universals', *J. Child Language*, *2*, 21-40

Dore, J. 'Conditions for the Acquisition of Speech Acts' in Markova, *The Social Context of Language*, Wiley, New York

Drach, K. M. (1969) 'The Structure of Linguistic Input to Children', Working paper No. 14, Language Behavior Research Laboratory, University of California at Berkeley

Freedle, R. and Lewis, M. (1977) 'Prelinguistic Conversations' in Lewis and Rosenblum, *Interaction, Conversation, and the Development of Language*, Wiley, New York, pp. 157-85

Halliday, M. A. K. (1973) *Early Language Learning: A Sociolinguistic Approach*, 9th Int. Congr. Anthropological and Ethnological Sciences, Chicago

Harris, A. E. (1975) 'Social Dialectics and Language: Mother and Child Construct the Discourse', *Hum. Dev.*, *18*, 80-96

Kaye, K. (1976) 'Toward the Origin of Dialogue' in Schaffer, *Interaction in Infancy — the Loch Lomond Symposium*, Academic Press, London

Kaye, K. (1977) 'Thickening Thin Data: The Maternal Role in Developing Communication and Language' in Bullowa, *Before Speech*, Cambridge University Press, Cambridge

Keenan, E. O., Schieffelin, B. B., and Platt, M. (1976) 'Questions of Immediate Concern', Dept. of Linguistics, University of Southern California, Los Angeles, unpublished manuscript

Lewis, M. and Cherry, L. (1977) 'Social Behavior and Language Acquisition' in Lewis and Rosenblum, *Interaction, Conversation, and the Development of Language*, Wiley, New York, pp. 227-45

Lewis, M. and Freedle, R. (1973) 'Mother-infant Dyad: the Cradle of Meaning' in Pliner, Krames and Alloway, *Communication and Affect, Language and Thought*, Academic Press, New York, pp. 127-55

Lewis, M. and Lee-Painter, S. (1974) 'An Interactional Approach to the Mother-infant Dyad' in Lewis and Rosenblum, *The Effect of the Infant on the Caregiver*, Wiley, New York, pp. 21-48

Moerk, E. (1974) 'Changes in Verbal Child-mother Interactions with Increasing Language Skills of the Child', *J. psycholinguist. Res.*, *3*, 101-16

Moerk, E. (1977) 'Processes and Products of Imitation: Additional Evidence that Imitation is Progressive', *J. psycholinguist. Res.*, *6*, 187-202

Nelson, K. (1973) 'Structure and Strategy in Learning to Talk', *Monogr. Soc. Res. Child Dev.*, *38*, Serial No. 149

Newport, E., Gleitman, H., and Gleitman, L. (1977) 'Mother, I'd Rather Do it Myself: Some Effects and Noneffects of Maternal Speech Style' in Snow and Ferguson, *Talking to Children*, Cambridge University Press, Cambridge, pp. 109-49

Osofsky, J. D. (1976) 'Neonatal Characteristics and Mother-infant Interaction in Two Observational Situations', *Child Dev.*, *47*, 1138-47

Pfuderer, C. (1969) 'Some Suggestions for a Syntactic Characterization of Baby Talk Style', Working paper No. 14, Language Behavior Research Laboratory, University of California at Berkeley

Richards, M. P. M. (1974) 'First Steps in Becoming Social' in Richards, *The Integration of a Child into a Social World*, Cambridge University Press, New York, pp. 83-97

Riegel, K. F. (1978) 'Psychology Mon Amour', Houghton Mifflin, Boston

Ryan, J. (1974) 'Early Language Development: Towards A Communicational Analysis' in Richards, *The Integration of a Child into a Social World*, Cambridge University Press, New York, pp. 185--213

Searle, J. (1965) 'What is a Speech Act?' in Black, *Philosophy in America*, Cornell University Press, Ithaca

Searle, J. (1969) 'Speech Acts', Cambridge University Press, Cambridge

Searle, J. (1975) 'Indirect Speech Acts' in Cole and Morgan, *Speech Acts*, Academic Press, New York

Shatz, M. (1977) 'On the Development of Communicative Understandings: An Early Strategy for Interpreting and Responding to Messages' in Glick and Clark-Stewart, *Studies in Social and Cognitive Development*, Gardner Press, New York

Snow, C. (1972) 'Mothers' Speech to Children Learning Language', *Child Dev.*, *43*, 549-65

Snow, C. (1977a) 'The Development of Conversation Between Mothers and Babies', *J. Child Language*, *4*, 1-22

Snow, C. (1977b) 'Mothers Speech Research: From Input to Interaction' in Snow and Ferguson, *Talking to Children*, Cambridge University Press, Cambridge, pp. 31-49

Snow, C. and Ferguson, C. A. (eds.) (1977) *Talking to Children*, Cambridge University Press, Cambridge

Soderberg, R. (1974) 'The Fruitful Dialogue', Stockholms Universitet, Project Child Language

Stern, D. (1971) 'A Micro-analysis of Mother-infant Interaction', *J. Am. Acad. Child Psychiat.*, *10*, 501-17

Stern, D. (1974) 'Mother and Infant at Play: The Dyadic Interaction Involving Facial, Vocal, and Gaze Behaviors' in Lewis and Rosenblum, *The Effect of the Infant on the Caregiver*, Wiley, New York, pp. 187-213

Stern, D., Jaffe, J., Beebe, B. and Bennett, S. (1975) 'Vocalizing in Unison and Alternation: Two Modes of Communication Within the Mother-infant Dyad', *Ann. NY Acad. Sci.* (*Devl Psycholinguist. Commun. Disorders*), *263*, 89-100

Tamir, L. (in press) 'Interrogatives in Dialogue: Case Study of Mother and child 16-19 Months', *J. Psycholinguist. Res.*

Watson, J. S. (1972) 'Smiling, Cooing and "the game" ', *Merrill Palmer Q.*, *18*, 323-9

SECTION II: EVOLUTIONARY AND DEVELOPMENTAL PERSPECTIVES

There are two main reasons for considering the evolution of language in the context of the development of language: both are related to a major difference between the two processes. That difference is the presence or absence of a language environment in which language has to be created or, as Branigan and Stokes (Chapter 1) put it in the developmental context, re-created. The first reason is that there is something unsatisfactory and incomplete about an account of language development that puts a lot of responsibility on factors in the learner's cultural environment. Since that environment is largely predicated on language use, we find ourselves in a circular regress concerning where that environment came from. Secondly, if we can get a handle on how language might have been created *de novo*, we may find ourselves being able to sharpen our perception of the nature of the problem facing the child. The papers in this section are all concerned with language construction, and the question of what we may learn about development from a study of evolution. The topic is given a more substantial consideration in the course text.

We believe that this is the first time the chapter by Romanes has been reprinted in the 100 years since it was written. Romanes was an early and enthusiastic student of Darwin, and devoted the major portion of his work to the study of intelligence from an evolutionary perspective. The main reason his work has been neglected stems from the adoption of Lloyd Morgan's famous canon by animal behaviourists early in the present century: in essence, that one should prefer the explanation that makes the fewest assumptions, and credits an animal with the simplest of abilities congruent with the activities it undertakes. If deciding between whether, for example, a herring gull feeds its chick because it knows it is hungry, or because the chick pecks at the appropriate part of the gull's bill, one should subscribe to the latter. Romanes' discussions of animal abilities are peppered with examples of the former. He marvels at the intellectual powers exhibited in the genius of a spider's web-engineering; is convinced that parrots can talk; catalogues a myriad of anecdotes about the mental abilities of domestic pets: in sum, he provides a *Wind in the Willows* account of animal life. For this reason his work has been quite comprehensively ignored. Yet in method, many of his scientific papers on animal behaviour reveal a highly skilled scientific mind; it is in his interpretation of phenomena that he lapses from orthodoxy.

While we would not wish to defend some of his wilder flights of fancy, we believe he had good reasons for his mode of interpretation. One of the great controversies in Victorian evolutionary theory was the status of human intellectual powers. Wallace, the co-founder of the theory with Darwin, was never able to accept that the human brain had arisen through the process of natural selection. Human capabilities appeared too different in quality from those of animals to be regarded as the result of quantitative additions of 'more of the same'. Wallace thus maintained a place for God in the process, infusing a qualitatively new spirit into human biology. Such a solution was not acceptable to Victorian biology, and Wallace lived out his later days in ostracised seclusion. A better explanation, however, was not really forthcoming: there certainly was something about human abilities that evolutionary theory found very difficult to get to grips with. Until, that is, Romanes. Romanes' solution finds an echo in recent work by Gauld and Shotter on the nature of an infant's capabilities. Considering the nature of human abilities, they argued that:

> the conceptual cannot be derived from the non-conceptual, the intentional from the non-intentional, action from non-action, rationality from the non-rational. [There can be] no 'behavioural reduction' of intention, action, concept-possession, rational thought. . . Thus there is no hope of our being able to exhibit the nascent intentions, actions, concepts, communicative endeavours, etc., of the young infant as arising from some synthesis of behavioural or mental elements that are not themselves intentional, conceptual, etc. We have to regard the infant as already possessing the rudiments (*not* the elements) of intention . . . etc. (Gauld and Shotter, 1977, pp. 199-200)

This is the course Romanes took 100 years ago. He took the evolutionary view and reversed its perspective. Rather than characterising animals, accepting that as the only legitimate interpretive theory, and then looking *forward* from animals, to find humans anomalous, he characterised human abilities, and then looked *backwards* to animals in the light of this interpretive framework, saw them in this new way, and then sought among them for the rudiments of human abilities. His 'anthropomorphism' was therefore scientifically motivated. While we would not defend some of his excesses, we leave the reader to judge the value of his approach in the thoroughly Victorian essay we reprint here.

The remaining two papers in this section are representative of more recent work, and show remarkable parallels with Romanes' approach. The first of these is the chapter by Lock. Lock's paper lacks the logical rigour of Romanes', but shows a similar concern in tracing the roots of language (and hence self-awareness) to their beginnings. Lock's approach is in the more social paradigm outlined in the introduction to the previous section: Romanes' is stolid Victorian individualism. There is, though, nothing in principle to prevent these two perspectives being brought together: many of the transitions that Romanes pointed to could be viewed as socially-assisted activities, rather than the products of individual insight. It is important to note that neither of these chapters offer us an explanation of language development. Rather, they both present descriptions of the process, and call on unspecified abilities as responsible for the process: in Romanes' case the child passes magically from one ability to the next; in Lock's, development is predicated on the unanalysed and unspecified process of explication. In a recent study of the theoretical adequacy of proposals about the way language does develop Atkinson (1982) argues that no current theories have any real explanatory power. Perhaps this weakness should be one of our major concerns in the coming years.

It would be quite possible to have included Chapter 11 by Goldin-Meadow and Feldman — on the development of language by children with only a minimal language environment — in this section. It has, however, been placed elsewhere for another purpose; but it can be profitably read at this time. Instead, this section concludes with a paper by Hewes. His paper contains a number of technical terms, and frequent reference to the glossary at the end of this volume may be necessary. The views he puts forward are not dissimilar to those of Romanes. Both have the same underlying logic: that the language system was built up slowly, and has some relation to cognitive capacity. There is, though, a change in emphasis brought about by a further 100 years of research. While one gets the same impression of a building up of an argument from first principles, Hewes is able to make more informed guesses about the channels and modes of communication, and to make some claims as to the evolutionary timing of these developments.

There are many points that emerge from these papers. The ones we must emphasise are that language may be viewed as the culmination of earlier developments. It is not yet clear how these earlier developments might contribute to the final components of language, but we can pick up an underlying thread concerned with how mental abilities are linked to ways of conceiving the world and, irrespective of its medium, that language is fundámentally involved in these conceptualisations. There is more to language, then, than is directly observable. In essence, what we have been looking at in this section is the evolution of the symbolic powers that provide the foundations on which the grammatical, phonological and other components of language are grounded.

References

Atkinson, M. (1982) *Explanations in the Study of Child Language Development*, Cambridge University Press, London
Gauld, A. and Shotter, J. (1977) *Human Action and its Psychological Investigation*, Routledge and Kegan Paul, London

Suggested Further Reading

Beyond that old standby, *The Encyclopaedia Britannica*, and the first chapters of Genesis, there is really very little widely available material on the topic of language evolution. Apart from Hewes' classic 1973 paper, 'Primate Communication and the Gestural Origins of Language', *Current Anthropology*, *14*, 5-32, the best place to look is in *Origins* (1977) by Richard Leakey and Roger Lewin (Macdonald and Jane's, London).

3 ORIGINS OF HUMAN FACULTY[1]

George John Romanes

Source: Lloyd Morgan, C. (ed.), *Essays by George John Romanes*, (Longmans, Green & Co., London, 1897), pp. 86-112.

Having been requested by the Council of the Neurological Society to read a paper on a recently published book of my own, for the purpose of raising a discussion on the psychological doctrines which are therein presented, I will begin by briefly stating the aim and scope of the book in question.

The title of the book is *Mental Evolution in Man*; but, as the work constitutes only the first member of a series which I intend to devote to this topic, its second or subsidiary title more accurately defines the limits of its subject-matter — namely, 'The Origin of Human Faculty.' The aim of this treatise is twofold. First, to meet upon their own ground those various writers — psychological and theological — who maintain that a great exception must be made in the case of the human mind to the otherwise uniform law of continuous evolution; and, secondly, to indicate the probable causes, and thus to trace the probable history, of the transition between the intelligence of the lower animals and the intelligence of man.

It appears to me that before the Neurological Society I may be allowed to adopt the first of these positions without argument; and will, therefore, assume that in some way or another the transition in question has taken place. On the basis of this assumption I shall be free to devote all the time at my disposal to a consideration of the probable causes, or method, of the transition. For this purpose it is needful to set out with a brief analysis of ideation.

If I look at any particular face now before me, I receive what is called a perception, or a percept, of that face. If I then close my eyes, or turn them away from that face, but still retain the memory of it before what Hamlet calls 'the mind's eye,' I have what is designated an image or an idea of the face which I had previously perceived. The idea which I should have in this case would be what Locke calls a Simple Idea — that is to say, the idea of a particular object, or the mere memory of a particular percept. But now

25

suppose that before shutting my eyes I had taken a general survey of all the faces at present before me, I should then have what Locke calls a Compound Idea, or the idea of a face in general, as distinguished from my previous simple idea, or the idea of a single face in particular. It is of great importance to note that these compound ideas are created by a fusion of a number of individual percepts, and thus differ from simple ideas in that they are something more than the mere memories of particular percepts. It is needless to say that animals possess compound ideas as well as simple ideas. For instance, a dog has a compound idea of Man, as distinguished from his particular idea of Master. But, lastly, when we come to what Locke calls General or Abstract Ideas, we find, as he says, 'that which puts a perfect distinction betwixt man and brutes.' Wherein, then, consists the difference between a compound idea and a general idea? It consists, according to the unanimous agreement of nearly all writers, in the idea having been named by a word, or other sign, which is designedly used as the mark or symbol of that idea. For instance, like my dog, I have a compound idea of Man, and a simple idea of some particular man; but, unlike my dog, I can name the one by the general word Man, and the other by the particular word John. A compound idea, when thus named, becomes what is called a conception, or a concept. Now, it will be observed that this conceptual order of ideation differs entirely from the other two orders which we have just been considering, in that a symbol is substituted for the mental image, so that the symbol may be used instead of the image, whether or not the image is present to the mind — or, indeed, whether or not any equivalent image admits of being formed at all. Consequently, the mind is now enabled to deal with symbols of ideas without requiring to call up the ideas themselves as memories of perceptions. Consequently, also, the mind is thus enabled to quit the sphere of sense and rise to that of what is called abstraction; furnished with the wings of language, human thought can soar far beyond the possibilities of any ideas which could be suggested by merely sensuous experience.

It will be further observed that the psychological condition to thus naming ideas, so as intentionally to treat the names as symbols of the ideas — the psychological condition required for this is the presence of what is called Self-consciousness. Unless an agent is conscious of itself as a mental agent, and of its own ideas as ideas, it is clearly not in a position to bestow upon them names as names. The mind must be able, so to speak, to get outside of itself, in order to contemplate its own states as such, before it can name these states with the conscious intention of using the names as symbols. In other words, the mind must be capable of introspection; and this power of introspection it is that goes to constitute the one and only distinction between the human mind and mind of lower animals, whether we call this distinction the faculty of Self-consciousness, of Abstraction, of Reason, of *Logos*, or by any of the other terms which are habitually used to signify this unique power of mind to turn in upon its own self and examine its own ideas.

Thus far psychologists of every school are agreed. But as a great deal of laxity has been displayed by responsible writers in the use of Locke's terms, and, moreover, as his intermediate division of compound ideas has been largely lost sight of, I have devised for this intermediate division what I think are more appropriate terms, viz. *Generic Ideas* or *Recepts*. Adopting, then, these terms, you will note that all ideas admit of being classified under one or other of three divisions — viz. Simple Ideas, Generic Ideas, and General Ideas; or, more briefly, Percepts, Recepts, and Concepts. Percepts and recepts are common to the lower animals and to man; but concepts belong to man alone. Moreover, while recepts are formed by an automatic fusion of percepts, without any intentional activity on the part of the mind itself, concepts can only be formed by the intentional activity of the mind in the act of naming a percept or a recept, for the purposes of symbolic abstraction. Thus, a recept is passively received into the mind, while a concept is actively conceived by it. For example, observation shows that waterfowl have one recept (or organized body of percepts) answering to water, and another recept answering to land. So has man. But, unlike the fowl, he is able to bestow on each of these recepts a name, and so to raise them both to the level of concepts. Now, in order to do this, he must be able to set his recept before his own mind as an object of his own thought; before he can bestow his conceptual names on these ideas, he must have cognized them as ideas. In virtue of this act of cognition, he has created for himself — and for purposes other than locomotion — a priceless possession; he has formed a concept.

Nevertheless, the concept which he has thus formed is an exceedingly simple one — amounting, in fact, to nothing more than the naming of some among the most habitual of his recepts, 'land' and 'water'. But it belongs to the nature of concepts that, when thus formed, they admit of being intentionally compared and grouped together into higher and higher concepts, which, in virtue of being successively named, become further and further removed from the sphere of sensuous perceptions. Thus there arises a kind of algebra of recepts. Now, it is in this algebra of the imagination that all the higher work of ideation is accomplished; and throughout it depends on the power of a mind to contemplate its own ideas as such.

The difference between a mind which is capable only of receptual ideation, and a mind which is capable, even in the lowest degree, of conceptual ideation, is usually taken to depend on the absence in the one and the presence in the other of the faculty of Language. Therefore, it is here necessary to say a few words upon this subject.

The faculty of language is, in the largest signification of the term, the faculty of making signs. Now, there is no doubt that the lower animals present the germ of this faculty. A dog wil bark significantly before a closed door as a sign to request that it shall be opened; a wise cat will pull one by one's clothes as a sign to come to her kittens if they are in danger; a parrot will depress its head as a sign to be scratched, and so forth. Nay, a parrot will even use verbal signs with a correct appreciation of their meanings, as proper names, substantives, adjectives, and verbs.[2] Where, then, is the difference between this kind of sign-making, which we may call receptual sign-making, and the sign-making which is peculiar to man, and which alone is conceptual sign-making? The difference is broad and deep. It consists in the power which the human mind displays, as already explained, not only of naming its ideas, but of making one idea stand before another as itself an object of thought. In other words, a man is able to think about his own ideas as ideas. Not only, like a parrot, can he name a particular man John (in consequence of having heard that particular man called John, and therefore associating the name with the man), but he is able to think about this name as a name. And similarly, in all other cases, the difference between naming a thing receptually by mere association, and naming a thing conceptually by intentional thought, is all the difference between knowing that thing and knowing that we know it. And the difference on the side of the talking or sign-making agent is all the difference between an agent that is conscious only, and an agent that is likewise self-conscious. For it is the faculty of self-consciousness which thus enables a mind to set one idea before another as an object of its own thought; by means of this faculty the mind is able, as it were, to stand outside of itself, and so to perceive objectively the ideas which are passing subjectively — and this just as independently as if it were regarding a external series of dissolving views. How it is that such a state of matters is possible, whereby a mind can thus, as it were, get outside of its own existence, and so regard its own ideas as objective to itself — this is the mystery of all mysteries, the bottomless abyss of personality. But, accepting the fact as a fact, all that we have at present to do is to note the enormous difference which the presence of this fact introduces with reference to the sign-making faculty. For it means that merely conscious or receptual sign-making is sign-making which is not thought about as such; while self-conscious or conceptual sign-making is sign-making that is thought about as such. Consequently, while a parrot can only learn words or phrases which are stereotyped in the frame-work of special associations, man, after having thus learnt his vocabulary, can afterwards use his words and phrases like moveable types, whereby to convey any number of different meanings by changes of their relative positions. Thus there are names and names; names receptual and names conceptual. In short, it is his super-added faculty of self-consciousness that has made man *par excellence* the sign-making animal; and therefore what we have to do to-night is to consider the genesis of this faculty.

First of all, however, I should like to say something more about the sign-making faculty, as this occurs before the rise of self-consciousness — that is to say, in the brute and in the human infant.

I distinguish four grades of the sign-making faculty. First there is what may be called the *indicative stage*. Long before it can speak, the infant will express its simple desires by means of intentionally significant tones and gesture-signs, such as pointing to objects in connexion with which it desires something to be done. Here the infant is obviously at the same level of sign-making as the cat which pulls one's dress to signify 'come', or the parrot which will depress its head to signify its desire to be scratched.

Next we find what I call the *denotative stage* of sign-making. Here names are bestowed receptually, or by special association, upon particular objects, qualities, actions, and states of feeling. This stage occurs in the child when it is first emerging from infancy, and is psychologically indistinguishable from that which obtains in the talking birds. Denotative names, then, are names which have been learnt by merely receptual association; they do not imply any self-conscious or conceptual thought.

Following upon the denotative stage is what I call the *connotative*. This consists in a receptual extension of the meaning of a name, from the thing which was at first denoted by that name, to other things which are seen to resemble it. Thus, for example, as M. Taine has remarked, a young child which has learnt the name *Bow-wow* for a house terrier will soon extend it to all other dogs, then to pictures of dogs, to images of dogs, to his elder brother when walking on hands and knees, and so on through ever-widening circles of connotative extension. Now I have observed that a parrot will do precisely the same. One of the birds which I kept under observation used to bark in imitation of a terrier in the same house. Soon the barking became the parrot's denotative name for the terrier, so that the bird would bark whenever it saw the terrier. After a time it ceased to do this, but would always bark when it saw any other dog. Thus the parrot resembled the child of which M. Taine speaks, in that it extended the significance of its name for a particular dog, so as to apply it to any other dog. Here, however, the connotative extension of the name ceased; the bird would not bark at pictures of dogs, no doubt because it was not intelligent enough to perceive the pictorial representations.

Lastly, there is what I call the *denominative stage* of sign-making, or the bestowal of a name consciously known as such. Here we arrive at what I mean by conceptual naming, and therefore this stage of sign-making cannot arise until the mind has attained to self-consciousness. Therefore, also, it only occurs in man, and first appears in the growing child between the second and third years. Then, of course, the child begins to predicate, or to arrange its names in the form of propositions.

Now, in connexion with our subject, it is of the highest importance to note, not only that the three first stages of the sign-making faculty are thus common to animals and human beings, but also that these three first stages advance very much further in the growing child than they ever do in any animal, even before the growing child attains to the fourth, or distinctively human, stage.

In other words, even while still moving in the purely receptual sphere, the growing child becomes much more intelligent, and much more proficient in the art of making signs, than any animal. Although not yet a self-conscious agent, and therefore not yet having attained to conceptual thought, a child between two and three years of age has already distanced every animal in respect of its purely receptual intelligence. But observe, thus far no difference of kind can be alleged by our opponents, because to allege any difference of kind between one order of receptual intelligence and another would be to vacate their whole argument. This argument depends on the distinction between ideation as receptual and conceptual — or between an agent that is, and an agent that is not, self-conscious. But a child up to its third year is not a self-conscious agent. This is proved by the fact that it never employs words having any self-conscious implication, and never gives evidence of even in the lowest degree thinking about its own ideas as such. In short, it cannot be disputed that the respects in which the intelligence of a child between two and three years of age distances that of the most intelligent animal have reference only to a higher advance of receptual ideation; the ideation has not yet become conceptual, and therefore cannot be alleged by our opponents to differ from the ideation of an animal in kind. The higher degree of intelligence which is displayed by a child of this age must therefore be taken to consist in a higher development of receptual intelligence, just in the same way as a dog is more intelligent than a bird. In order to distinguish this higher degree of receptual intelligence, which only occurs in man, and in the growing child immediately precedes the first appearance of conceptual intelligence, I will call it *pre-conceptual* intelligence.

It is of importance to note how far this higher receptual, or pre-conceptual, intelligence can go, and therefore I will briefly consider the kind of language or sign-making (*a*) which leads up to it, and (*b*) by which it is expressed when attained.

The indicative stage of language in the infant is at first below that of the more intelligent animals. But very soon it becames equal to that of the most intelligent. The child will then point to objects in connexion with which it desires something to be done, in just the same way as a dog will beg before a water-jug, etc. It will pull one's dress in the same way as a cat does to signify 'Come'; and, lastly, it will use its voice to make significant — although inarticulate — sounds, after the manner of all the more intelligent of the higher animals. Thus far, then, the child is still moving in the same levels of receptual ideation as the higher animals. But very soon its receptual ideation begins to distance that of even the most intelligent animal: the ideation of the child has therefore entered upon what I call its pre-conceptual phase. From this point onward its gesture-signs become correspondingly more and more significant, so that in children who are late in beginning to talk it may develop into regular pantomime. But now note, it is impossible that as yet there can be any conceptual ideation, because as yet there are no names, and therefore an absence of so much as the condition to the performance of any act of introspective thought.

Thus much, then, for the indicative phase of language in the receptual and pre-conceptual levels of human ideation. Passing on now to the next, or denotative phase (which the indicative phase may largely overlap in children who are late in talking), we find that when a child first begins to use articulate signs it learns the use of them in just the same way as a parrot does; that is to say, it learns the name of particular objects, qualities, actions, and states by special association — in other words, receptually. So far, then, as the beginning of the denotative stage of language is concerned, there is no difference at all between the child and the parrot. Neither is there any difference with regard to the beginning of the connotative stage; for, as I have already said, a parrot will extend its denotative name for a particular dog to all other dogs the resemblance of which one to another it is able to perceive — just in the same way as a young child will extend its name of *Bow-wow* from a terrier to a mastiff. And, although the bird will not follow the child where the child takes the further step of extending the name from living dogs to pictures of dogs, this is plainly due to the intelligence of the bird not advancing far enough to perceive the resemblance of pictures to the objects which they are intended to represent. Many dogs, however, and certain monkeys are able to do this, and, therefore, if a dog or a monkey were able to articulate, there can be no doubt that the brute would follow the child through this further step in the connotative extension of a name. Indeed, when we remember the extraordinary degree in which monkeys are able to understand the meanings of words, as well as the extraordinary propensity which they show in the way of imitating the actions of mankind, there can be no question that, if it were not for the anatomical accident of monkeys being unable to articulate, they would follow a child through what would probably seem a surprising distance in the use of denotative names and receptually connotative words. The chimpanzee now at the Zoological Gardens, which I have taught to count as far as five, displays in a perfectly marvellous degree the power of understanding language — so that one can explain to her verbally what one wishes her to do, in just the same way as we explain this to an infant about eighteen months old. Therefore, if this animal had been able to articulate, there can be no doubt that it would answer us in the same way that a child answers us when first emerging from infancy.

But here we come to an important point in our comparison between the two cases. After a child does emerge from infancy, its receptual intelligence continues to grow; and it continues to grow until it has left far behind the receptual intelligence of any brute. That is to say, between the time that a child first parts company with the brute in the matter of sign-making, up to the time when it first begins to use denominative words, or words which are used with a true conceptual appreciation of their significance, there is an immensely large interval which is filled by advancing stages of receptual development. Before it has attained to even the earliest dawn of self-consciousness — and therefore before it has attained to the possibility of thinking about names as names, or of ideas as ideas — the child has made a prodigious advance in its receptual intelligence, and therefore in the sign-making whereby this intelligence expresses itself. Now, as already stated, in order to distinguish this large and important territory of ideation, which is occupied by the mind of a child between the time that its receptual intelligence parts company with that of the most intelligent animal, up to the time when it first reaches the truly conceptual or self-conscious intelligence of a human being. I call this intervening territory of ideation by the name pre-conceptual. Pre-conceptual ideation, then, is the order of higher receptual ideation which is not presented by any brute, but which is presented by the growing child between the time that its developing intelligence parts company with that of even the most intelligent animal, up to the time when the dawn of self-consciousness begins to convert this higher receptual ideation into ideation that is truly conceptual.

I will now briefly consider the kind of sign-making which is distinctive of this pre-conceptual stage of ideation. The child has now acquired a large number of denotative words, which it has learnt by special association to regard as significant of certain objects, qualities, actions, and states. Suppose, then, that it sees its little sister crying. Its denotative name for this sister is *Dit*: its denotative name for the action of crying is *Ki*. Now the object and the action which these two names severally denote happen to occur together before the child's observation; by the mere force of special association, therefore, the child denotes them both simultaneously — that is to say, brings them into *apposition*. This apposition in consciousness of two habitual recepts with their corresponding denotations is thus effected *for* the child by what may be termed 'the logic of events'; it is not effected *by* the child in the way of any intentional or self-conscious grouping of its ideas, such as goes to constitute the distinguishing feature of the logic of concepts. Therefore, when, on seeing its sister crying, the child says *Dit Ki*, although in one sense we may say that the child is making a proposition, in another and a stricter sense we must deny that this is a true proposition. The proposition, if so it may be called, is pre-conceptual, not conceptual: it is of the psychological kind that we might have expected a monkey to make, if a monkey had been able to pronounce denotative names as well as it can understand them. For the proposition is made by an agent which is not yet a self-conscious agent, and therefore cannot possibly have been thought about as a proposition. That is to say, it lacks the very element of conceptual or introspective thought on which our opponents rely as proving a difference of kind between the brute and the man. Therefore, without argumentative suicide, our opponents cannot afford to maintain that a pre-conceptual proposition of this kind is a genuine proposition, in the sense of being a proposition that implies for its construction any of the distinctively human powers of introspective or abstract thought.

Now, it is needless to say that at this age a child is incessantly making these pre-conceptual propositions; and, of course, the important thing to notice about them is that as yet they are not, and cannot possibly be, conceptual propositions. It is not until the child has attained to self-consciousness, and therefore is able, not only to denote, but to denominate — not only to name, but to think the names, not only to make statements, but to contemplate its statements as such — it is not until the child has taken this further step that it has the peculiar quality of ideation on which our opponents rely for their psychological distinction between the brute and the man. No doubt these pre-conceptual propositions are strongly suggestive of a near approach to true or conceptual propositions: but the point is that as yet they do not present the very feature which it is necessary that they should present, if they are to conform to the distinction of kind between animal and human intelligence which our opponents have endeavoured to institute. They are always evoked by the external logic of events bringing into apposition objects, qualities etc., the denotative names of which are called up in the child's mind by immediate association — and, therefore, are necessarily called up in apposition. Thus the apposition which here gives to the two denotative names the outward form of a proposition is, as I have before said, an apposition which is furnished *to* the child by the external logic of events; not an apposition which is formed *by* the child through any internal operations of introspective thought. So far, therefore, as any question of kind is concerned, it is manifestly impossible for our opponents to argue that these pre-conceptual propositions betoken anything further than the gesture-signs which characterize the earlier stages of a child's intelligence, and which, as we have before seen, serve to connect its growth with the indicative stage of sign-making as this occurs in the lower animals.

The whole issue, then, here becomes resolved into a inquiry touching the subsequent rise of self-consciousness in the child, or the appearance of the psychological condition to a child thinking about its own ideas as ideas — the psychological condition to its thinking about names as names, and therefore the psychological condition to its raising a merely pre-conceptual statement of a fact which it perceives into a conceptual statement of that fact with an introspective knowledge of it as a fact.

Now, in considering this final stage, or the rise of self-consciousness in the child, it is of importance to note that even the lower animals present some of the earliest psychological conditions to the subsequent appearance of self-consciousness in the more gifted intelligence of man. Thus, in the minds of brutes, as in the minds of men, there is a world of images or recepts; and this image world, even in brutes, displays a certain amount of internal activity, which is not wholly dependent on sensuous associations supplied from without. The phenomena of dreaming, hallucination, home-sickness, pining for absent friends, and so forth, amply demonstrate that in our more intelligent domesticated animals there may be an internal (though unintentional) play of ideation, wherein one image suggests another, this another, and so on, without the need of any immediate associations supplied from present objects of sense. Furthermore, receptual ideation of this kind is not restricted to the images of sense-perception, but is largely concerned with the mental states of other animals. That is to say, the logic of recepts, even in brutes, is sufficient to enable the mind to establish true analogies between its own subjective states and the corresponding states of other intelligences. Now, at this stage of mental evolution the individual — whether an animal or an infant — so far realizes its own individuality as to be informed by the logic of recepts that it is one of a kind, although of course it does not recognize either its own or any other individuality as such.

Nevertheless, there is thus given a rudimentary or nascent form of self-consciousness, which up to the stage that it reaches in a brute or an infant may be termed receptual self-consciousness, while in the more advanced stages, which it presents in young children who have just emerged from infancy and are therefore beginning to talk, it may be termed pre-conceptual self-consciousness. Pre-conceptual self-consciousness, then, is exhibited by all children after they have begun to talk, but before they begin to speak of themselves in the first person, or otherwise to give any evidence of realizing their own existence as such. Later on, when true self-consciousness does arise, the child of course is able to do this, and then only is supplied the condition *sine qua non* to a reflection upon its own ideas — hence to a knowledge of names as names, and so to a statement of truths as true. But long before this stage of true or conceptual self-consciousness is reached — whereby alone is rendered possible true or conceptual predication — the child, in virtue of its pre-conceptual self-consciousness, is able to make known its wants, and otherwise to communicate its ideas, by way of pre-conceptual predication, as I have previously shown. Now, if I had time, I could further show that the pre-conceptual self-consciousness, of which this is the expression, amounts to nothing more than a practical recognition of self as an active and feeling agent, without as yet any introspective recognition of that self as an object of knowledge.

Given, then, this stage of mental evolution, and what follows? The child, like the animal, is supplied by its logic of recepts with a world of images, standing as signs of outward objects; with a practical knowledge of processes going on in other minds; and with that kind of recognition of self as an active and suffering agent to which allusion has just been made. But, over and above the animal, the child has now at its command a much more improved machinery of sign-making, which, as we have before seen, is due to the higher evolution of its receptual ideation. Now, among the contents of this ideation is a better apprehension of the mental states of other human beings, together with a greatly increased power of denotative utterance, whereby the child is able to name receptually such mental states on the part of others as it thus receptually apprehends. These, therefore, severally receive their appropriate denotations, and so gain clearness and precision as images of the corresponding states experienced by the child itself. 'Mamma pleased to Dodo' would have no meaning as spoken by a child, unless the child knew from its own feelings what is the state of mind which it thus attributes to another. Hence we find that at the same age the child will also say, 'Dodo pleased to mamma'. Now, it is evident that we are here approaching the very borders of true or conceptual self-consciousness. The child, no doubt, is still speaking of itself in objective phraseology; but it has advanced so far in the interpretation of his own states of mind as clearly to name them, in the same way as he would name any external objects of sense-perception. Thus, he is enabled to fix these states before his mental vision as things which admit of being denoted by verbal signs, although as yet he has never thought about either the states of mind or his names for them as such, and, therefore, has not yet attained to the faculty of denomination. But the interval between denotation and denomination has now become so narrow that the step from recognizing 'Dodo' as not only the object, but also the subject of mental changes, is rendered at once easy and inevitable. The mere fact of attaching verbal signs to mental states has the effect of focussing attention upon those states; and, when attention is thus focused habitually, there is supplied the only further condition which is required to enable a mind, through its memory of previous states, to compare its past with its present; and so to reach that apprehension of continuity among its own states wherein the full introspective consciousness of self consists.

In confirmation of this my general argument, I must now conclude by observing that, although the advance to true self-consciousness from lower grades of mental development is no doubt a very great and important matter, still it is not so great and important, in comparison with what this development is afterwards destined to become, as to make us feel that it constitutes any distinction *sui generis* — or even, perhaps, the principal distinction — between the man and the brute. For even when self-consciousness does arise, and has become fairly well developed, the powers of the human mind are still in an almost infantile condition. In other words, the first genesis of true self-consciousness marks a comparatively low level in the evolution of the human mind — as we might expect that it should, if its genesis depends upon, and therefore lies so near to, those precedent conditions in merely animal psychology to which I have assigned it. But, if so, does it not follow that, great as the importance of self-consciousness afterwards proves to be in the development of distinctively human ideation, in itself, or in its first beginning, it does not betoken any very perceptible advance upon those powers of pre-conceptual ideation which it immediately follows? There is thus shown to be even less reason for regarding the first advent of conceptual self-consciousness as marking a psychological difference of kind, than there would be so to regard the advent of those higher powers of conceptual ideation which subsequently — though as gradually — supervene between early childhood and youth. Yet no one has hitherto ventured to suggest that the intelligence of a child and the intelligence of a youth display a difference of kind.

I have condensed as much of my main argument as I have found to be possible within the limits of a paper. But, of course, it is needless to say that I am very far from having given the whole.

Notes

1. A paper read before the Neurological Society on Thursday, 28 Feb. 1889.
2. All such statements on matters of fact, here and elsewhere, rest upon evidence which is furnished in my book.

4 THE EMERGENCE OF LANGUAGE: ON BEING PICKED UP

Andrew Lock

Source: Lock, A. J. (ed.), *Action, Gesture and Symbol: The Emergence of Language* (Academic Press, London, 1978), pp. 3-10

A relatively short time ago humans stood apart from the rest of the animal world by virtue of the pillars of culture and language. But in recent years these cornerstones of our conceived humanity have been greatly eroded. The attack on the uniqueness of our cultures has arisen from recent Japanese reserch on the transmission of patterns of life in the Japanese Macaque monkey (Kawai, 1963, 1965). There they have observed behaviour which shows a distinct likeness to a cultural tradition. They have seen the development of 'cleanliness' — the primate society having adopted what was originally the discovery of one individual. That individual discovered that eating clean food was better than eating it covered in sand. And cleanliness is next to Godliness.

Almost simultaneously an American chimpanzee learnt a language. Maybe not very well, but well enough (Gardner and Gardner, 1969). The interest which this finding has generated stems partly from its effect on the old adage concerning how many monkeys, with how many typewriters and so much time, would be needed to produce a Shakespearian play. Their chances may be only one in 10 million, but, with a little help from their friends, they have taken that chance.

In both cases questions concerning the evolutionary implications of these findings have arisen. Are we witnessing the beginning of the evolution of language and culture, beginnings similar to those of our own? Are we seeing these processes beginning for the *second* time? The importance of these questions is often dismissed by pointing at the one great difference between the evolution of our languages (and culture), and its acquisition by chimpanzees: the difference that prompts the question, 'Who were the friends who gave language to us?' Ignoring such supernatural speculations, I wish to propose instead that we have not *given* language to a chimpanzee, but have rather provided one with conditions which have enabled her to discover language for herself. Further, I am implying that this is the case with our own infants: that they discover language through the conditions provided by their interactions in the social world. Many writers treat 'language' and 'grammar', 'learning', 'acquisition', 'discovery' and 'invention' as virtually synonymous. For example, Chomsky (1968, p. 75) summarizes a line of argument thus: 'In short, the language is "reinvented" each time it is learned, and the empirical problem to be faced by the theory of learning is how this invention of grammar can take place.' I will retain this ambiguity at present, and summarize my argument here with a slogan: *children discover language through a process of guided reinvention*.

My line of thought is as follows: the major problem for any theory dealing with the possible evolution, or development, of language is that of reference. There are very few traces of this ability in the affective communicative systems of either primates (Goodall, 1968; Itani, 1963; Marler, 1969; Reynolds, 1968) or human infants. The ontogenetic gulf between communicating with emotional expressions and communicating with propositional ones thus seems vast: but I wish to argue that this vastness is illusory. It is the Russian psychologist L. S. Vygotsky who provides the ideas that change the scale of our perceptions. He puts forward a 'general genetic law of cultural development' as follows: 'any function in the child's cultural development appears on the stage twice, on two planes, first on the social plane and then on the psychological, first among people as an intermental category and then within the child as a intramental category' (1966, p. 44).

If he is correct, it follows that symbolic systems have their first expression in the social transactions that go on between us, and in the case of infants, these are initially emotively-based. The implication of this now takes the argument in the reverse direction: if we have evolved from similar stock to our primate initiates, these transactions used to be solely emotional. Thus in some way, language of a referential nature must be implicit in earlier affective, non-referential communicative actions. A theory of either the evolution or development of language would then be aimed at elucidating how what is implicit in prelinguistic communication is given an explicit form (cf. Popper's account (1972) of the development of world 3 and objective knowledge). In the Chomskyan paradigm, the child's problem is 'to determine which of the [humanly] possible languages is that of the community in which he is placed' (1965). Here instead, his problem is cast as having to use the language of his community to give an explicit form to the 'language' implicit in his own transactions with that community. By using examples of three infant's early dealings with the world I will outline how three of our own contemporaries accomplished this task.

None of us are born with the ability to raise our arms to assist another in lifting us up: an activity that infants are often partners to. Thus in early occurrences of this activity the child's arms only get raised by the physical consequences of the mother pushing her hands under his armpits: he himself shows no active adjustment to her behaviour. But fairly quickly the child becomes familiar with being picked up, and he begins to recognize his mother's actions towards him. This is evidenced by the fact that he now shows anticipation of her reactions: he raises his arms himself, and does not rely passively on her efforts.

At first he responds to the physical stimulation of his mother's hands: as she touches him he adjusts his position, and she very easily slides her hands under his arms. As he grows, he anticipates sooner and sooner in the interaction until his mother only has to stand in front of him for him to raise his arms. At this point in his development a new element creeps into the situation. Because he is able to anticipate his mother's actions so far in advance, he can make a 'wrong guess' at what she is going to do: and making a 'wrong guess' has a very important consequence. As an example, consider Paul at 9 months and 6 days of age:

> Paul is in his baby-walker. His mother comes into the room holding a pair of scissors and stands 'absent mindedly' in front of him. She looks at Paul and he raises his arms.
> Mother: OK, just a minute.
> She puts the scissors down and comes back to him. Paul has not been watching her, but is scooting across the room. She stops in front of him, and before she starts to bend down and move her arms out toward him, he raises his arms.

This incident was recorded on videotape, and was played back to the mother afterwards. She confirmed that when she came into the room she had no intention of interacting with Paul: she was wondering what she had done with a piece of material. It was only because Paul 'signalled' to her that they subsequently became involved together. Thus Paul by his behaviour can create an intention for his mother where previously she had none. But while he has stumbled upon this ability, he cannot use it with any deliberateness. He has created an intention for his mother, communicating something to her, quite fortuitously. In Vygotsky's terms his ability exists at the intermental level, and not at the intramental one. Yet similarly, there are few of his innate, as opposed to acquired, abilities that can be executed with any deliberateness at this time. His bladder, his crying and his laughing are still patterned largely by the spontaneous rhythms of a primate's nervous system. (This is an obvious oversimplification: see, for example, Emde and Harrison, 1971.)

But around the time that he shows such sophisticated behaviour as this, the patterning and employment of most of these early actions begins to change. In the case of arm-raising it is initially possible to describe these changes in terms of anticipation again. Thus far the child has shown anticipation within the act of being picked up: his mother must be 'physically in the process of doing' for him to raise his arms. But being picked up occurs in the wider context of everyday life. Infants are picked up to be fed, washed, bathed and comforted; and the preparations for these activities occupy a large part of his day. Food is prepared and cooked, tins are opened; baths are drawn: all these activities culminate in being-picked-up. The child now begins to move his arms in anticipation of these: not in response to his mother's actions, but to the sights, smells and sounds of these events. For example, Mary aged 10 months and 15 days:

> Mary is on the kitchen floor while mother is preparing her dinner. Every time mother walks past her or turns towards her Mary raises her arms. Eventually she is picked up and put in her chair ready for feeding.

The final development of this communicative 'gesture' can be seen in the next example. Here arm-raising is used by Paul, not in anticipation of being picked up, but in the pursuit of that goal — he makes a request:

> Paul; age 10 (6): Paul crawls to his mother and scratches her leg while she is ironing.
> Mother: What do you want?

Paul raises his arms.
Mother: No, I can't pick you up now.

Not only does he make a request of his mother, he leaves her in little doubt as to what that request is. This specificity in the meaning conveyed by arm-raising is important. For example:

Mary; age 10 (16): Mary crawls after her mother as she leaves the room. She manages to jam her fingers in the door as it closes. She screams. Mother comes back, immediately Mary sees her she lifts her arms.

It may be argued that the action of lifting the arms is irrelevant on this occasion: a crying child would be lifted anyway. But cries on their own are notoriously inefficient:

Paul; age 6 (19): Paul is sat alone in the middle of the living-room. He starts to cry. Mother comes into the room.
Mother: Oh, now what's up, hey? Oh dear, Oh dear, what's the matter? She picks him up.
Mother: Are you thirsty, is that what it is? Do you want a drink? She goes and picks up his bottle and offers it to him. He refuses it and continues crying.
Mother: Hungry? Are you? Do you want something to eat? No? Sleepy then, do you want to go to sleep?
She puts him in his pram but he continues to cry. She picks him up again and walks about comforting him. She stops at the window. Paul apparently looks out but continues crying. Mother tries to attract his attention, and then to direct it.
Mother: Look, there's a pussycat, can you see him? Do you know what pussycats say? Do you? They said 'miaow' don't they, yes, of course they do. Paul stops crying during this speech.
Mother: There, that's better, down you go then. She places him back on the floor.

Crying on its own leaves too much of the message 'unsaid', too much to be supposed by the hearer. Apparently in response to this problem the developing infant begins to modify his crying, complementing it with other, more specific, communicative actions, each with its separate developmental history. A dramatic example of this is:

> Paul; age 14 (23): Mother enters the room holding a cup of tea.
> Paul turns from his play in her direction and obviously sees the
> cup of tea.
> He cries vestigially and so attracts mother's attention;
> immediately he points toward her and smacks his lips
> concurrently.
> Mother: No, you can't have this one, it's Andy's.

Here crying functions both to attract attention and convey the
message of the child's wanting something. Pointing directs that
attracted attention and informs the mother what that something is.
For this child, the roots of the pointing gesture can be traced back
to earlier direct attempts to pick objects up. Lip-smacking has
resulted from a stylization of actually eating or drinking, and its
use here leaves the mother in little doubt as to why the child wants
the cup.

Similarly, when the crying child runs to his mother with
outstretched arms, he conveys a specific message to her through
the combination of these different actions: *and to do this is to have
mastered one of the fundamental skills of language.* Sentences
convey specific messages through the combination of different
actions. If we look at the developmental history of the child's
ability to combine gestures we find three phases. One in which the
ability to use single gestures is developed; a second in which single
gestures occur in sequences — the child cries . . . and then points
or raises his arms, say; and finally a period in which two or more
gestures occur together — the child cries and points 'at the same
time'. A similar sequence is found in language development: the
so-called holophrastic period of one-word-at-a-time; the
occurrence of two words in a sequence; and that of true multiword utterances. This is another hint that the two processes — of
language and gesture — are very similar. And they are alike in
further ways. As noted earlier, the great chasm to be bridged in
both speculations on the evolution of language and those on its
development is that between affective and referential
communication. Here it should be noted that in these gestural
combinations the child displays an ability which is transitional
between the two. Crying is no longer solely affective: it now both
attracts the mother's attention and conveys information. Similarly,

pointing directs that attention, and also 'refers' to an object. Functionally there is little difference between the child crying and pointing at an object — gestural use, and later saying the name of that object with a whining intonation while pointing at it — language use. What difference there is would seem to be enshrined in the concept of symbolism. Yet the removal of lip-smacking from its original sphere of application to this one of interpersonal communication 'smacks' of symbolism itself.

I would suggest that at this stage in his development the child has *mastered* the fundamentals of language: but I would not wish to go as far as saying he now *possesses* language. Whilst he can communicate his intentions in an unambiguous and structured manner, the messages he conveys are not objective in nature, nor are they propositional, and neither are they capable of being judged true or false. Language is still only implicit in his activities, and will remain so until he becomes able to name objects.

This latter ability *seems* to have a totally separate history to the communicative ones I have been discussing thus far. And for 2 or 3 months after they appear in his repertoire, words stay separate from, and are not used in, the communicative pursuit of the child's intentions. During this period they seem to be used only 'for the fun of it', in social games with the mother:

Mary; age 11 (28): Mary is sat on the floor with her mother, who is sat facing her.
Mother: (holding duck out to Mary) What does the duck say? What does he say?
Mary: (reaching towards duck) Argh
Mother: Yes, I know you want it. What does he say?
Mary: Woraghagh
Mother: He doesn't, he says 'quack quack quack quack'.
Mary: Gh, gh
Mother: Yes he does. And who's this? (holding out Teddy)
Mary: Aah
Mother: And that aah is it, that's aah Teddy.
Mary: Aah

It is only after words have been practised in this context for a few months that they are found being used communicatively — and for this purpose they are used in conjunction with the older gestural ability:

Peter; age 14 (4): Mother is playing with Peter, getting him to fill a box with all his toys. He gathers every object in reach and puts them in the box. He turns to me (I am about four feet away), looks at the toy dog at my feet, waves his arm (a gesture peculiar to Peter, used communicatively to make demands; cf. Lock, 1976) and says 'darg'. I throw it across to him.

Perhaps, though, this apparent developmental separateness of gesture and word, communicative function and referential function, is illusory. Certainly the child's ability to respond with different noises to differing objects arises from roots other than those underlying his gestural attainments. But how does he make the transition from this primitive level of perceptual discrimination and associative responding to that of actually naming objects, to the level of reference? This transition surely depends on factors involved in his earlier communicative use of gestures and actions. As already noted, pointing, lip-smacking and arm-raising show the rudiments of both reference and symbolism well in advance of the appearance of a linguistic system. When sound and object are associated, these rudiments are capitalized upon, and referential language emerges (cf. Bruner, 1975; Edwards, 1978; Lyons, 1973).

Further, in this period of the emergence of spoken words, the language and gestural systems interact to such an extent that any separateness they may have is immediately lost. Edwards (1978) notes that in the naming of objects, the importance of 'reference' is obvious. But, he points out,

object-naming also has a social relational and cognitive structure which underlie the nature of reference itself. Object-naming typically occurs in the context of what Brown (1956) called 'the original word game', in which child and caretaker (usually mother) supply each other with names for pointed-at objects and pictures, or point out things named by the other. Typically the 'game' is linguistically mediated by much more than mere object-names; it is full of questions and answers, locative and deictic expressions like 'What's that?', 'there it is', 'that's a kangaroo', 'it's a box', 'it's over there', and so on. Moreover these expressions are integrated into a context of sequenced looks and gestures which are crucial to their function in the total communication setting . . . The game has two complementary versions. In object-naming the child supplies a name for a located object. In pointing at named objects he indicates their location. (Edwards, 1978, pp. 3-7)

Reference, gesture and communication are all obviously intertwined. Finally, certain two-word utterances can be traced back directly to gestural origins. It would be a bit simplistic to say that gestures are translated into words, that words begin to replace gestures in the child's communicative system: but it would not be too simplistic. Consider the utterance 'mommy up' reported by Greenfield and Smith (1976) being used by an 18-month-old child. Here 'mommy' does not refer to mother, but seems to have developed from the total stylization of crying into a repeated nasal phrase. It retains the same function as crying, that of attracting attention and making a demand. 'Up' specifies the child's intention, and thus functions to the same end as arm-raising did earlier. The two-word utterance 'mommy up' has thus both the same form and use as the two-gesture communicative act of crying and arm-raising, and developmentally the two abilities appear very closely related.

Through looking at the emergence of language in this way the evolutionary perspective is opened up. Gestures arise in the interactions between people, in the communicative acts they share. At the height of their development these gestures show all the rudiments of language and at least in some cases, patterned speech results from the internalization of the structure of these shared acts — as, in similar vein, Piaget argues that thought arises from the internalization of action. Likewise, meanings initially exist between the interactants — Vygotsky's 'intermental level' — and only later with the development of symbols are they internalized and simultaneously given explicit form — Vygotsky's 'intramental level'. George Mead (1934) maintains similarly that meaning is objectively present in any social conduct between individuals, and that 'language simply lifts out of the social process a situation which is logically or implicitly there already' (1934, p. 79). Implicitly there, *both functionally and structurally*, in the interactions between chimp and chimp, chimp and man, or man and child: and given explicit form, first through the gesture and then through the symbol.

Gestures and words may thus be thought of as tools which enable an individual to accomplish the task of making explicit meanings. It is a task that chimpanzees have just started upon, but one which is always set before our own infants. But these tools are not given by us to either chimp or child: rather, we provide the social context in which they fashion them for themselves. From here it is only a short distance to saying that in our own evolutionary past we created the social context in which we, as a species, could fashion these tools for ourselves. Thus, being picked up is a part of every primate's childhood: but being a being being picked up is an integral part of picking up language.

References

Bruner, J.S. (1975) 'The Ontogenesis of Speech Acts', *Journal of Child Language*, 2, 1-20

Chomsky, N. (1965) *Aspects of the Theory of Syntax*, MIT Press, Cambridge, Mass.

Chomsky, N. (1968) *Language and Mind*, Harcourt, Brace and World, New York

Edwards, D. (1978) 'The Sources of Children's Early Meanings' in I. Markova (ed.), *Language and the Social Context*, John Wiley, London

Emde, R.N. and Harrison, R.J. (1971) 'Endogenous and Exogenous Smiling Systems in Early Infancy', *Journal of Child Psychiatry*, 11, 177-200

Gardner, R.A. and Gardner, B. T. (1969) 'Teaching Sign Language to a Chimpanzee', *Science*, 165, 664-72

Goodall, J. (1968) 'A Preliminary Report on Expressive Movements and Communication in the Gombe Stream Chimpanzees' in P. Jay (ed.), *Primates: Studies in Adaptation and Variability*, Holt, Rinehart and Winston, New York

Greenfield, P. M. and Smith, J. (1976) *Communication and the Beginnings of Language: The Development of Semantic Structure in One Word Speech*, Academic Press, New York and London

Itani, J. (1963) 'Vocal Communication of the Wild Japanese Monkey', *Primates*, 4, 11-66

Kawai, M. (1963) 'On the Newly Acquired Behaviors of the Natural Troop of Japanese Monkeys on Koshima Island', *Primates*, 4, 113-15

Kawai, M. (1965) 'Newly Acquired Pre-cultural Behavior of the Japanese Monkeys on Koshima Islet', *Primates*, 6, 1-30

Lock, A. J. (1976) 'Acts instead of Sentences' in W. von Raffler-Engel and Y. Lebrun (eds.), *Baby Talk and Infant Speech*, Swets and Zeitlinger BV, Lisse, Holland

Lyons, J. (1973) 'Deixis as the Source of Reference', *Work in Progress*, 6, 92-115. Department of Linguistics, Edinburgh University

Marler, P. (1969) 'Vocalisation of Wild Chimpanzees: An Introduction', *Proceedings of the Second International Congress of Primatology*, Atlanta, Vol. 1, 94-100

Mead, G. H. (1934) *Mind, Self and Society*, University of Chicago Press, Chicago

Popper, K. R. (1972) *Objective Knowledge: An Evolutionary Approach*, Clarendon Press, Oxford

Reynolds, P. (1968) 'Evolution of Primate Vocal-auditory Communication Systems', *American Anthropologist*, 70, 300-8

Vygotsky, L. S. (1966) 'Development of the Higher Mental Functions' in *Psychological Research in the USSR*, Progress Publishers, Moscow

5 THE INVENTION OF PHONEMICALLY-BASED LANGUAGE

Gordon W. Hewes

Source: Paper given at Interdisciplinary Symposium on Glossogenetics (UNESCO, Paris, 1981).

For some years I have been studying ideas about the origin of language, and I have been especially impressed by the arguments and evidence for the notion, so prominent in eighteenth century debates on the subject, that language originated in the visual — gestural mode, and not as speech. Since spoken language is now clearly predominant over gestural communication, a gestural origin theory must explain how the shift to vocal language occurred, and as part of such an explanation, why and when this happened. Here I shall address that later stage of language, which several writers have placed with the first appearance of fully modern *Homo sapiens* populations. Following a recent paper by Grover S. Krantz, a physical anthropologist who links the emergence of specifically sapiens features of the skull, face, and jaws to 'phonemic' language, I shall explore that hypothetical connection in greater detail than Krantz, whose focus was on cranial and facial traits rather than language as such.

If we assume that language originated in gestural signs, it is difficult to imagine why it would have shifted over so completely to speech, so that gestural languages (as distinct from the use of gesture as an accompaniment of speech) exist marginally, mainly in communities of deaf people, or as auxiliary systems for ritual purposes, for inter-tribal communication, and the like. For the primates in general, and certainly for man, vision is much more important than hearing, except for the special case of spoken language. The *glottogenic model* I support suggests that gesture language began with simple *ostension* or *deixis*, as it still seems to begin in infants. There are several advantages in spoken language over visible language, to be sure. Speech can be used in the dark, and passes around nearby environmental barriers to vision, and it allows its users to continue using their hands for other activities. But it would be absurd to contend that spoken language is always

49

more efficient than visible language, or else written languages would not have developed. Reading, if not writing, is far faster than speech for well-trained individuals, and writing has the great advantage of non-fading, or relative permanence.

It is worth stating early on that I do not intend to insist that language is either primarily innately based, nor that it is wholly learned or conventional. As with so much else having to do with human behavior, both genetic dispositions and learning are involved. Work with apes shows that by now human beings surpass apes in being able to learn to speak, and that even where language is offered to apes in the visual-gestural mode, their levels of achievement remain much lower than those of quite retarded children. It is plausible to assume that a significant reason for the large brains of *Homo sapiens* lies in our language capacities, and further that the marked increase in hominid brain size over the past million and a half years corresponds in some ways to improvements in the language-handling capacities of our lineage. Language was probably not the sole cause of hominid cerebral expansion. While human language has a biological foundation, the development of language must rest on a long succession of cultural innovations or inventions, each successful step initiating a new adaptive level against the background of which natural selective processes relating to survival of populations had to operate. That language, in the hominids, has had survival advantages seems incontestable. That nothing else much resembling it has ever arisen in any other line of organisms on this planet is interesting, but there are biological parallels to the emergence of features limited to one or a small group of closely related species. That our most devoted and by no means unintelligent commensal, the dog, which has been closely associated with speaking human beings for a dozen millennia, still cannot speak, and has achieved only limited understanding of speech, shows that it takes more than an alert brain, good hearing, and a good vocal capability to acquire language.

I would place the beginnings of language (as something distinct from other forms of animal communication), about three million years ago, by which time our ancestors had achieved bipedal locomotion, with the requisite modifications in the pelvis and feet. If gestural language came first, the freeing of the hands from locomotor functions was probably a contributing factor in glottogenesis. It is at this point that I would begin the scenario for language formation. I am not committed to the support of any part of this hypothetical model, and if contrary evidence demands its alteration, or the jettisoning of the entire reconstruction, so be it.

The roots of language may lie in the limited gestural behavior seen in the modern apes, notably the chimpanzee, although this could be the result of later convergent evolution. In a previous paper, I argued that the first step might have been simple ostension or deixis, as Trân Duc Thao (1973) explained. Hominid brain size was still at the *anthropoid ape level*, around 400 to 500 cc, and there is so far no evidence for the making of stone tools, nor any evidence for the regular hunting of large animals. The only reason to suppose that a slight amplification of a gestural communication system might have been underway so early is that little else in the reconstructible behavioral repertoire of the *australopithecine hominids* seems able to explain their survival in what must have been an otherwise unfavorable environment for survival. A minimal gestural proto-language would have favored the food-quest, not yet involving significant hunting, through exchange of propositional information about the location of seasonal food resources and their possible transport and shared consumption. Anatomical evidence, such as it is, gives no warrant for attributing articulate speech to these creatures, whereas the recent studies of language-like behavior induced in chimpanzees, gorillas, and orang-utans permits us to credit the early Australopithecines with manual signalling capabilities. Similar analogies with modern apes would compel us to credit the australopithecines with a developed vocal call system as well, innately programmed and involuntary. The neurological evidence relating to the production of a set of such closed vocal calls makes it unlikely that the later phenomenon of speech arose in involuntary calls, little subject to learned modification.

After a long period marked by quite modest increments in brain size, and a gradually increasing manufacture and use of extremely crude stone tools, probably accompanied by tools of wood and other perishable materials, the hominids came to occupy a very wide range, from Southern Africa to Southern and Central Europe, and east to the Pacific, in forms now classified as *Homo erectus*. Brain-size had risen to 400 to 500 cc, and around or not long after one million years ago, the use of fire had been added to the cultural inventory of these now regularly hunting and gathering groups, and the stone tools began to show manufacture to a pattern, and some regional diversity. It seems reasonable to suppose that this cultural enrichment entailed improvements in social communication by means of language, although as yet little change had occurred in the face and jaws, suggesting that adaptive pressures connected with articulate speech were not yet significant, if indeed such speech does entail changes of the lower part of the face and jaws. On the other hand, there could be no reason to deny *Homo erectus* populations a developed gesture-language capability. If gesture-language had appeared a million or two years earlier, and if such language is reflected in the archaeologically documented elaborations of the later Lower Paleolithic, we might guess that a gestural lexicon of a few hundred to a thousand word-like signs had been attained in the several thousand small local social groups into which the *Homo erectus* populations were divided. Since such languages were, in my view, formed by cultural processes — invention and social learning, and to some extent by means of inter-group diffusion, rather than by some mysterious general biological process, I would also assume that considerable linguistic diversity already existed. Indeed, it would be precisely in such local linguistic diversity that the potential for steady enrichment and enlargement of conceptual communication would lie. As to the rate of such changes, the surviving artifactual record may provide a rough indication for the overall rate of cultural change from perhaps 1,500,000 to 300,000 years ago. The long-standing difference in stone artifacts, dividing East and South-east Asia from the other *Homo erectus* populations to the west and into Southern Africa may indicate that there was very little cultural diffusion between the two main bodies of *Homo erectus*, and perhaps this was also manifest in their language systems.

The accelerated enlargement of the cerebral hemispheres in the latest *Homo erectus* and so-called 'Pre-Neanderthal' populations perhaps represents the attainment of some voluntary control over vocalizations. The artifacts do not, except for some refinement of handaxe-making in certain regions, in themselves seem to require significantly bigger brains. In any case, it seems highly unlikely that voluntary control over vocalizations came overnight, or produced more than a few 'spoken words'.

The innovation of voluntary vocal sound production as part of a language system still mainly gestural might well have ushered in a stage during which vocal language elements constituted the '*paralanguage*', much in the way that at present, manual gestures are the paralanguage, and are dispensable under some conditions. I would also suppose that the earliest vocal accompaniments of gesture language were *motivated*, not arbitrary. Some may have been *onomatopoeic*, or deliberate imitations of the older involuntary emotional calls and cries. We may imagine that over the vast geographic range of the *Homo erectus* populations, and their pre-Neanderthal successors, different sets of vocal signs would be coming into use. Over the course of two to three hundred thousand years, given the contacts between neighboring social groups, there would be diffusion of the new acoustic elements, from initially very small sets of two or three such voluntary vocal signs to several dozen. These would not yet be classifiable as *phonemes*, but rather '*phememes*' (Foster, 1978).

These developments would take us up to the start of the Middle Paleolithic, a comparatively short period exhibiting, in several regions, radically accelerated cultural growth attributable in part to more effective language, moving from a mainly gestural system with very few vocal signs to a mixed system involving twenty to thirty or more such vocal elements, and several hundred or more gestural signs. The vocal signs, like the manual gestures, would be fully meaningful, and without much evidence either way, I tend to think of them as consonants rather than vowels, following many previous speculations. Vowels would then have emerged as *euphonic* elements, lacking concrete meanings aside from some onomatopoeic functions.

Why would one put this kind of linguistic advance in the early Middle Paleolithic, rather than earlier? The artifactual record shows a sharp upturn in complexity in many regions of the Old World, with the practice of deliberate burial of the dead (not necessarily everywhere), and brain size not only reaches modern *Homo sapiens* levels, but even exceeds it in some populations, which may of course be an effect of small sample size. Lieberman and his colleagues, moreover, have shown that whereas some earlier hominids were probably incapable of articulate speech, the Neanderthalers, along with such forms as Rhodesian Man, could have spoken, although with a voice quality unlike that of modern speakers, and perhaps at slower speeds (especially with respect to decoding spoken messages). If gestural language had long existed as the chief vehicle for human communication, it should have by this period attained some syntactical rules, probably mostly of the word-order variety, but such rules could also be readily applied to the enlarging lexicons of vocal language. In general I am skeptical of those linguists who assert the primacy of syntactical structures at earlier stages of glottogenesis. With accompanying gestures capable of making agent and object clear, and limitation to short sentences without embedded clauses, a language for everyday use in simple hunting and gathering cultures of the kind we can reconstruct for Neanderthal Man, could well get along with minimal syntax.

We now come to the transformation of phememes into phonemes — that is, the reduction and loss of semanticity in vocal signs, save for some residual sound-symbolism, which is with us still, evidently worldwide but usually subliminal. Ultimately, say by the close of the Middle Paleolithic, the balance might have finally tipped toward spoken rather than gestural language for everyday use. Gesture might have persisted in special circumstances — for communication while stalking game, for rituals, and because of its higher iconicity, for inter-tribal communication, just as it existed in far later times among many North American or Australian aboriginal groups.

Krantz, in his remarkable article (1980), has credited the attainment of fully phonemicized speech to the distinctive features of the *Homo sapiens sapiens* skull, face, and jaws, as mentioned earlier. In brief, these changes include considerable reduction in supraorbital ridges, marked maxillary and mandibular shrinkage, reduction in molar tooth size, enlargement of the mastoid processes, the appearance of a projecting, bony chin, thinning of the cranial bones, and an overall increase in the gracility of the skull, reducing its absolute weight. The forehead bulges out, the occipital bun diminishes, and so on. To be sure, Krantz could not explain all of these changes in terms of 'phonemic language'; he overlooks or neglects the role of food-processing on jaw and tooth size, although most of the advances in cookery would have come later than the Upper Paleolithic, such as the use of stone milling implements and pottery cooking vessels (for boiling and stewing), and were far from culturally universal in Post-Pleistocene times.

Homo sapiens sapiens status was accompanied by all sorts of indicators of conceptual elaboration, at least in some important areas of the world. Various forms of Paleolithic art appear, along with body ornaments, and the shift was quite sudden — a matter of a few millennia — roughly from about 40,000 to 35,000 years before the present. The human morphological transformation affected all parts of the inhabited world, even in regions without spectacular archaeological evidence for art, ritual, and so on. Some time within this short period, man began to settle in Australia, and the American continents.

That the foundations of spoken language of fully phonemic type had been reached by 20,000 to 10,000 years ago is further supported by the existence of such languages (unfortunately poorly documented) on the remote island of Tasmania, the inhabitants of which were seemingly cut off from contact even with the Australian mainland by 10,000 BC or so, when the post-glacial sea-level rise occurred. Fully modern phonemic speech existed on Tasmania when that island was rediscovered by Europeans in the seventeenth and eighteenth centuries, which, unless we assume that the Ancient Tasmanians had independently invented it after their arrival there, must provide a *terminus ad quem* for the formative stage of phonemicization.

The *terminus a quo*, of course, is one of the main questions of this paper, and my inclination is to put it somewhere in the course of the Middle Paleolithic, so that it came to be a nearly universal human attribute by the time that worldwide sapienization was going on. Whether these were causally connected seems probable, but not demonstrable in detail.

Now to the question of the *raison d'être* for phonemes, above and beyond the obvious point that their use permits an easier lexical expansion than a phememe-based system. I doubt that the critical factor at the start of phonemicization was the potential for immense vocabulary growth. Instead, I shall argue that phonemes — sound units shorn of their former semanticity, aside from lingering sound-symbolism, are much more effective for the very rapid retrieval of word-units composed of them, both by speakers about to employ them in utterances, or by hearers seeking to decode the spoken words uttered by others. The presence of meaning in any filing system, paradoxically, detracts from its efficiency, particularly since for any large set of items, there are no obvious or unambiguous rules for sorting according to meaning categories. *Polysemy* is a characteristic of things in the external world, where almost any item that can be perceived can fall simultaneously, into several possible categories. Most things, as any compiler of a catalogue knows, can be filed under competing headings. An analogy with the utility of alphabetic or numerical filing is appropriate here. The virtue of filing entries alphabetically, or according to arbitrary numerical headings is precisely that one does not have to worry about what the filing sequence means. Secondly, such filing by alphabetical order or by numbers (in such a case, decimally separated), provides a branching system, so that one does not have to file only by initial letter or initial number, but letter by letter or number by number throughout the signs forming the item.

Phonemes function, as their linguist-discoverers in modern times realized, very much like the letters of the written alphabet, as meaningless signs from which longer and meaningful sequences can be constructed without paying attention to the original meaning, if any, inherent in the sound of the letter or phoneme. My point is that long before there were any written languages, alphabetical or other, speakers were unconsciously classifying and filing their words by reducing them to their phonemic constituents, in the order of their production and reception, that is from initial to final sound.

All I am saying here is that something very roughly analogous to alphabetic filing exists in the brain, for phonemicized speech; there is scattered evidence from psycholinguistics and neurolinguistics for something like this, having to do with word-storage and word-retrieval, by both normal and deviant speakers, which accounts for some kinds of systematic speech-errors, and which is much more apparent in the early stages of language acquisition by young children. The acquisition of this kind of phonemic filing system, rather than a pressing need to expand the lexicon, would have been of immediate value to speakers just emerging from a pre-phonemic stage of language use, and in which gestural signs may still have been very important for everyday communication. With vocabulary size held fairly constant, say, from 50,000 to 40,000 years ago, the introduction and spread of a far more efficient cortical filing system, unconscious to be sure, as it still is with us, based on phonemes as indices or filing tags, largely bereft of syntactic loading, should have meant a dramatic rise in the ability to handle complex, conceptual thought at high speeds. One effect would have been to permit more complex sentences and syntactic rules, since these entail the need for rapid verification of meanings. With a more efficient word-meaning retrieval system, we can go back and forth many times, in the course of a verbal exchange, to check and recheck on the meanings our interlocutors are using. If we had to make such searches by means of the precise semantic associations of each sign, the process would be much slower and more frequently in error. It can be assumed that considerable individual differences in the ability to handle phonemes as filing tags or indices would exist, with dysphasias analogous to some of the current forms of dyslexia.

I am sure that this scenario is far from convincing, and I offer it mainly as a topic for discussion. It is possible that I have ignored some other important pathways to fully phonemicized speech, and that the periodization presented, linking particular phases of the prehistoric record, fossil and artifactual, is far too precise, given the sketchiness of our knowledge of hominid biological and cultural evolution.

References

Allott, R. (1973) *The Physical Foundations of Language*, 2 vols., ELB Printers, Seaford
Foster, M. LeCron (1978) 'The Symbolic Structure of Primordial Language' in S. L. Washburn and E. R. McCown (eds.), *Human Evolution: Biosocial Perspectives on Human Evolution*, vol. IV. Cummings, Menlo Park, pp. 77-121
Johannesson, A. (1952) *Gestural Origin of Language*, H. F. Leiftur, Reykjavik and B. H. Blackwell, Oxford
Krantz, Grover S. (1980) 'Sapienization and Speech', *Current Anthropology, 21(6)*, 773-92
Limber, J. (1981) 'What Can Chimps Tell us about the Origin of Language?', University of New Hampshire, Durham. (Unpublished MS)
Paget, R. A. S. (1930) *Human Speech*, Kegan Paul, Trench, London
Stopa, R. (1979) 'Clicks, their Form, Function and their Transformation', Krakow, *Uniwersytet Jagiellonskiego*, 561
Trân Duc Thao (1973) *Recherches sur l'origine du langage et de la conscience*, Éditions Sociales, Paris

SECTION III: EARLY DEVELOPMENT OF LANGUAGE

In this section we first present McShane's views of the early stages of language. Different theorists may use a different terminology, but the honest ones tend to end up in McShane's position: that the early breakthrough into language rests on some process, he terms it insight, that we are, as yet, at a loss to comprehend. One of the legacies of the Chomskyan revolution in psycholinguistics has been the problem of creativity, which occupies a central position in our current views of language. Explaining the processes involved in creativity is like trying to account for genius: difficult to say the least. It is one of psychology's great tasks for the future to strive for a better grip on what one hopes does not turn out to be a facet of 'the peace of God, which passeth all understanding'.

Macnamara turns the spotlight to an aspect of language development that has often been overlooked in recent years in our enthusiasm to locate language in its prelinguistic precursors: the fact that language is a system of sounds, and that system has to be 'cracked' if one is to speak. What is interesting in this account is how so many of the processes at the crux of what we have recently learned about the non-verbal aspects of language development are apparently involved in the infant's learning of the sound system. When one breaks down language development into its parts, one finds that none of them are entirely independent of any other. In terms of reaching an understanding of language development, we do not know whether this is a cause for cynicism, optimism or pessimism.

Finally, Gopnik's paper looks at the emergence of words that do not refer to 'things'. The main points her analysis establishes are that: children's early words have to be understood from the child's point of view; early words are a part of the child's larger cognitive development; and that language is intimately bound up with the process Piaget has termed 'decentration' — a growing ability to deal with the world from a standpoint other than one's own. We will be taking up the relationships between language and cognition in more detail in the course text.

Suggested Further Reading

At the time of writing, textbooks tend not to be very good in their coverage of this phase of language development. We would therefore suggest two useful sources of further information that are of a slightly more specialised nature. First, two of the above authors have recently published full-length works: J. McShane (1980) *Learning to Talk*, Cambridge University Press, London; J. Macnamara (1982) *Names for Things*, MIT Press, Cambridge, Mass. Secondly, there have been a number of edited volumes on the topic: H. R. Schaffer (1977) *Studies in Mother-Infant Interaction*, Academic Press, London; A. J. Lock (1978) *Action, Gesture and Symbol: The Emergence of Language*, Academic Press, London; M. Bullowa (1979) *Before Speech*, Cambridge University Press, London; E. Bates *et al.* (1979) *The Emergence of Symbols*, Academic Press, New York. An early paper on the transition into language that is still one of the clearest statements of psychology's approach to the problem is J. Macnamara (1972) 'The Cognitive Basis of Language Learning in Infants', *Psychological Review, 79*, 1-13.

6 THE DEVELOPMENT OF NAMING

John McShane

Source: Linguistics, 17, 1979, pp. 879-905

Joint Attention and Naming

One of the principal general arguments concerning language development in recent years is that particular communicative acts do not arise *de novo* but develop from more primitive means of preverbal communication. As an example consider the behaviour of requesting. There is a considerable amount of recent theory and evidence relating to the prelinguistic origins of the behaviour itself (Bates, Camaioni and Volterra, 1975; Sugarman-Bell, 1978; Trevarthen and Hubley, 1978) as well as documentation of its initial linguistic expression (Greenfield and Smith, 1976; Halliday, 1975; McShane, 1980). It seems obvious that there is no direct sense in which naming could be carried out without the use of words. Nevertheless, it has been argued that there are preverbal developments that contribute to the development of naming.

Bates *et al.* (1975) argue that the communicative precursors to 'declaratives' are the child's preverbal attempts to direct the attention of an adult to some object or event in the world. Following Parisi and Antinucci (1973) they regard the declarative as:

> a particular kind of imperative which commands the unique epistemic act of 'assuming' some proposition . . . [it is] a command for the listener to attend to or assume some piece of information. (1975, p. 208)

Bates *et al.* use the terms 'declarative' and 'imperative' to refer to speech acts rather than sentence-types, a possibly unfortunate choice of terminology (see Lyons, 1977, pp. 30, 748). It is clear that their declarative subsumes naming. Their main argument is that declarative and imperatives have a common intentional component in being commands. If a declarative is a command to attend to some piece of information then perhaps its origins can be traced to preverbal commands to attend. It is argued that declaratives have some element of functional continuity with certain types of preverbal behaviour, in particular pointing. However, there is little evidence to link declaratives with commands to attend as the continuity from preverbal pointing to verbal expression seems to lie elsewhere. McShane (1980) has found that utterances that are used to direct attention during the initial stages of language development most commonly involved either saying *look* or *that* or calling the name of the person whose attention the child wished to direct. Names were used very infrequently to direct attention suggesting that directing attention is not the main use of object names. But, although such a direct link between attention and naming must be discounted it is nevertheless possible that the development of joint attention and reference are less directly linked.

Bruner (1975a, 1975b) has claimed that the development of joint attention creates an intersubjective framework where there is implicit social agreement about an activity, attending, that is a necessary part of reference. Bruner further argues that the topic-comment structure of language reflects the processes of attention. Following Neisser (1967) he regards the process of attention as one of analysis-by-synthesis:

> a process of positing wholes (topics) to which parts or features or properties may be related and from which the new wholes may be constructed. The predicational rules of natural language are surely a well-adapted vehicle for expressing the results of such attentional processing: topic-comment structure in language permits an easy passage from feature to its context and back, while topicalization provides a ready means for regrouping new sets of features into hypothesized whole to be used as topics on which to comment. (Bruner, 1975b, pp. 4-5)

Let us first consider how joint attention develops and then its relevance to the development of reference. Studies of the development of joint attention have revealed that visual co-orientation is initially due largely to the efforts of the mother. Collis and Schaffer (1975) and Collis (1977) have shown that with infants of 10 months, mothers allowed their attention to be directed by the infants' behaviour and continually monitored the infants' focus of visual attention. However, there was no evidence that the infants tended to follow the mothers' direction of gaze more often than would be expected by chance (Collis, 1977). The finding conflicts with the results reported by Scaife and Bruner (1975) where there was a clear tendency for infants from 8 months old to follow another's direction of gaze. The differences may be due to differences in experimental technique. In Scaife and Bruner's experiment an experimenter established eye contact with an infant and then looked to one side, either right or left. In the Collis and Schaffer (1975) and Collis (1977) experiments mother and infant were engaged in unrestrained interaction in a laboratory. Mutual gaze did not necessarily precede a line of gaze in this situation. These experiments seem to show that from 8 months onwards infants are capable of following the line of gaze of another person provided eye-contact is first established. In the absence of initial eye-contact infants do not appear to consistently follow another's gaze at this age.

Other studies of joint attention have focused on the use of pointing in mother-infant dyads. Murphy and Messer (1977) found that by the time infants were 9 months old mothers used the pointing gesture to attract the infants' attention. When these 9-month-old infants were compared with 14-month-old infants it was found that the mothers of the 9-month-old group often supplemented their pointing gesture with additional cues. The abilities of the two groups of infants to follow a point differed. The 9-month-old infants were best at following a point where the relevant object was in the same visual field as the pointing hand. Most infants of this age failed to follow a point across their midline (i.e. where the infant would have to turn through 90 degrees, having observed the pointing hand, in order to locate the object). Infants of 14 months had no difficulty in following either type of point and many of these infants were also observed to point themselves. Collis and Schaffer (1975) noted that mothers not only looked at the same toy as the infant but often went on to label it verbally and comment on it. However, they did not present any systematic data on this point. Collis (1977) did present data on the incidence of naming by mothers. He found that when a mother named a toy the infant was much more likely to be looking at the toy that was being identified than at any other toy but the number of occurrences of naming was also small. On the other hand Murphy and Messer (1977) reported that only five out of 428 points were unaccompanied by maternal vocalizations and over 40 per cent of these vocalizations consisted of naming. However, these studies may not tell us very much about the relation between joint attention and naming outside the laboratory for it must be rare for a mother and an infant to sit down and be confronted, as they were in these studies, by a carefully arranged array of novel toys.

Studies by Murphy (1978) and Ninio and Bruner (1978) added the desired element of realism. Both studies report data from sequences of picture-book reading, an activity that mothers and infants commonly engage in. Murphy's is a laboratory study in which the mother was asked to look at the book with her infant and the subsequent behaviour was recorded. Ninio and Bruner report a longitudinal study of one mother-infant dyad between the ages of 8 and 18 months. The data in this study are naturalistic in that book-reading was spontaneously engaged in by the mother-infant dyad.

Naming, by the mother, is not a random affair. In Ninio and Bruner's study 76 per cent of all observed naming by the mother occurred in picture-book sequences. Within these sequences several other regularities were apparent. The mother's utterances were remarkably consistent over the period studied. They consisted of four key utterance-types: a call for attention from the infant, e.g. *look*; a query to the infant, e.g. *what's that*; a name, e.g. *it's a dog*, and feedback to a response from the infant, e.g. *yes*. Some, or all, of this sequence of utterances was regularly observed. Murphy also found that for all age-groups in her study a call for attention (*look/see*) was a frequent accompaniment of naming and pointing by the mother.

How did the infants' participation develop? At the beginning of Ninio and Bruner's study the infant was 8 months old and his participation in the dialogue while looking at picture-books was minimal by adult standards. However, in common with Snow's (1977) findings, Ninio and Bruner report that the interaction was structured by the mother as a well-regulated conversation with any minimal participation by the infant accepted as a turn in the conversation. Initially the mother accepted her infant's vocalizations as attempts at labelling, confirming his attempts by supplying the correct label. But, when instances of naming by the infant began at 14 months other vocalizations were now challenged with a *What's that*? query, where previously they had been accepted and unchallenged. When the infant at this age pointed to an object the mother still tended to name the object for the infant. Murphy's study reports similar results for infant pointing and maternal naming at 14 months. By 20 months things were different: the child tended to both point and name and when it was the mother who pointed she was likely to ask the child to name the object pointed at (in contrast to the behaviour of mothers of 14-month-old infants who were likely to provide the name themselves).

Is joint-attention the preverbal behaviour from which naming develops? I believe it is, provided that the joint attention occurs in the context of a ritual naming game. In the next section I will elaborate on this. But first I want to put one other issue in context. There are many ways of referring to an object, an object can have many names. As Brown (1958) has pointed out one object could be called 'dime', 'coin', 'money', 'change', 'it', 'that', and so on. In the face of the proliferation of possible referring expressions for any one object a number of writers (Harrison, 1972; Olson, 1970; Rommetveit, 1974) have been concerned to point out that the expression chosen on any particular occasion is one that serves to identify the referent in question from alternative objects. The central point of such accounts of reference is that the relation between a referring expression and a referent is not one of simply attaching an inevitable name or a description to an object but of choosing an expression that is both intersubjectively and contextually unambiguous. This fact has sometimes been used to dispute the importance of naming (cf. Bruner, 1975a; Olson, 1970). If the point is that things do not have *a* name then that point is well taken and an adequate theory of reference must specify how the relations between the different possible names any object may have actually develop. But that should not obscure the point, as it sometimes does, that the concept that things can be named still requires a developmental explanation. I now turn to that explanation.

A Theory of Naming

Looking at picture-books maximizes joint attention and it also appears to maximize naming by the mother as Ninio and Bruner (1978) have shown. Do children therefore learn the names of objects due to the fact that they repeatedly hear the same objects named while looking at picture books? Before answering that question, let us reconsider the words 'name' and 'naming'. In the situations discussed above I have implicitly regarded any word we would recognize as a noun in the adult language as a name, whether it was used by the child or the mother and I have regarded instances of the use of the word as instances of naming. I have no doubt that this is an accurate characterization of the mother's behaviour but it is not necessarily an accurate characterization of the child's behaviour because nothing has been done to show that the child possesses the concept that words name objects. I would suggest that the child does not possess the concept of naming when he or she first learns to pair words with objects in rituals such as story-book reading. My further suggestion is that the words the child initially learns in these situations are learnt as a means of participating in a ritual activity that concerns talking about objects. The child first learns the words and later learns that these words are names. The key element in learning that words are names is an insight by the child that *the behaviour previously engaged in* in ritual situations (such a picture-book reading) can be taken to constitute a special type of language-use: naming.

The appeal to the concept of insight is quite deliberate. Insight is a psychological process of common experience (though much ignored theoretically, with a few exceptions, notably Kohler, 1925). The basic achievement of an insight is a relatively sudden realization of some previously unseen structural relationship. While the environment can supply the child with names for objects and a context appropriate to the learning of these names it cannot supply the concept of naming. This the child must construct out of his or her own experience in the environment. We know very little about that construction process; indeed it has been frequently ignored in accounts of the development of naming. However, the product of the child's attempts to construct an understanding of the relation between words and objects I suggest to be a relatively sudden realization that the words are names for the objects. On the antecedent side the appeal to insight is motivated by the fact that the ritual nature of many naming games will be such that the child's use of names will have the characteristics and context appropriate to naming even if the activity is not conceptualized by the child as one of naming. (And even if the child learns to utter very few words in these situations the role of his or her comprehension of the mother's utterances must not be ignored.) The fact that children's initial use of names has often been regarded as referentially idiosyncratic (Bloom, 1973; Leopold, 1939-49; Piaget, 1945; Vygotsky, 1934; Werner and Kaplan, 1963) lends support to the view that the concept of naming does not precede the use of names. On the consequent side the appeal to insight is motivated by the sudden increase in naming that is frequently observed towards the middle of the second year (Halliday, 1975; Leopold, 1939-49; Nelson, 1973). Many of the names learnt during this period are the names of objects that are of no functional significance to the child. The child acts as if he or she had discovered that things have names by seeking to discover the names of objects encountered.

This account of naming raises a number of further issues. The first concerns the generality of the hypothesis. Not all children are observed to rapidly increase their vocabularies and undoubtedly not all children receive environmental support in the form of ritual naming games. The two facts may be related. The achievement of the concept of naming, I have suggested, crucially depends on the nature of the child's previous experience and one of the consequences of the attainment of the concept is a sudden increase in the vocabulary of names. But language is not only about naming, however crucial naming may be, and a child who does not learn many names will nevertheless learn to talk. If there are referential and expressive speakers as Nelson (1973) has suggested then the referential speakers may be the children who have played ritual naming games and the expressive speakers those who have not. That, at least, is what the present account predicts. This is not to say that expressive speakers learn to talk by bypassing the concept of naming but rather that the achievement of that concept will be slower and its manifestation less dramatic than in referential speakers.

A second issue concerns the development of grammatical structure. Rapid increases in naming are usually quickly followed by the emergence of two-word utterances (Halliday, 1975; Leopold, 1939-49; Nelson, 1973). There is little difficulty in accounting for this. If objects have words to represent them then, by generalization, so should actions, attributes, and so on. And as objects act, or are acted upon, then the child's description of these events will necessarily need to encode the different aspects of the event for which he or she has separate words. It is central to this account that the development of names for objects precedes the development of both structured speech and the development of words that describe actions and attributes. McShane (1980) in a longitudinal study of six children during their second year confirmed these predictions. All of the children's initial statements consisted of names. For four of the six children a sudden increase in naming occurred in the latter part of the second year and was followed, within a few weeks, by the development of words describing attributes and actions, both alone and in combination with names.

The account of naming offered above has concentrated its emphasis on the ritual interactions that may help a child to conceptualize the relationship between a name and an object. It is commonly held that the ability to conceptualize this relationship is dependent on the symbolic capacity that characterizes Stage VI of Piaget's theory of sensorimotor development. If this argument is valid then the conceptualization that I have characterized as insight may itself depend on more general processes of cognitive development.

References

Bates, E., Camaioni, L. and Volterra, V. (1975), 'The Acquisition of Performatives Prior to Speech', *Merrill-Palmer Quarterly*, *21*, 205-26

Bloom, L. M. (1973) *One Word at a Time*, Mouton, The Hague

Brown, R., (1958) 'How Shall a Thing be Called?', *Psychological Review*, *65*, 14-21

Bruner, J. (1975a) 'From Communication to Language', *Cognition*, *3*, 255-87

Bruner, J. (1975b) 'The Ontogenesis of Speech Acts', *Journal of Child Language*, *2*, 1-19

Collis, G. M. (1977) 'Visual Co-orientation and Maternal Speech' in H. R. Schaffer (ed.), *Studies in Mother-Infant Interaction*, Academic Press, London

Collis, G. M. and Schaffer, H. R. (1975) 'Synchronization of Visual Attention in Mother-infant Pairs', *Journal of Child Psychology and Psychiatry*, *16*, 315-20

Greenfield, P. and Smith, J. (1976) *The Structure of Communication in Early Language Development*, Academic Press, New York

Halliday, M. A. K. (1975) *Learning How to Mean*, Edward Arnold, London

Harrison, B. (1972) *Meaning and Structure*, Harper and Row, London

Kohler, W. (1925) *The Mentality of Apes*, translated by E. Winter, Routledge and Kegan Paul, London

Leopold, W. (1939-49) *Speech Development of a Bilingual Child*. Vol. 1: *Vocabulary Growth in the First Two Years*; Vol. 2: *Sound Learning in the First Two Years*; Vol. 3: *Grammar and General Problems in the First Two Years*; Vol. 4: *Diary from Age Two*, Northwestern University Press, Evanston, Ill.

Lyons, J. (1977) *Semantics*, Vols. 1 and 2, Cambridge University Press, Cambridge

McShane, J. (1980), *Learning to Talk*, Cambridge University Press, Cambridge

Murphy, C. M. (1978) 'Pointing in the Context of a Shared Activity', *Child Development*, *49*, 371-80

Murphy, C. M. and Messer, D. J. (1977) 'Mothers, Infants and Pointing: A Study of Gesture' in H. R. Schaffer (ed.), *Studies in Mother-Infant Interaction*, Academic Press, London

Neisser, U. (1967) *Cognitive Psychology*, Appleton-Century-Crofts, New York

Nelson, K. (1973) 'Structure and Strategy in Learning to Talk', *Monographs of the Society for Research in Child Development*, *38*, (1-2, serial no. 149)

Ninio, A. and Bruner, J. (1978) 'The Achievement and Antecedents of labelling', *Journal of Child Language*, *5*, 1-15

Olson, D. (1970) 'Language and Thought: Aspects of a Cognitive Theory of Semantics', *Psychological Review*, *77*, 257-73

Parisi, D. and Antinucci, F. (1973) *Essentials of Grammar*, translated by E. Bates, Academic Press, New, York, 1976

Piaget, J. (1945) *Play, Dreams and Imitation in Childhood*, translated by C. Gattegno and F. M. Hodgson, Routledge and Kegan Paul, London, 1951

Rommetveit, R. (1974) *On Message Structure*, Wiley, New York

Scaife, M. and Bruner, J. (1975) 'The Capacity for Joint Visual Attention in the Infant', *Nature*, *253*, 265-6

Snow, C. E. (1977) 'The Development of Conversation Between Mothers and Babies', *Journal of Child Language*, *4*, 1-22

Sugarman-Bell, S. (1978) 'Some Organizational Aspects of Pre-verbal Communication' in I. Markova (ed.), *The Social Context of Language*, Wiley, New York

Trevarthen, C. and Hubley, P. (1978) 'Secondary Intersubjectivity: Confidence, Confiding and Acts of Meaning in the First Year' in A. Lock (ed.), *Action, Gesture and Symbol*, Academic Press, London

Vygotsky, L. (1934)· *Thought and Language*, translated by E. Hanfman and G. Vakar, MIT Press, Cambridge, Mass., 1962

Werner, H. and Kaplan, B. (1963) *Symbol Formation*, Wiley, New York

7 SOUND SENSE

John Macnamara

Source: Macnamara, J., *Words for Things* (MIT Press, Cambridge, Mass., 1982), pp. 85-100

No belly and no bowels,
Only consonants and vowels.
— John Crowe Ransom, 'Survey of Literature'

Why do foreigners speak so quickly and indistinctly? It can hardly be that aside from English speakers the world is full of gabblers and mumblers. The explanation must be a perceptual one; over years we have learned the sounds of English and the words, and we can recognize them rapidly and easily. But even though we know a little French, we find we cannot keep pace with those who speak and perceive French as their native language. Foreigners, therefore, only seem to mumble, and any other explanation must sound parochial. Now there is a real sense in which we must sound to our infants as foreigners sound to us. Doubtless the parallel is not exact, since we have learned perceptual biases in learning English whereas the infant is, auditorily, a *tabula rasa*. Nonetheless, the infant has not as yet grown accustomed to and mastered the sound patterns of English, and until he does, much of what we say to him must sound like gibberish. Since names are part of this gibberish, learning them involves among other things sorting out those sound patterns that are names. In this chapter we shall be concerned with how he does it, and we shall begin with the question how sharp are the infant's ears? Is he able to detect all those contrasts in sound that are important in English, or do some of them have to be thrust upon him, in the way that the Scots and Irish thrust on the English the distinction between *loch* (lake) and *lock*. Part of the Englishman's trouble is that he doesn't seem to hear the difference.

The study of such phonological problems is of central importance to cognitive psychology. Failure to come to grips with them has led the two main branches of contemporary philosophy — phenomenology and the logical analysis of language that stems from Frege — into seriously simplistic proposals about concept formation. The standard position is that the problem of how to categorize objects is solved for the child by the names he hears applied to them. That presupposes that the problem of categorizing those phonological entities that we call names is psychologically simpler than that of categorizing nonlinguistic objects. To examine this presupposition will require a detailed analysis of phonological learning.

The first question we will ask is this: In learning the set of sound contrasts of English is the infant learning mainly to ignore certain auditory distinctions of which he is capable and settling for those that are essential in the system? Or is it the other way about; does he have to increase his acuity so that he can detect them all? Put this way, it is evident that the question is about the capacity for distinguishing among speech sounds that nature endows a child with. Is the capacity too sharp or too blunt initially?

Before answering, we may wonder that the question arises at all; why do we suppose that the capacity is not exactly right for English? The answer is that children of English-speaking parents are just as capable of learning Chinese or Tagalog as English. The sounds of English match those of other languages only in part. It follows that the set of speech sounds that the child learns depends on which language he learns. Nature, then, could not equip a child equally well to learn any natural language and at the same time set him up with a linguistic capacity to distinguish all and only the sounds of his mother tongue.

Experiments on Auditory Acuity in Infants

The past fifteen years or so have seen a remarkable increase in ingenious techniques for studying the abilities of very young infants in their first months. Some of the ingenuity has been applied to the infant's acuity in distinguishing speech sounds. The first studies were carried out by Peter Eimas and his colleagues (see Eimas, Siqueland, Jusczyk and Vigorito, 1971), and others have followed. Several were carried out at McGill by Sandra Trehub, and since I had the good fortune to witness some of these, I will describe them.

The main item of apparatus was a special nipple which was attached to a pressure transducer. This enabled the automatic recording of the number of times it was sucked in a given space of time. The nipple was placed in an infant's mouth and a pair of headphones over his ears. The infant's sucking controlled a tape recorder and determined whether or not he heard anything in the headphones. He heard a single speech sound until he grew tired of it and stopped sucking. Then came the interesting part of the experiment. At that point the tape recorder was started again. Some infants heard the same sound as before, but some heard a different sound. Interest attached mainly to whether the new stimulus provoked more sucking than the old one.

In one experiment Trehub & Rabinovitch (1972) contrasted the syllables *bah* and *pah*, and *dah* and *tah*. There were 30 experimental infants and 30 control ones aged between one and four months. Sucking patterns subsequent to the change of sound showed that the experimentals responded differently to the new sound. Infants who heard the same sound sucked little, those who heard a new one sucked vigorously. They must have noticed the change. Of course much more technical skill in phonetics is required to run this experiment successfully than this brief description suggests. Nevertheless the method does enable us to explore differences in sound to which infants are sensitive, and the experiment just described shows that they are sensitive to whether an initial consonant is voiced or not.

Even more interesting, this sensitivity was probably not learned in the brief period during which the infants had been hearing English. Streeter (1976) repeated the experiment with Kikuyu infants and obtained very similar results. The Kikuyu are a Bantu tribe whose language does not make the same voiced-voiceless contrast as English. Moreover, Trehub (1976) found that infants in English-speaking homes were sensitive to the contrast between [ža] and [ra] that is made in Czech, but not in English. Infants were highly sensitive to the contrast, though adult English speakers find it difficult to detect. The result is interesting, but there are difficulties with its interpretation. Perhaps adults could detect the distinction if there was some way of getting them to believe it wasn't speech, so that they did not attempt to bring their speech perception rules to bear.

So far the results suggest that the infant comes to speech with more acuity than he needs. However, there is a study by Eiler and Minifie (1975) in which infants did not react to the difference between [sa] and [za], a contrast that their native language would require them to attend to later. So the overall result is that infants appear to have more acuity than they need in some acoustic regions and perhaps less than they need in others. It would follow that they must be able to increase their acuity in some regions. There are only two ways in which this could happen. One is that their auditory systems become more sensitive with time. This happens because we know that the sound-frequency range to which infants are sensitive increases with age, perhaps owing to developments in the bone formations of the ear. The only other way is that they attend to finer differences. We know that this happens in the visual domain. Not everyone can read a thermometer at first, for example. Presumably infants must learn to attend to differences in certain sounds that their ear registered but that escaped their attention. (For a much more complete review of the literature on infant speech perception, see Jusczyk, 1980).

What about those acoustic regions where the infant appears to have more acuity than he needs? One might be tempted to say that in learning his mother tongue he has to blunt the acuity. But this may be a mistake. After all, as we grow older we do not lose our ability to detect slight differences in accent, and we can even recognize our friends by the sounds of their voices. There is something puzzling about this, but at the same time we must reocognize that the difference between, say, an Irish /r/ in the word *girl* and that of a Scotsman, though detectible, forms no part of the phonological system that we call English, or even of an Irishman's English, because that distinction is not built into the system.

The point is subtle, but it comes up again and again in psychology. For example, Corballis and Beale (1976) have written about the ability of various animals, including humans, to discriminate between simple figures and their mirror images, e.g., the letters *b* and *d*. They draw a sharp distinction between the ability to notice that the two are different when they are presented together and the ability to tell which is which when they are shown one at a time. Ability to *tell* which is which is difficult to pin down. For example, one could train an animal to seek food on the right when he encountered an arrow in this orientation →, and to seek it on the left when he encountered one like this ←. But he might merely learn to move to the side where the arrowhead is, without really knowing which is which. By varying his behavior consistently, he shows that he is responding to differences in the arrows, but he may have nothing equivalent to such labels as our 'right pointing' and 'left pointing.' True discrimination, then, as distinct from merely noticing differences, involves knowing which is which. It seems to involve some sort of cognitive labels that attach absolutely to the different stimuli, though the perceiver need not be conscious of the label.

To speak English with an Irish accent does not involve knowing the difference between an Irish /r/ and a Scottish one. It merely demands the ability to pronounce /r/ in the Irish fashion and to discriminate between it and all the other sounds that form the phonological system of an Irishman's English. Of course matters may be complicated in several directions. An Irishman may learn to mimic a Scottish accent and may know very well which pronunciation of *girl* is which. In that case he is clearly able to discriminate between the two.

An infant is not much concerned with accents, but he must learn the set of sound contrasts that are made in his mother tongue. It is not enough to learn to distinguish between them; he must learn to discriminate and know which word is which. For example, he must learn to tell which his mother is saying, *bad* and *pad*. When he talks, though at first he is allowed much latitude, he must eventually produce the appropriate sounds.

By the example I gave of accents, we must not be misled into supposing that within a particular accent the child's task presents no theoretical complications. His trouble, in a way, is the opposite — of discriminating between an Irishman's /r/ and a Scotsman's. He must learn to discount, phonologically, variation in speech sound that is accidental. He must, for example, discount difference in pitch, so that he does not assume a word is different just because his father pronounced it an octave lower than his mother. He must not assume that he is dealing with two different words because once a sound pattern was pronounced slowly or loudly and once quickly or softly. This is not to say that he cannot notice whether his mother spoke to him sharply or softly, and that he does not know what the difference means; neither is it to suggest that he cannot discriminate between his father's and mother's voices. The point is that he must not build such discriminations into the phonology of English, i.e., that system of speech sounds intrinsically involved in deciding which words are which in English. In other languages, like Chinese and

Vietnamese, certain differences in pitch are built into the phonological system; not in English. The child's task in learning the phonemes of English is much more complicated than that of discriminating figures and their mirror images. The child must discriminate among discriminations; he must keep the discrimination of his father's and mother's voices separate from the discrimination of the phonemes.

What I have to say is made awkward by the fact that the word *discriminate* tends to suggest an awareness of differences, and I am uneasy about the notion that infants become aware of phonemes. In fact I very much doubt that they do, since phonemes are theoretical constructs in linguistics. For example, the English phoneme /p/ has several allophones or different phonological realizations. At the beginning of a stressed syllable, it is heavily aspirated, as in *pit* or *appear*. In a consonant cluster it is almost entirely unaspirated, as in the word *spit*. The phoneme /p/ is a construct to explain the similarity between $[p^h]$ and $[p]$, the aspirated and unaspirated forms respectively, and to explain too the fact that English phonology does not employ the differences between the two to discriminate among words. Doubtless some readers will not remember having adverted to the difference between the two, and thus illustrate the perceptual collapsing of the two sounds into a single phoneme. However, what children must become aware of is which words are which, and presumably it is only at the level of words, or perhaps syllables, that awareness enters. The mechanisms of articulation do recognize the distinction, but they are largely unconscious in their operation.

The illustration just given serves a second purpose in drawing attention to a type of variation that, if he noticed it, an infant must discount in mastering the phonemic system of English. It is distinctly possible that the infant at first notices the difference, because in Hindi /p/ and /pʰ/ are phonemically distinct. The ability to detect the difference would help a baby learning Hindi, but if the same baby were learning English, he would have to learn to ignore it.

The Role of Meaning

Hitherto I have represented the child as pitting his auditory system against the phonology of English more or less in a vacuum. This is misleading because — certain maternal urgings to pronounce words aside — he encounters the words only in attempts to communicate. His mother's speech is usually trying to tell him something, or to do or stop doing something. Usually the environment, distinct from her words, provides a clue to what she means, and so can guide him to the phonemic system.

Take a Spanish speaker who is trying to learn English. He provides a lot of fun, and some embarrassment, in being unable to tell which word an English speaker is saying: *slip* or *sleep*, *dip* or *deep*, *pip* or *peep*. Unlike English, Spanish does not contrast /i/ as in *ship* and /I/ as in *sheep*. In view of what we know about the infant's auditory acuity, it seems that the Spanish speaker has learned to discount variations in the pronunciation of the Spanish /I/, and he has learned it so well that he now has difficulty in detecting a contrast that seems so clear to us. It is not just that he is unwilling to make a phonemic contrast between /i/ and /I/; he does not notice the difference that we make. I would like to claim that one good reason he does not is that it is never associated in Spanish with a difference in meaning, and luckily Roger Brown (1958, pp. 213-16) reports an experiment that gives some support.

Brown performed an experiment on the salience of vowel length for two groups of adult subjects, one in whose native language, English, vowel length is not phonemic and one, Navaho, in whose it is. There were fifteen subjects in each group, and the task was to classify colored chips as described by nonsense syllables. There were eight chips which varied by gradual degrees from red to blue. There were four nonsense words: [ma], [ma:], [mo], and [mo:]. It was believed that English speakers would readily notice the change from [a] to [o], but not the change in vowel length (increase in vowel length is denoted by a colon placed after a vowel). As expected, the English speakers made two classes of the chips corresponding to what they heard. The Navahos generally made four classes, corresponding to the four nonsense words.

When the English speakers had completed their task, Brown rejected their classification as erroneous. They then set to work again and all, eventually, made four classes corresponding to the four words. That is, they began to discriminate between words on the basis of vowel length. It is tempting to conclude that infants can hear many discriminations but tend to ignore those that do not make some difference to sense. The early discrimination would explain the accuracy of production; the collapsing of distinctions in perception would be a function of meaning. This seems highly probable, though we remind ourselves of what we have already noted, that difference in meaning does not always imply phonemic difference. *Stop* pronounced softly may mean something quite different from *stop* shouted, yet loudness is not phonemic in English; the word is the same.

I will conclude the case for meaning as a guide to phonology with some examples from Irish. I list some nouns under the headings nominative, genitive, and dative, and indicate changes in the initial sound that, granted certain syntactic conditioning, regularly occur in those cases:

Nominative	Genitive	Dative		English
[pobal]	[fobail]	[bobal]	=	people
[bád]	[váid]	[mád]	=	boat
[tarv]	[hairv]	[darv]	=	bull
[daul]	[g^{h}auil]	[naul]	=	blindman

The phonetic representation is rough but it will suffice for my purpose, which is to show that the infant who sets about learning Irish encounters a great deal of phonological variation in the sound of initial consonants. How does he cope with it? I suggest that he will be helped by the fact that he often knows what is being spoken about, whether because of some action of the speaker or of something in the environment. In other words, he is able to guess that the speaker is talking about the same thing and using the same word, though its sound changes quite a bit. For example, his father may say to him, 'Look at the boat [bád]', and go on to speak of 'the size of the boat [váid]' and of 'the sail on the boat [mád]'. Surely the meaning will be a clue that there are phonological rules at work on what is basically the same word. The form of the rule for the dative, for example, is roughly: change an unvoiced consonant to the corresponding voiced one: [p] → [b]; [t] → [d], and replace a voiced consonant by the homorganic nasal: [b] → [m]; [d] → [n].

The Irish examples are particularly interesting in that on the one hand [p] and [b] are phonologically (actually morphophonemically) related in the foregoing examples, and on the other hand they can also be phonemically distinct. For example, [paul] = *hole* and [baul] = *limb* are different words. The same holds for each of the other pairs in the set of examples as well as for many other pairs. It follows that the child must learn, on the basis of nonphonological cues — such as syntax and context — whether [baul] is the nominative of the word which means *limb* or the dative of that which means *hole*. He must learn to treat a single sound contrast now as a syntactically conditioned variation, now as a phonemic contrast. To a lesser extent the same is true of English. *Leaves* may be the present tense, third person, singular of the verb *leave*, or the plural of *leaf*. So we must not regard Irish as extraordinary in the demands it makes on infants.

The role of meaning must not be exaggerated, however, because if a child were guided by it alone he would soon be in serious trouble. *Small* and *little* mean very nearly the same thing, but a child who for that reason attempted to derive one from the other phonologically would be a phonological anarchist. Presumably, the child is endowed with a phonological similarity metric that tells him that *small* and *little* are too different to be related phonologically, but *leaf* and *leaves* are not. So both sound and meaning play a part in guiding the child to the phonology of his language.

One may wonder why I have so far ignored the many studies of phonological development in infants. The reason is that all the studies of child phonology that I have come across deal with the sounds that children produce, not with the sounds they can cope with when they are listening. These are quite different matters. If one is taking violin lessons, one can hear perfectly the sounds that the master plays but fail miserably to reproduce them. The perception and production of violin music are, alas, related by a tortuous chain of events. And so with speech sounds. We will not delay over their production, important though that may be in its own right. However, I feel compelled to draw attention, fleetingly, to one development in child phonology.

Kiparsky and Menn (1977) studied theories of how children learn to pronounce the speech sounds of their native language. The theories they studied had in common the belief that development is deterministic; that development follows a predetermined path. Kiparsky and Menn showed that the data refute all such theories. All children in a speech community do not follow the same path. An individual child will progress and backtrack in a curious manner. They cite, for example, Werner

Leopold's daughter, Hildegarde, who when still very young learned the word *pretty* and pronounced it correctly, initial consonant cluster and all. Though she continued to pronounce that word correctly, for a long while she pronounced no other consonant clusters. All words with such clusters she simplified in pronunciation. It was as though she could manage such clusters, but only with great difficulty, and so she adopted a strategy of simplifying.

Kiparsky and Menn (1977), and in a more detailed form Menn (1977) and Ferguson (1977), propose a highly 'cognitive' theory of the development of skill in phonology. The data lead them to conclude that phonology presents children with a set of articulatory puzzles, and children achieve temporary solutions of great ingenuity and originality.

Segmenting the Sound Stream

One of the problems that confronts the infant word learner in any language is that words are not normally given him distinctly in the flow of parental talk. What I mean is that the words are dovetailed together without clear indications of when one begins and ends. Nothing in speech corresponds to the spaces between words in print. There are short pauses, but they are occasioned by the stop consonants like /d/ and /b/. In pronouncing them we stop the airstream for a brief period that shows readily enough in a sonographic printout of speech. But such pauses are as likely to appear in the middle or end of words as at the beginning, so they are not much use as guides to segmentation. Indeed a speaker who is not being artificially pedantic normally modifies the end of each word and the beginning of the following one, so that the transition from one to the other can be effected without a pause and as effortlessly as is compatible with the requirement of being interpretable by his listener. Pauses are not a likely means of segmentation into words.

In some languages that stress the initial consonant of a word, stress can be a clue to the beginnings and, by implication, the ends of words. But English, to take just one language, provides the baby with no such regularity. Stresses can occur almost anywhere: e.g., *possible, impossibility, political, politics*. So English babies must have some other clue to words.

One possible clue has been explored by Hayes and Clark (1970). They followed up a suggestion of Harris (1955) that there are more constraints on phoneme combinations within a word than across words. The idea, which they call clustering, is simply this. The phonemes that occur within a word must always be pronounced together. There is not an equal obligation to place words side by side. It should follow that the number of different phonemes that can follow a particular phoneme within a word should be smaller than the number that can follow the final phoneme of a word. Hayes and Clark constructed a language of unutterable sounds, without syntax or meaning, but with just the constraints that they call clustering. They asked adults to segment continuous strings into wordlike segments. And they found that adults could, within the space of about three quarters of an hour, do so. It seems likely, then, that human beings come equipped with a system for using clustering effects for segmenting speech strings.

In an unpublished experiment Professor A. L. Bregman of McGill Psychology Department studied a different type of clue. He wondered whether frequently repeated patterns of sound, without clustering characteristics, are not readily detectible. He composed a sequence of eight pure tones as the pattern to study. To make sure they did not form a tune and thus exhibit clustering characteristics, the intervals between the tones were not those of any known musical scale. To make the pattern continuous and in that sense similar to speech, the tones were all connected. He embedded the pattern hundreds of times in a long series of randomly chosen pure tones. The intervals between occurrences of the pattern were random; each repetition of the pattern fitted into the stream without obvious trace.

The entire tape, about an hour in length, was played to listeners who were told that there was an eight-note pattern repeated at frequent intervals. Their task was to press a button every time they identified the pattern. There were some very slight indications of learning after long periods of listening, but it is virtually true that no subject identified the pattern.

However, if Bregman made one slight change, nearly everyone identified the pattern right off and continued to do so. If he played the pattern a few times in isolation, people had little difficulty in detecting it in the continuous string. In fact the effect is so powerful that Bregman has frequently used his tape for demonstration purposes in lecturing and whole audiences react as he expects them to.

Suppose a mother wants her child to say *cat*, it is very likely she will go through some such routine as the following:

Look at the cat, pet.
Look at the cat.
This is a cat.
A Cat.
Say, *cat*.
Cat.
Cat.

All the time the mother is narrowing down the context until the word is isolated. Most of us know from experience that mothers go on like this, but recently there has been intensive study of how mothers modify their speech when talking to young children, and it has been observed, not surprisingly, that they do single out words in the manner illustrated — see Snow (1976). In my opinion this combines well with Bregman's work to show that infants must be greatly aided by such isolation. It remains a problem, however, that the same words sound different when isolated and when embedded in speech. There was no such contrast between Bregman's isolated and embedded patterns. Still his work suggests a partial solution of how the child solves the problem. He must have a remarkably tenacious memory for patterns of speech sounds, and a remarkable skill in detecting them even though modified to fit into speech contexts.

For an excellent account of how adults manage to recognize familiar words in fluent speech, see Cole and Jakimik (1978). The interest of such work in the present context is that it shows the end product of the learning process — competence — that the child must eventually acquire.

References

Brown, R. (1958) *Words and Things*, Free Press of Glencoe, New York
Cole, R. A., and Jakimik, J. (1978) 'Understanding Speech: How Words are Heard' in G. Underwood (ed.), *Strategies of Information Processing*, Academic Press, New York
Corballis, M. C., and Beale, I. L. (1976) *The Psychology of Left and Right*,

Lawrence Erlbaum, Hillsdale, NJ

Eilers, R., and Minifie, F. (1975) 'Fricative Discrimination in Early Infancy', *Journal of Speech and Hearing Research*, *18*, 158-67

Eimas, P. D., Siqueland, E. R., Jusczyk, P., and Vigorito, J. (1971) 'Speech Perception in Infants', *Science*, *171*, 302-6

Ferguson, C. A. (1977) 'Words and Sounds in Early Language Acquisition', Papers and Reports on Child Language Development, Department of Linguistics, Stanford University

Harris, Z. S. (1955) 'From Phoneme to Morpheme', *Language*, *31*, 190-22

Hayes, J. R., and Clark, H. H. (1970) 'Experiments on the Segmentation of an Artificial Speech Analogue' in J. R. Hayes (ed.), *Cognition and the Development of Language*, John Wiley, New York, pp. 221-34

Jusczyk, P. W. (1980) 'Infant Speech Perception' in P. D. Eimas and J. L. Miller (eds.), *Perspectives in the Study of Speech*, Lawrence Erlbaum, Hillsdale, NJ

Kiparksy, P. and Menn, L. (1977) 'On the Acquisition of Phonology' in J. Macnamara (ed.), *Language Learning and Thought*, Academic Press, New York, pp. 47-78

Menn, L. (1977) 'Pattern, Control, and Contrast in Beginning Speech: A Case Study in the Development of Word Form and Word Function', Unpublished PhD thesis, Department of Linguistics, University of Illinois at Urbana-Champaign

Snow, C. E. (1976) 'Mothers' Speech to Children' in W. von Raddler-Engel and Y. LeBrun (eds.), *Baby Talk and Infant Speech*, Swets and Zeitlinger, Amsterdam

Streeter, L. (1976) 'Language Perception of 2-month-old Infants Show Effects of Both Innate Mechanisms and Experience', *Nature*, *259*, 39-41

Trehub, S. E. (1976) 'The Discrimination of Foreign Speech Contracts by Infants and Adults', *Child Development*, *47*, 466-72

Trehub, S. E., and Rabinovitch, M. S. (1972) 'Auditory-linguistic Sensitivity in Early Infancy', *Developmental Psychology*, *6*, 74-7

8 WORDS AND PLANS: EARLY LANGUAGE AND THE DEVELOPMENT OF INTELLIGENT ACTION

Alison Gopnik

Source: *Journal of Child Language, 9,* 1982, pp. 303-18

Introduction

A number of authors have noted that, in addition to using names, children use other, non-nominal, expressions when they begin to speak (Bloom, 1973; Nelson, 1973; Halliday, 1975). Moreover, the same non-nominal words appear again and again in accounts of early language, e.g. such words as *gone, there, oh dear, no more* and locative expressions like *down, up, in, out, on* and *off.* However, theoretical accounts of early meaning have concentrated on names (Nelson, 1974; Clark, 1974; Bowerman, 1978) or else have been concerned with the functions of early language or with the child's communicative intent (Greenfield and Smith, 1976; Halliday, 1975; MacShane, 1980) rather than with the meaning of individual words.

The suggestion has been made in a general way that some non-nominal words are 'expressive' or 'social' (Nelson, 1973) or that they encode cognitively significant concepts (Bloom, 1973). However, we do not know which concepts these expressions encode. Do they encode perceptual features, sensory-motor schemes, actions, events or relationships? We also do not know how the meanings of these expressions change as the child grows older. Finally, we do not know why children choose to use these expressions when they begin to speak and why they only use them in certain types of contexts. This article tries to answer these questions. First the results of a longitudinal study of nine English-speaking children between 1 and 2 years will be reported. The contexts in which these children used *gone, down, up, in, out, on* and *off, there, oh dear, no* and *more* were studied in some detail. By looking at the way in which children used and did not use these expressions it was possible to discover what concepts the expressions encoded and how the meanings of the expressions changed. I will argue that children initially used these expressions

83

to encode the aims of their actions or to encode abstract relationships between their actions, their aims and the world. In both cases they seemed to be concerned with PLANS, i.e. courses of action that are intended to achieve aims. Later, the children extended their use of some of these expressions so that they referred to events or relationships as well as plans.

In order to explain these results we need to look beyond the linguistic data. In the second part of this article some relevant work on cognitive development in infancy is reviewed. This literature suggests that infants come to understand the relationships between actions and aims in their first two years. More significantly, the child's understanding of these relationships changes at about the time he begins to use the non-nominal expressions.

Method

Three children were audio-taped in their homes for one hour every two weeks from the time they began to speak until they reached the two-word stage. Six more children were videotaped in their homes for a half-hour every month for six months. Three of these children were 1;3 when recording began, the other three were 1;6 when recording began. (For further details of this study see Gopnik (1980, 1981).)

The contexts in which each expression was produced were compared. It was assumed that if some common factor was present in all the contexts in which a child used an expression, the expression encoded that common factor. (Sometimes no single factor could be found, and the expression was assumed to be ambiguous.) The fact that the child used the same expression in different contexts was taken to indicate that he noticed some similarity between those contexts. He had some general concept that was exemplified in all those contexts. His word encoded that general concept. We could then say that concept was the meaning of the word for the child. For example, if the child always said *down* when objects moved downwards, we could assume that he had some general concept of downward motion, that this concept was encoded by his word *down* and that the word *down* meant 'downward motion' for the child.

Results

'Gone' and 'down', 'up', 'in', 'out', 'on' and 'off'.
Gone and the locative expressions, *down, up, in, out, on* and *off*
were usually used in the early period when the child tried to bring
about a certain kind of result.

All 9 children used *gone* 154 times to comment on
disappearances. (*Gone* was also used in some other ways.) In 121
of these contexts (78%) the children themselves made or tried to
make the object disappear. If we consider only the first half of the
period in which *gone* was recorded, 56 of 61 (92%) of the
utterances of *gone* occurred when the child made or tried to make
an object disappear. All the children used *gone* when they made
objects disappear before they used *gone* to comment on
disappearances they did not cause (see Table 1).

All 9 children used *down, up, in, out, on* or *off* 573 times in
locative contexts. In 401 (70%) of these contexts the children
made or tried to make an object move in a particular direction. In
the other contexts the children commented on the movement of
objects, or later, noted the spatial relationship of stationary
objects. In the first half of the recording period, 92 of 116 (79%) of
the utterances occurred when the children made or tried to make
objects move.

All the children used locative expressions when they made
objects move before they used them to comment on spatial
relationships. Seven of the children used locative expressions
when they made objects move before they used them to comment
on movements they did not cause. The remaining two children,
who were both in the oldest group, used the expressions in both
ways for the first time in the same session (see Table 1).

Gone and locative expressions were applied to a wide variety of
actions on a wide variety of objects. One child said *gone* when he
hid a ring under a pillow, turned away from a boring game and
turned over a piece of paper. Another child said *down* when he
knocked over a pile of blocks, sat on the floor and pulled down the
door of a toy cage. Also, the children used these expressions 83
times before they actually performed an action, 87 times when
they tried unsuccessfully to make an object disappear or move,
and 53 times when they tried to get someone else to make an
object disappear or move.

Table 1: Appearance of Expressions in Various Contexts[a]

Disappearance expressions (*gone, go gone, all gone*)
Group I

Jonathan	Henry	Rachel
Action +	Action +	Action +
Disappearance (5)	Disappearance (47)	Disappearance (3)
	Disappearance (16)	Disappearance (7)

Group II

John	Christian	Harriet
Action +	Action +	Action +
Disappearance (23)	Disappearance (15)	Disappearance (14)
		Disappearance (6)

Group III

Paul	Hannah	Anna
Action +	Action +	Action +
Disappearance (7)	Disappearance (2)	Disappearance (5)
	Disappearance (3)	Disappearance (1)

Direction expressions (*Down, up, in, out, on, off*)
Group I

Jonathan	Henry	Rachel
Action +	Action +	Action +
Movement (146)	Movement (70)	Movement (38)
Movement (66)	Movement (26)	Movement (13)
Position (12)	Position (21)	Position (9)
Other (4)	Other (4)	Other (2)

Group II

John	Christian	Harriet
Action +	Action +	Action +
Movement (40)	Movement (16)	Movement (29)
Movement (4)	Movement (2)	Movement (2)
Position (1)	Other (1)	Position (3)
		Other (2)

Group III

Paul	Hannah	Anna
Action +	Action +	Action +
Movement (26)/	Movement (8)	Movement (28)/
Movement (1)	Movement (4)	Movement (4)
Position (3)	Position (1)	Other (2)
Other (9)	Other (3)	

Success expressions (*there*,[b] *did it, good, right*)
Group I

Jonathan	Henry	Rachel
Success (111)		Success (71)

Group II

John	Christian	Harriet
Success (2)	Success (4)	Success (23)

Group III

Paul	Hannah	Ann
Success (29)	Success (5)	Success (4)

Failure expressions (*oh*[b] *dear, oh dash, oh no, can't, oh, come off*)
Group I

Jonathan	Henry	Rachel
Failure (90)	Failure (29)	Failure (21)

Group II

	John	Christian	Harriet
	Failure (11)		Failure (75)

Group III

	Paul	Hannah	Anna
	Failure (35)	Failure (26)	Failure (33)

No

Group I

	Jonathan	Henry	Rachel
	Refusal (32)	Refusal (52)	Protest (40)
	Failure (32)	Protest (33)	Refusal (10)
	Protest (24)	Failure (14)	Failure (14)
	Change of mind (32)	Propositional	Propositional
	Propositional	negation (5)	negation (7)
	negation (32)	Other (8)	Other (1)

Group II

	John	Christian	Harriet
	Refusal (2)		Protest (7)/
			Failure (3)
			Refusal (8)
			Change of mind (4)
			Other (1)

Group III

	Paul	Hannah	Anna
	Refusal (15)/	Protest (20)	Refusal (21)/
	Protest (5)	Refusal (7)/	Protest (20)/
	Failure (7)	Failure (6)	Failure (21)/
	Change of mind (1)	Change of mind (3)	Change of mind (15)
	Other (1)	Propositional	Propositional
		negation(15)	negation (6)

More

Group I

	Jonathan	Henry	Rachel
	Repeated actions	Repeated actions	Repeated actions
	on objects (30)	on objects (69)	on objects (11)
	Other (2)	Requests (3)	Object similarity (1)
		Other (1)	

Group II

	John	Christian	Harriet
			Repeated actions
			on objects (6)
			Object similarity (1)
			Other (1)

Group III

	Paul	Hannah	Anna
	Repeated actions	Repeated actions	Repeated actions
	on objects (4)	on objects (6)	on objects (22)
		Requests (1)	Requests (3)
		Object similarity (5)	Object similarity (9)
			Other (3)

Notes: a. Beside each context is the number of utterances that appeared in that context. The contexts are listed in the order in which they appeared.
b. *There* and *Oh* were sometimes ambiguous. Some children used *there* to indicate location and *oh* to indicate surprise as well as success and failure (for discussion, see Gopnik, 1980). Utterances in these contexts are not listed here.

The common factor in all these contexts was not the performance of a particular type of action. Any action might lead to the disappearance or movement of an object and the expression could be used before an action was performed. On the other hand, the common factor was also not simply a particular type of event, a disappearance or a movement. At least in the early period the event had to be the result of the child's action, although later the expressions were extended to events the child did not cause. Moreover, in some contexts, e.g. when the child tried unsuccessfully to bring about the event or tried to use someone else as an intermediary, the event might not take place at all. The common factor in these contexts was an aim, a possible future state of affairs that the child could act to bring about. The children commented on the fact that an event was the aim of their action, rather than commenting on the event or the action by itself.

Success and Failure Expressions

Another group of expressions were used to encode success and failure. Eight children used some expression, usually *there*, 240 times when they brought about an event successfully, e.g. when they placed a block on a tower without knocking over the other blocks or fitted a puzzle piece into a space. Eight children used some expressions, usually *oh dear*, 320 times in similar situations when the tower fell or the pieces did not fit. Like the other expressions I have described, these expressions were applied to a wide variety of actions and objects. However, unlike those expressions, they were also applied to actions with a wide variety of aims. Instead of picking out the aim of an action, these expressions picked out the relationship between an action and its aim. They encoded the fact that an action did or did not lead to its intended consequence.

No

Eight children used *no* in ways that also seemed to involve relationships between an action and its aim. Like *oh dear*, *no* was used 97 times when the child failed to achieve his aim because objects did not behave as he expected them to. However, *no* was also used 149 times when the child could not achieve his aim because of the actions of other people. For example, one child said *no* when the observer closed the lid of a tape recorder he was trying to open. Another child said *no* when her mother put one lid on a box and she wanted to put a different lid on the box. In these cases the child seems less concerned with the particular actions he performs or other people perform than with the conflicting consequences of those actions. The children also used *no* 157 times when they refused to bring about an event suggested by someone else. One child said *no* when he refused to give a toy to his brother, when he refused to go to the bathroom to have his hands washed, and when he refused to put a puzzle piece in a particular space. Finally, *no* was used 33 times when the child began to perform an action in order to bring about a certain result and then changed his mind. One child had a game in which he shook a container of dice and then uncovered the container so that the dice fell out. On one occasion he started to uncover the container, said *no*, and recovered the container and shook the dice some more.

What does the child mean when he uses *no* in these ways? What is the common factor in all these contexts? The child cannot be concerned solely with his actions. When the child fails, he acts, but his action does not achieve its aim. When other people's actions conflict with his aims, he may be unable to act. When he refuses to act or changes his mind, he is able to act but decides not to. *No* cannot simply encode the fact that the child's action fails, or that he wants to act but cannot, or that he decides not to act. None of these hypotheses will explain the use of *no* in all these contexts.

However, if we consider actions and aims instead of just actions, we can see that there is a common factor in all these contexts. In each case an aim could be achieved but is not. The reasons for this may vary — the objects may not behave as expected, other people may interfere or the child may simply decide not to act. In all these cases, the child notes the mismatch between a possible future state of affairs, a state of affairs he could bring about by acting in a certain way, and the actual state of affairs. The jigsaw piece could go in the space, the recorder lid could be open, the child's hands could be washed and the dice could fall out of the box. All of these events would be the result of the child's actions. However, none of these events actually happens.

Eventually, *no* came to be used 65 times to negate propositions. One child commented on the fact that he did not wear clothes at the swimming pool by saying *John-John clothes on no*. However, the children only used *no* in this way after they used *no* to comment on actions and aims (see Table 1).

More

Seven children used *more*. *More* was used 148 times when children acted on an object and then repeated or tried to repeat that action on the same object or on a similar object. One child said *more* after she had placed a piece in a jigsaw puzzle as she went to place another piece in the puzzle. Another child said *more* after he had closed the tape recorder lid as he went to close it again. Sometimes children said *more* when they repeated a complex series of actions leading to a particular result. One child said *more* after she had built a tower of dominoes and knocked it down as she went to rebuild the tower. Children also said *more* when they tried unsuccessfully to repeat an action on an object. One child said *more* after he had eaten a piece of candy as he searched for another piece of candy to eat. Children used *more* 7 times when they request that someone else repeat an action on an object. One child said *more* as he asked his mother to mark his face with an eye pencil after she had done so once

What does the child mean when he uses *more* in these contexts? *More* cannot encode just the fact that an action is repeated. Children did not use *more* when they simply repeated an action or when they repeated an action on a different type of object. The actions had to be similar, but the objects that were acted upon also had to be similar. On the other hand, in the early period the children used *more* only when they acted on similar objects, not just when objects were similar. If we think in terms of aims of actions, rather than in terms of actions, objects or events this pattern of use makes more sense. Suppose *more* encodes the fact that the child has achieved an aim, and now wants to achieve a similar aim. In order to do this he must not only repeat his action, he must repeat it on an object that is similar to the object he acted on before. He can ensure that his action will succeed only by acting in this way. The fact that children used *more* before they acted, when they acted unsuccessfully, when they used an intermediary and when they repeated a complex series of actions also suggests that they were concerned with aims of actions rather than actions or events by themselves.

I am arguing, then, that when the child says *more* he is concerned with the aims of his actions, just as he is when he says *gone*, *down*, *there*, *oh dear* and *no*. He is concerned with a possible future state of affairs that he can act to bring about. Here, however, he does not mark what his aim is, as he does when he uses *gone* and *down*, but instead notes that this possible future state of affairs is like a past state of affairs, a state of affairs he has already brought about, and that it will be brought about by similar actions on similar objects. *More*, like *no*, *oh dear* and *there* marks a rather abstract relationship between the child's aims, his actions and the real world.

Five children eventually used *more* 22 times to comment on the similarity of objects, even though they did not repeat actions on those objects. One child said *more* as she placed a green pencil next to another green pencil. However, the children only used *more* in this way after they had used it when they repeated actions on objects (see Table 1).

Discussion

The meaning of 'gone', 'down', 'up', 'in', 'out', 'on', 'off', 'there', 'oh dear', 'no', and 'more'. We can begin to answer our first question, i.e. what concepts *gone*, locative expressions, success and failure expressions, *no* and *more* encode. These expressions are not simply social devices, they do encode aspects of the world, but they do not solely encode actions, objects or events, or even relationships between objects. Perhaps the best way to characterize the meaning of these expressions is to introduce the notion of a PLAN. A plan is an action or a series of actions that are performed in order to bring about a certain event. We can contrast plans with actions on the one hand and aims on the other. We may act [, but] without acting in order to bring about an event. Or we may wish to bring about an event without knowing how to go about it. When we have a plan, we want to bring about an event, and we believe that we can do this by acting in a certain way. In plans, actions and events are related. The action is the means by which a certain end, namely the occurrence of an event, is achieved.

Plans can be classified in terms of aims. For example, we can classify together all plans that will lead to the disappearance of an object or to a movement of the object. Expressions like *gone* or *down* encode classes of plans of this sort. Plans can succeed or fail. Expressions like *there* and *oh dear* mark these aspects of plans. Plans may not be successfully implemented, either because the planner simply decides not to implement them, or because he rejects the consequence of a plan, or because they conflict with the plans of others or simply because they fail. *No* marks this aspect of plans. *More* encodes the fact that a plan is to be repeated.

In addition we have plans before we implement them, which helps to explain why *more*, *gone* and *down* are used before an action is actually performed or its intended consequences ensue. Plans may involve other people; we may decide that the most effective way of producing a certain result is to get someone else to act in a particular way. This might explain the occasional use of these expressions in contexts that involve requests.

We can also begin to answer our second question: there seems to be a general pattern in the development of these expressions. The expressions are applied to plans at first, but later their meaning is extended. They come to encode events or relationships that are not involved in plans. *Gone* and locative expressions were eventually used to refer to events that were not the result of the child's actions and locative expressions also eventually referred to relationships between objects. *No* was eventually used to negate propositions and *more* was used to mark the fact that two objects were similar. It is interesting that *no* and *more* which initially marked abstract aspects of plans, came to mark equally abstract aspects of objects.

However, in order to answer our third question — why do these expressions encode these concepts? — we will have to digress and consider the development of these concepts.

The Development of Plans

We have seen that we can infer the existence of plans from the child's linguistic behaviour. We must assume that certain expressions encode aspects of plans if we are to explain the way children use these expressions. But we might also infer the existence of plans from the child's non-linguistic behaviour. For instance, when a child completes a jigsaw puzzle, trying each piece in different spaces, turning a piece that does not fit at first and searching for missing pieces, we feel that he is performing these actions in order to bring about the completion of the puzzle. We feel that he is implementing a rather complex plan. Psychologists have tried to use these kinds of observations to construct an account of the development of intelligent action. Piaget (1953, 1954, 1962) has provided the most extensive and complete account of the development of plans, but his work has been supplemented and altered by the work of writers like Bower (1974), Bruner (1966), and Papousek (1969). The following account tries to integrate Piaget's observations and theories and the more recent work.

Even when they are only a few weeks old infants notice that their actions are followed by events. They will then reproduce an action in order to reproduce the event that followed it. If a picture appears every time the infant sucks, or a set of flashing lights is activated every time he turns his head, he will rapidly learn to suck or turn his head appropriately and he seems to anticipate the result of his action (Lipsitt and Kaye, 1964; Papousek, 1969). In some ways these early behaviours look like plans. After all, the infant is acting in order to bring about an event. However, his actions at this stage are severely limited in two respects. First, he can only reproduce actions that he has produced spontaneously, like sucking or turning his head. If his original action is unsuccessful, he will not alter it or try something new. Second, he does not seem to understand the connection between his action and the event that follows it. He is perfectly willing to accept the arbitrary connection between head-turning and flashing lights. Also, very young infants do not seem to be disturbed if the contingencies in an experiment are changed so that an action that was effective becomes ineffective and another action produces the interesting event (Lipsitt, 1969; Monnier, 1977).

While this acceptance of arbitrariness can improve the infant's performance on experimental tasks, it is a disadvantage in the real world. Piaget (1953) and Bower (1974) have noted that young infants tend to use 'magical procedures'; they inappropriately generalize successful actions. They seem to believe that if an action produced an event once, it will produce the event in entirely different circumstances and it will also produce other interesting events. When Jacqueline learns that pulling a string makes the hood of her pram move, she pulls the string to get a watch and a book to move (Piaget, 1953, p. 202). Nine-month-olds who have learned how to pull on a support to get an object on top of it will also pull on the support when the object is placed to one side of it (Piaget, 1953, p. 285; Bower, 1979, p. 130). Nine-month-olds who have found an object under a cup once will search under the cup when the object is hidden in another container (Piaget, 1954, p. 53; Bower, 1974, p. 211). In short, young infants seem to link particular actions and particular events rather arbitrarily. They do not seem too understand how their action brings about the event, or that a variety of different actions could bring about the event, or that some actions could not possibly bring about the event.

There are several developments in the first year that allow the infant to overcome the limitations of his early actions. First, he begins to generate new actions on objects. Seven-month-olds systematically apply all the actions they can think of to new objects (Piaget, 1962; Bruner, 1973). Twelve-month-olds also systematically vary the actions they perform on objects. They hit a toy hard and then hit it gently, they drop it close to the ground and then drop it from a height (Piaget, 1962). In this way the infant finds out about the effects of actions in different circumstances and the effects of different types of actions. He is no longer limited to reproducing actions he has produced in the past.

At the same time the infant learns more about the world, and he becomes less willing to consider action–event sequences that do not fit his theories of objects. This change can make some tasks more difficult for older infants than for younger ones. For example, Bower (1979, p. 131) reports that infants less than nine months old can easily learn to kick, in order to break a light beam so as to make a picture appear, although from the infant's point of view there is no connection between his action and the event that follows it. Older infants have much more difficulty learning this arbitrary connection. Similarly, Monnier (1977) reports that infants older than nine months have trouble dealing with changed circumstances. If an infant explores the experimental apparatus thoroughly and discovers that a certain action leads to a certain event, he will not change his behaviour when the experimenter changes the apparatus so that a new action becomes effective. Young infants can deal with such changes. The older infants seem to feel that they have discovered a real connection between the action and the event that follows it and they are not willing to give up this theory easily. This change also leads to the gradual disappearance of 'magical procedures'. Children begin to understand that their actions will only produce an event if there is some connection between the action and the event.

These two developments lead to an important change in the child's actions. Some time after he is a year old he becomes able to produce an action in order to bring about an event, even if he has never seen that action to that event before. He does this by using a kind of experimental sub-routine. When he wants to produce an event, he tries a variety of different actions on objects, just as he does when he plays with new objects. However, he would not get very far if he had to try all the possible actions before he discovered the correct one. Fortunately, his theory of the world allows him to consider only some action–event sequences. He tries only those actions that have some connection with the event he is trying to produce. Moreover, he monitors the effects of his actions, and this information shapes his subsequent attempts. In short, he solves problems by trial and error.

This change in the child's behaviour is nicely demonstrated in an experiment done by Koslowski and Bruner (1972). The infant is presented with a rotary lever which has a toy placed at one end. In order to get the toy he has to swivel the lever so that the far end moves towards him. In order to produce an event — the movement of the toy towards him — he has to produce an action, swivelling the lever, even though he has never experienced the action–event sequence before. Children who were less than a year old could not solve this problem. They would only try actions that had brought about the desirable event in the past, like grabbing the toy or pulling the lever directly towards them. Older children seemed to realize that a variety of actions might produce the event. They would try manipulating the lever in various ways, and swivelling it to different positions, watching the effects of their actions. Eventually, they figured out how to get the toy.

Piaget (1953, p. 298) describes similar changes in the child's problem-solving behaviour at a similar age. When she is a year old, Lucienne cannot use a stick to draw a distant object towards her. She will only try strategies that have succeeded in the past like pulling the support the object rests on. Four months later she sees a distant toy, picks up a stick and begins to experiment. She touches the toy with the stick, pushes it back and forth, pushes it further from her and pulls it towards her. Finally, she uses the stick to get the object.

What are the conceptual prerequisites for this sort of behaviour? First, the infant has to understand that a variety of different actions, including new actions, could lead to the event. At the same time he must be able to consider and to reject certain actions that do not lead to the event. He does this before he acts, when he decides which sorts of actions to try, and after he acts, when he abandons unsuccessful strategies. He must also note the success or failure of specific attempts, i.e. note that certain actions do or do not bring about the event, and use that information to shape subsequent attempts. He must also be able to compare action–event sequences and decide whether or not they are similar. He must calculate whether an action that had a certain effect once will also have that effect in slightly different circumstances or on a slightly different object.

The three-month-old's behaviour, on the other hand, does not seem to require these abilities. The three-month-old does not consider alternative actions and decide whether or not to try them. Instead he simply produces the action that has succeeded before. Success and failure only affect the frequency of his actions, not their shape. If he fails, he goes on trying the same action less and less enthusiastically until he gives up altogether. Nor does he need to consider the similarity of action–event sequences, since each event is only linked to one action.

After the child is 18 months old, his behaviour changes again. Now he can sometimes skip the experimental sub-routine and immediately produce the new action that will produce a new event. In the Koslowski and Bruner experiment, the older infants would immediately swivel the lever towards them. Similarly, Piaget (1953, p. 335) reports that Laurent immediately used a stick to obtain an object without a period of trial and error.

We do not know exactly how the child moves from solving problems by trial and error to solving them by using insight. The most plausible explanation is that he reflects on his own behaviour and experience and constructs a model of the world which includes his own actions. This model allows him to consider hypothetical actions and to predict the outcome of those actions. In this way he can do experiments with his head rather than his hands. This change in the child's plans seems to be part of a general shift that takes place when the child is about 18 months old. Before this age the child's cognitive system appears to be firmly rooted in perception and action. After 18 months he develops a more conceptual and reflective system. Piaget (1953) has described this change in terms of a shift from the sensory-motor period to the pre-operational period; Bruner (1966) has described it in terms of a shift from enactive to ikonic representation; and Bower (1979) has talked of a shift from a perceptual to a conceptual view of the world.

The Development of Plans and Early Words

How are these cognitive developments related to the development of the early expressions I have previously described? The plans that are the subject of these expressions are more like the structures that appear after the child is a year old than like the three-month-old's structures.

The first group of expressions, e.g. *gone* and *down*, encode the fact that a wide variety of different actions, including new actions, are intended to bring about the same type of event. In order to develop such concepts, the child must be able to understand that an event may be brought about by many different actions, not just by actions that led to the event in the past. This ability is one of the things that make the one-year-old's plans so different from the three-month-old's. For the three-month-old, only one particular type of action is linked to each event, he tries only the action that led to the event in the past. The one-year-old tries a variety of different actions and variations on actions in order to bring about the event.

The concepts that are encoded by the second group of expressions — success and failure expressions, *no* and *more* — also concern plans, but they are more abstract. In order to plan effectively, the one-year-old has to note whether or not an action led to the event he was trying to produce; he has to note the success or failure of particular actions. But in order to develop general concepts of success and failure — the sorts of concepts encoded by *there* or *oh dear* — he must generalize about these particular observations of success and failure. He must see that the same thing is going on when he tries to fit a square block in a round hole, and when a tower topples as he places a large block on top of it.

Similarly, in order to plan effectively the one-year-old has to consider alternative actions and reject those actions that do not lead to his particular goal. He has to decide not to perform certain actions because of the consequences of those actions. He must also decide not to repeat actions that he has tried but which have failed. The concept encoded by *no* involved a generalization across all these cases. When he refuses to act, or changes his mind about acting, he does not perform a certain action because of its consequences; when he fails, or his plans conflict with the plans of others, his actions fail to achieve their goal.

Finally, in order to plan effectively the one-year-old must be able to compare different action–event sequences and decide whether they are similar. In order to develop a general concept of repetition, like the concept encoded by *more*, he has to be able to compare these comparisons. He has to understand that two action–event sequences that are similar are like two other action–event sequences that are similar

In short, while the one-year-old has to compare actions and events and make decisions about them, he does not have to generalize about those comparisons and decisions. But expressions like *there*, *oh dear*, *no* and *more* encode just these sorts of generalization. In order to use expressions in this way the child must at least have reached the 12- to 18-month-old stage in the development of intelligent action; he must have developed a fairly sophisticated planning system. But he must also be able to do something more difficult — he must be able to step back and consider the workings of that system and make generalizations about it. The development of the higher-level concepts encoded by *there*, *oh dear*, *no* and *more* could depend on some of the same changes that allow the child to develop insight after he is 18 months old. In both cases the child has to be able to reflect on his plans and to operate on a model of his plans. In one case this allows him to construct hypothetical action–event sequences and to make predictions. In the other case it allows him to make generalizations about his plans.

I am arguing then, that the concept of a class of different actions leading to the same consequence — the sort of concept encoded by *gone* and *down* — is the sort of concept that is developed between 12 and 18 months, and that this is the sort of concept that underlies the development of trial-and-error problem solving. The more abstract concepts encoded by success and failure expressions, *no* and *more*, are more like the reflective concepts that develop after 18 months — the concepts that underlie the development of insight. Unfortunately, there was no way of knowing exactly what stage of cognitive development the children in this study had reached. However, most of these expressions were recorded for the first time when the children were between 1;3 and 2;0 (see Table 2). In fact, some of the children, especially the three 18-month-olds (who were already speaking at the start of their study) had probably begun to use the expressions some time before the expressions were first recorded. This suggests that the children used *there*, *oh dear*, *no* and *more*, and perhaps even *gone* and direction expressions, to encode new concepts (concepts they were in the course of developing) rather than simple and well-established concepts. For example, I have argued, on the basis of the cognitive literature, that children do not develop the general concept of the success of a plan until some time after they are 18 months old. But the children in this study began to use a term to encode this concept between 16 months and 20 months, that is, at just about the same time we would expect them to be developing such a concept.

Table 2: Age in Months of Children when Each Expression was First Recorded

| | Group I | | | Group II | | | Group III[a] | | | |
	Jonathan	Rachel	Henry	John	Christian	Harriet	Paul	Hannah	Anna	Mean
Gone	24	22	20	17	18	15	18	18	18	18.9
Down	12	18	23	16	18	15	20	18	19	17.7
No	22	19	13	20	–	16	18	18	18	18
More	22	20	20	–	–	17	23	21	18	20.1
Failure expressions	21	22	26	19	–	17	20	19	18	19.6
Success expressions	19	17	–	20	19	16	18	19	19	18.4

Note: a. The children in Group III were first recorded at 18 months. Expressions recorded at that age may have appeared earlier.

This relationship between cognitive development and the development of these early words may help to explain why children use these expressions and why they use them in particular types of contexts. The concepts encoded by these expressions are rather different from the concepts encoded by these expressions in the adult language. The children are not simply acquiring the adult meanings. Nor do these concepts play a central role in the semantic system of the adult language in the way that, say, temporal concepts or concepts of agency do. While some of these expressions, particularly *no* and *more*, are used to achieve social ends, they are also used in non-social ways. However, the psychological literature suggests that these concepts are cognitively significant for 1- to 2-year-olds. In their second year, children explore the ways that their actions can bring about events.

Other authors, such as Bloom (1973), Sinclair (1973) and Clark (1974), have suggested that early words encode cognitively significant concepts. However, these authors have generally argued that the expressions encode relatively simple and well established concepts. In fact, Clark has suggested that early names encode aspects of an innate perceptual system. The force of their arguments has been that the child can develop expressions that encode concepts only if he has already developed the concepts themselves.

The classical cognitive view of early language treats the child's acquisition of language as if it were like an adult's acquisition of a second language. The child had already developed a cognitive 'language', and he maps the terms of the adult language on to the concepts of his cognitive system, as an English speaker might map the words of French on to the English words he has already acquired. This model leaves open the question of why the child chooses to translate some parts of the cognitive language rather than others. However, if the child's early words encode new and difficult concepts rather than simple and well-established ones, another analogy might be more appropriate. The child might learn at least some early words in the way that an adult learns the terms of a science. Scientific terms do not map directly on to the terms of ordinary language. Instead they encode new concepts — concepts the adult is in the process of trying to understand. The acquisition of scientific terms and scientific concepts go hand in hand. Moreover, an adult learning a science is motivated to acquire terms that encode concepts that are at the frontiers of understanding, rather than terms that simply rephrase what he already knows, or terms that encode totally unintelligible concepts. Children between 15 and 24 months old are trying to understand the nature of intelligent action — how plans succeed or fail, how to reject certain courses of action, and how to ensure that a plan that succeeded once will succeed again. I would suggest that they use words like *gone*, *down* and especially, *there*, *oh dear*, *no* and *more* because they are relevant to these problems.

References

Bloom, L. (1973) *One Word at a Time: The Use of Single-word Utterances Before Syntax*, Mouton, The Hague

Bower, T. G. (1974) *Development in Infancy*, Freeman, San Francisco

Bower, R. G. (1979) *Human Development*, Freeman, San Francisco

Bowerman, M. (1978) 'The Acquisition of Word Meanings: An Investigation of

Some Current Conflicts' in N. Waterson and C. Snow (eds.), *Development of Communication: Social and Pragmatic Factors in Language Acquisition*, John Wiley, London

Bruner, J. S. (1966) 'On cognitive growth' in J. Bruner, R. Olver and P. Greenfield (eds.), *Studies in Cognitive Growth*, John Wiley, New York

Bruner, J. S. (1973) 'The Organisation of Early Skilled Action', *ChDev*, *44*, 1-11

Clark, E. (1974) 'Some Aspects of the Conceptual Basis for First Language Acquisition' in R. Schiefelbusch and L. Lloyd (eds.), *Language Perspectives: Acquisition, Retardation and Intervention*, University Park Press, Baltimore

Gopnik, A. (1980) 'The Development of Non-nominal Expressions in One to Two Year Old Children', unpublished doctoral dissertation, Oxford University

Gopnik, A. (1981) 'The Development of Non-nominal Expressions: Why the First Words Aren't About Things' in D. Ingram and P. Dale (eds.), *Child Language: An International Perspective*, University Park Press, Baltimore

Greenfield, P. and Smith, J. (1976) *Communication and the Beginnings of Language: The Development of Semantic Structure in One-word Speech and Beyond*, Academic Press, New York

Halliday, M. (1975) *Learning How to Mean: Explorations in the Development of Language*, Edward Arnold, London

Koslowski, B. and Bruner, S. (1972) 'Learning to Use a Lever', *ChDev*, *43*, 790-9

Lipsitt, L. P. (1969) 'Learning Capacities of the Human Infant' in R. J. Robinson (ed.), *Brain and Early Behaviour*, Academic Press, London

Lipsitt, L. P. and Kaye, H. (1964) 'Conditioned Sucking in the Human Newborn', *PsychonScience*, *1*, 29-30

MacShane, J. (1980) *Learning to Talk*, Cambridge University Press, Cambridge

Monnier, C. (1977) 'La genèse de l'expérimentation', unpublished doctoral thesis, Free University of Brussels, cited in Bower, 1979

Nelson, K. (1973) *Structure and Strategy in Learning to Talk. Mongr.Soc.Res.Ch.Dev*, *38*, Nos. 1-2

Nelson, K. (1974) 'Concept, Word and Sentence: Interrelations in Acquisition and Development', *PsychRev*, *81*, 267-85

Papousek, J. (1969) 'Individual Variability in Learned Responses in Human Infants' in R. Robinson (ed.), *Brain and Early Behaviour*, Academic Press, London

Piaget, J. (1953) *The Origins of Intelligence in the Child*, Routledge & Kegan Paul, London

—— (1954) *The Child's Construction of Reality*, Routledge & Kegan Paul, London

—— (1962) *Play, Dreams and Imitation in Childhood*, Routledge & Kegan Paul, London

Sinclair, H. (1973) 'Language Acquisition and Cognitive Development' in T. E. Moore (ed.), *Cognitive Development and the Acquisition of Language*, Academic Press, New York

SECTION IV: SOCIAL FACTORS IN EARLY DEVELOPMENT

A number of chapters in this collection have presented reviews of the early stages of communicative development: here Reilly *et al.* consider the topic again, but this time from a more social perspective. There has been an increasing acceptance over the last ten years that what an infant understands at any given time is going to be of crucial importance to the course of her development in the sphere of language. It is patently obvious that any mute representative of the higher mammals has some non-verbal grasp of the relation between itself and objects and events in its environment (although it is only following the discussion opened by Griffin in his book *The Question of Animal Awareness* (1976) that the academic world has come into any agreement with the lay-person's idea of animal abilities). Animals 'know' certain things, and this knowledge guides their activities: infants 'know' certain things, and this guides what they try to code into words when they begin to speak. This is, in essence, what people are referring to when they talk of 'the cognitive basis of language development': language codes knowledge. Much of mainstream American and Piagetian developmental research has emphasised the individual prowess of the infant. The infant is viewed as an hypothesis-tester, devising solutions to problems encountered in the environment, and then acting on the bases of these solutions (hypotheses) until proved incorrect, whereupon new hypotheses (solutions) must be devised. The current state of solutions (knowledge) will provide the basis for whatever the infant attempts to express (code) when she uses a word. In this approach, the social environment is seen as an appendage. It may determine what kinds of things the infant may make hypotheses about, and what opportunities the infant may have to make hypotheses. An institutionalised child, for example, may show a delayed development through being presented with fewer opportunities to exercise her hypothesis-generating abilities, either because her social environment is not very rich in the opportunities it presents her (environmental deprivation hypothesis), or because it affects her emotional state (maternal deprivation hypothesis) and so 'turns her off making hypotheses'.

Reilly *et al.* provide us with research in a different mould. They do not see the infant as self-reliant in the creation of her knowledge, but rather as a part of society. Society, represented by her mother, actively enters into development in the way it presents problems to the child. In the same way that a mother in a non-technological society will begin to wean her child on to solid food by first chewing that food before passing it on to the child who lacks sufficient teeth, so a mother will transact the world to a child who lacks the intellectual capacity to get her 'teeth' into a complex problem. Adults can act towards their children in ways that barely present them with problems to hypothesise about. It is not that the infant, confronted with an immensely complex problem, bravely hazards a guess at the solution dredged from her own resources: rather, we as informed adults simplify the problem for her as much as we can. The child's resources are pitted against the world in conjunction with those of her immediate cultural ambassadors. As her knowledge increases, so her parents change their mode of transacting. Reilly *et al.* document this change in one sphere of development relevant to language. But they are not documenting *child* development, they are documenting *mother-child* development: the environment does not begin as a complex one for the child to cope with on her own, it starts off as a simple one due to the mediance of the mother, and gets more complex as the child appropriates more and more of her mother's problem-solving abilities to her own repertoire. This is a concrete instance of the abstract points made by Macmurray (see introduction to Section I).

Service, in a more general and speculative paper, considers the possible differences in the adult's abilities to 'simplify' the world to a child through interaction. She points to a very broad theoretical view in which the ability to articulate the world to oneself is set in the context of the social world. Roughly, if the social ecology of an adult's interactions with others requires taking the other person's point of view as a consistent strategy for effective communication, then that adult will be well practised in breaking down information to be transferred into its component parts. This practice will facilitate the adult's ability to simplify the infant's task, because she will take the infant's view into account, and try to pitch what she does with the child at what she perceives the child's level to be. Doubtless all adults attempt this, but on the basis of what they take to be the abilities of their children (Tulkin and Kagan, 1972) and their facility in breaking tasks down, they will differ in their goal of making the child's task more manageable. While we will be taking up this theme again in relation to Robinson's paper (see Section V), we should note that the breadth of Service's view makes its empirical substantiation very difficult. It falls into a potentially emotive area, and it could be argued that its implications are open to a great deal of political misuse and misinterpretation. Hence, given its speculative nature, it might not have been included here. While we will be dealing with these issues at more length in the course text, we may note here that broad, synthetic views should be welcomed in any area: thus we include it.

The final paper in this section, by Goldin-Meadow and Feldman, may appear rather odd in this context. On the face of it, it argues for a high innate component to language development, such that grammar may emerge without any input at all. We would suggest there is another interpretation: that these children's abilities reflect the demands of social interaction, and that those demands can be seen most clearly because of the magnifying effect of their handicap. Remember that the only handicap disadvantaging these children is their inability to hear what is said to them; there is no reason to suppose that they cannot see what is 'said' to them with any less proficiency than the younger children in the study by Reilly *et al.* Further, we have looked at the formidable problems facing the hearing child in decoding the sound system of spoken language (Macnamara, Section III). Early attempts at speaking are certainly very creative efforts, pursued within the constraints of the child's abilities. Hearing children, then, are essentially creating ways of expressing themselves, using the resources they possess. It is not surprising that deaf children do the same. In fact, the majority of hearing children will undertake some elaboration of their non-vocal gestural system at the same time as they are learning to articulate vocal 'gestures'. Some hearing children will even annoy their parents by being very reluctant to speak, and conduct much of their conversation by a pantomime similar to that described in the chapter. And what adult, holidaying in a foreign land, has not had occasion to fall back on the same resources?

The more difficult question posed here is to do with the apparent grammatical abilities of the children. Are we seeing particular 'word orders' being chosen that reflect the hypothesised innate capability for grammar, or is there another possible explanation? We will be considering functional approaches to grammar in the course text. In essence, these argue that inherent constraints to word order exist in any communicative task. These may stem from the demands of communication and/or the demands of our information-processing capacities. (Make clear what it is you are talking about before saying anything about it being an example: both demands conspire to push the topic of an utterance to first position.) It may be such constraints that lead children to go for certain word orders rather than others, and thus provide themselves with a good platform from which to break into the more abstract and esoteric subtleties of adult grammar. This is the stage what we may well be seeing in the language of these deaf children. If so, we again see the beauty of Bates' approach to the study of language development. Here we do not have a deliberate experiment aimed at elucidating the component parts of the developing language system. Rather we have a natural state of affairs in which one component is missing. If the interpretation we have offered above is anywhere near correct, we begin to see the spoken component of language, which in our common-sense view we would assume to be its essential ingredient, being relegated almost to the role of icing on the cake. Further, grammatical knowledge may be something that comes to the child relatively late, rather than being there from the beginning as a guide to the whole process of language development.

References

Griffin, D. R. (1976) *The Question of Animal Awareness*, Rockefeller University Press, New York
Tulkin, S. R. and Kagan, J. (1972) 'Mother-child Interaction in the First Year of Life', *Child Development*, *43*, 31-41

Suggested Further Reading

This issue is well treated in the previous collection of readings for this Course: V. Lee (1979) *Language Development*, Croom Helm, London. The recent publication of results from the Bristol Child Language Project, G. Wells (1982) *Learning through Interaction*, Cambridge University Press, London, is firmly located in a social view. A fuller account of the Goldin-Meadow and Feldman study may be found in A. J. Lock (1978) *Action, Gesture and Symbol: The Emergence of Language*, Academic Press, London.

9 FACILITATING THE TRANSITION FROM SENSORIMOTOR TO LINGUISTIC COMMUNICATION DURING THE ONE-WORD PERIOD

Judy Snitzer Reilly, Patricia Goldring Zukow and Patricia Marks Greenfield

Source: Paper presented at the International Congress of Child Language, Tokyo, August, 1978.

How do children who are able to communicate successfully in sensorimotor-interaction acquire the ability to transact a successful linguistic communication? To study this transition, we selected what is undoubtedly the most basic and well-established of all interactive routines in the infant's sensorimotor repertoire — the adult-initiated offer. The prototype for this interaction is, of course, the original feeding situation, in which the mother offers a nipple to the newborn infant. Our hypothesis was that a mother could utilize this well-understood interactive context to help the baby progress to the comprehension of offers presented on a purely linguistic level. We thought, furthermore, that the processes which ultimately lead to the comprehension of linguistically communicated offers might provide a prototypical core for the general transition from sensorimotor to linguistic communication. The specific focus of our research was to examine how the caregiver works to provide a shared context that is sensitive to the child's abilities at different points in the developmental process.

Successful communication rests on shared knowledge of the world (Bates, 1976; Keenan and Klein, 1975), notions about the orderliness of interactions (Goffman, 1974; Minsky, 1975; Watson, 1977), and methods of accomplishing negotiated activities (Cicourel, 1977; Grice, 1975; Sachs, Schegloff, and Jefferson, 1974) that are taken for granted (Garfinkel and Sachs, 1969; Searle, 1975a). Rarely do we make explicit these common presuppositions. Only when there is a failure in interaction, a violation of our expectations, do we even become aware that there is an intricate, invisible framework that is taken for granted and upon which we depend to guide us in our everyday activities. One way to uncover

107

these devices is to examine in careful detail instances that fail, deviate from the expected outcomes (Wikler, 1976).

Because not all offers initiated by an adult caregiver achieve their expected communicative result, a data base of videotaped caregiver–child interactions provided material for a naturalistic experiment. We could compare successful and unsuccessful offers of different types and analyze the verbal and nonverbal information required at different points in development to elucidate the transition from sensorimotor to linguistic communication. Our results show that, at first, the caregiver must explicitly provide on a sensorimotor level what, among adults, everyone already knows (Schultz, 1971), so that a collaborative interpretation of what is going on can be achieved or negotiated. Then, as the child comes to know more and more, first on the sensorimotor level, then on the level of symbolic representation, the caregiver's burden of responsibility for successful communication gradually decreases.

Different Approaches to the Problem

Working in language acquisition and infant-mother interaction, researchers have approached the transition from sensorimotor to linguistic communication from several empirical/theoretical per-spectives, perforce from different chronological vantage points. Psycholinguists studying language acquisition, have approached this transition from the top down. Development psycholinguists inspired by Chomsky (1965) ignored the transition, conceiving of language structure as apart from other facets of cognitive and social competence (e.g., Braine, 1963; Miller and Ervin, 1964; Brown and Bellugi, 1964). They began their accounts with the earliest multiword utterances, analyzing them in terms of formal syntax. Schlesinger (1971) presaged a new approach by pointing out that grammatical relations actually encoded the language learner's conceptualization of real-world events. Other writers became concerned with the cognitive and semantic aspects of language acquisition (Brown, 1973; Macanamara, 1972). Later, presyntactic speech was analyzed in relation to the extra-linguistic context (Bloom, 1973; Greenfield and Smith, 1976; Greenfield, Smith and Laufer, 1972) and to discourse history (Greenfield and Smith, 1976; Keenan, Schieffelin, and Platt, 1976). Researchers also began to consider the function as well as the form of child language and turned to speech act theory (Core, 1975). Precursors to speech acts were found in prelinguistic communication (Bates, 1976; Bruner, 1974/5, 1977; Carter, 1975; Dore, 1975).

Another approach has been to examine the effect of the caregiver's linguistic input on the child's acquisition of language (Newport, Gleitman, and Gleitman, 1977). The evidence for a direct link between syntactic input by the caregiver and acquisition by the child has been disappointing and tenuous at best. Our hypothesis is, that because the child acquires new linguistic forms by relating unknown language input to familiar nonlinguistic forms (Greenfield, Laufer, and Smith, 1972; Greenfield and Smith, 1976; Macanamara, 1972), the nonlinguistic or sensorimotor input of the caregiver is as crucial as the linguistic in the language learning process. During the transition from sensorimotor to linguistic communication, one would expect that the simultaneous presence of a message on *both* the sensorimotor and linguistic levels would be a key to the child's comprehension and acquisition of the new linguistic forms. From this analysis, it follows that linguistic studies of caregiver input which fail to consider whether or not a sensorimotor translation of the unknown linguistic form is available to the child would generally fail to find a strong connection between adult input and the child's progress.

Our study was designed to explore the interrelated roles of nonverbal and verbal input in the child's transition from sensorimotor to linguistic communication. As our focus we selected the comprehension of one particular type of communicative act, the offer. The method relies on holding communicative context (offers) constant over time and observing developmental changes in the forms that can be comprehended. It is a variant of a method suggested by Braunwald (1978) where nonverbal context is held constant over time and changes in the child's means of linguistic expression are observed.

In studying nonverbal input provided by the mother, we were in effect learning about the creation of shared world knowledge, upon which successful communication depends (Bates, 1976; Keenan and Klein, 1975). Part of this knowledge is of a general sort, not specific to offers. It relates to the nature of social and communicative interaction. Development of this knowledge in the first year of life is summarized in the next three sections, since this knowledge is prerequisite to the specific acquisition with which our study is concerned. For more detailed summaries of communicative development during the first year, the reader is referred to reviews by Schaffer (1977) and Lieven (1977).

Development of Interactional Skills

Interaction requires a variety of skills, and many of these have been found to exist in very young infants. Stern (1977) has shown how infants can initiate, maintain, terminate, and avoid interaction; caregivers have different repertoires to achieve the same ends. Trevarthen (1977) has discussed the origins of communicative behaviors, observing that, as early as two months of age, both caregivers and infants initiate exchanges and mutually work at sustaining them. Trevarthen proposes that the first six months are devoted to the development of intersubjectivity, i.e. a commitment to conveying and sharing a mental state with the coparticipant at this level. The exchanges have no content nor are they directed toward objects other than the participants themselves. At about six months of age the infant-caregiver exchanges begin to incorporate things from the objective world. That is, the interactions can now be focused on some topic outside of the interactants themselves.

Snow (1977), who has explored the development of vocal and conversational turn-taking between caregiver and infant, corroborated Trevarthen's findings. These same transitions are reflected in the content of the caregiver-infant 'conversations': 'At the earliest age, the mothers were talking a great deal about the children's feelings and experiences (their being tired, hungry, bored), what they are looking at, etc., and at later ages about their activities and about objects and events in the immediate environment' (p. 7). The change begins at about 5-7 months of age. Apparently at 5-7 months the infant can only interact with the caregiver or with an object, but not both simultaneously. That is, the infant can play with a ball or the mother, but not both. Only later can the infant play ball *with* the mother (Schaffer, 1977).

Communicative Intention

In caregiver-child interactions, intention on the part of the child has been defined as using the communicative value of behavior to purposefully affect the action of others, bringing about some desired goal. Trevarthen (1977) attributes the intention to initiate and sustain intersubjectivity to infants of two months. Bruner (1977) also describes the development of communicative intention during the first year, as reflected in the exchange of objects. Somewhat later, near the end of the first year of life, children manifest the intention to communicate by means of what Bates (1976) calls protodeclaratives and protoimperatives. Bates shows how children begin to use objects to get the attention of adults to interact with them, i.e. to make sensorimotor assertions, proto-declaratives. Adults are also used as a means to get objects, i.e. protoimperatives. Protodeclaratives and protoimperatives are considered to be the precursors of the corresponding speech acts, declaratives and imperatives.

Development of Reciprocity

Brazelton, Koslowski, and Main (1974) have discussed the genesis of reciprocity, i.e. the sensitivity of the coparticipants to each other, that is exhibited in the pacing of alternation in interactions. The turn-taking system observed in conversation (Sachs *et al.*, 1974) requires similar interactional skills. Conversational analysts (Sachs *et al.*, 1974) have developed concepts that are useful in studying the development/acquisition of the turn-taking system. Among the concepts is the notion of recipient design. Recipient design explains the management of turn size and turn order in conversation. According to Sachs *et al.* (1974), the talk of a speaker is designed to display the speaker's orientation and his sensitivity to the other coparticipants.

Speaker selection (in conversation) can be accomplished by the current speaker continuing or selecting a new speaker, and by a new speaker self-selecting. A common way for the current speaker to select a next speaker is with a device called an adjacency pair. Adjacency pairs such as Question/Answer, Summons/Response, Greeting/Greeting, have first pair parts, e.g. Question, Summons, and Greeting, which by their nature demand a response or second pair part, e.g. Answer, Response, and Greeting.

Snow (1977) has investigated the acquisition of these specific conversational skills in adult-infant dyads. In interactions with very young infants, the caregiver's major goal is characterized as getting the child to take a turn. At three months, caregivers and children participate in pseudo-dialogues; the mother responds to the infant as if the child's vocalizations have communicative significance. If the child fails to respond, the caregiver provides the response herself, i.e. she takes the child's turn. At about seven months the child is a more active interactant. The child can initiate an exchange by smiling, burping, laughing or with a protest cry. These serve as the first pair part of an adjacency pair since caregivers regularly respond to them. At this level, the caregiver does not have to fill in the child's part and the frequency of speaker switching is markedly increased. By 12 months the child initiates and responds more consistently, while the caregiver expands or explains the child's babbling. At 18 months the children in Snow's study were able to take turns appropriately and substitute words for babbling. The mother's criteria for an acceptable response became a closer and closer approximation to the adult form.

Interactive Routines

With the development of intentionality and reciprocity, plus the skills to interact (including intersubjectivity and turntaking), interactive routines are constructed by the prelinguistic child and the caregiver. These interactive routines are developed in the carrying out of everyday activities and especially in play activities, such as peek-a-boo (Bruner and Sherwood, 1976; Greenfield, 1972), and give-and-take (Bruner, 1977).

Since our study of the transition from sensorimotor to linguistic communication focuses on adult-initiated offers to children in the one-word period, the earlier development of the give-and-take routine described by Bruner (1977) documents the existence of the prerequisite sensorimotor framework. Bruner found that at three months the infant and his or her caregiver participated in a giving and grasping routine. At this age, the mother is the sole initiator, fitting her actions into and between the child's. A great deal of work is done by the caregiver, both verbaliy and non-verbally, to get the infant's attention: the object is maneuvered in front of her to catch her gaze, and questions such as 'Do you want X?' are posed to secure her attention. The caregiver manipulates the interaction so that the baby has a turn. For example, these sequences often end with the caregiver actually shoving the object into the baby's fist-shaped hand.

A relevant concept developed by Wood, Bruner, and Ross (1976) is scaffolding. This refers to the mother's structuring an interaction by building on what she knows the child can do. For example, if an object is dropped, the caregiver waits for the baby to pick up the object. If the baby does not pick it up, she may hold it just out of reach. Bruner found that at six months the baby takes his turn as the mother scaffolds the interaction; she may offer the object by holding it just out of reach so that the baby has to signal the intent to take it by a reaching gesture. At this stage (six months) the routine can be more aptly referred to as (mother) offering and (baby) taking. By 10 or 11 months, the baby inserts vocalizations into the game at regular intervals, thus segmenting the interaction. By 12 months, the child can dominate the game by both showing and offering the objects he possesses. The sensori-motor system has become reversible.

The ability to interact, the development of intentionality, and reciprocity in interactions and the establishment of stable interactive routines provide a base from which the child-caregiver pair can progress from sensorimotor to linguistically transacted communication. The infant-caregiver research recognizes the child as an integral and important partner in transacting or negotiating the outcome of interactions. However, the notion that, despite personal intention on the part of each coparticipant, interactions are collaborations whose outcomes are not predictable from individual intentions alone has not been made explicit. Ethno-methodologists suggest that interactants have procedures for making situations intelligible and that common understanding is an 'artful accomplishment' (Garfinkel, 1972). Meaning is seen as a dynamic process; it is constructed in a specific context by actors who actively interpret what they hear and see to make sense of the interaction (Cicourel, 1977; Garfinkel, 1967, 1972; Garfinkel and Sachs, 1969).

Braunwald and Brislin (1979) have recently demonstrated the importance of the caregiver's role of inferring the child's 'here and now' in order for the child to be understood. The complement of the situation studied by Braunwald and Brislin is one in which the caregiver wants to be understood. Her attempts to make herself understood highlight the crucial nature of creating a context in which communication can be interpreted by the coparticipants.

Children who are limited to saying one word at a time operate at the perceptual sensorimotor level, that is, in the 'here and now' (Greenfield and Smith, 1976). Thus, presupposed information, knowledge common to both coparticipants, is automatically available only to the extent to which it is tangibly present and being attended to. With children just beginning to talk the shared knowledge of the world that can be assumed is, therefore, severely limited. While most language development research has treated the nonverbal context as a static given, a 'background' to the interaction, the creation of the nonverbal situation may actually be 'foreground,' a part of the interaction itself. Thus, while the caregiver may sometimes passively use a pre-existing nonverbal situation in communicating, he or she may also take an active role in constructing a shared context on the sensorimotor level.

Method

Sample

The six children selected for this study are part of a larger longitudinal sample of babies made available through a private pediatric practice in Los Angeles. The children whose interactions were analyzed come from middle-class families. All the parents were college educated with the exception of one mother. Parents of each child were trained to keep a record of the child's language development. Each lexical item was entered on a separate form designed to record specific verbal as well as nonverbal information describing each speech event. The diary keeping procedure emphasized the acquisition of semantic functions presented in Greenfield and Smith (1976). Since the diary was longitudinal, the changes over time in the use of each lexical item were naturally incorporated into the diary record. Slightly before or just after the child's first meaningful word, diary keeping was initiated.

Videotapes were used to collect data. Two half-hour naturalistic videotapes were taken in the home of each caregiver-child pair. Caregivers selected interactive settings in which the most communication could be expected. Not surprisingly, these situations involved mealtime, play, diaper changing, and bathing. Bathing was excluded because of obvious technical difficulties due to water and available light.

Children were selected for the study who had attained an appropriate level of semantic development. Within the one-word period children at each of three levels of semantic development were chosen to participate in this study. The productive use of the following semantic functions served as criteria for classifying children at one of three levels. *Level I:* children were restricted to the simplest communicative acts characterised by minimal propositional content. An example of a semantic function at Level I is *indicative object* in which the child typically names something he or she is pointing at. Pointing indicates the child's relation to the object pointed at. In this case, the only propositional content is the object pointed at. At *Level II:* children were also able to communicate semantic functions implying simple predicate-argument relations. In this case, the child may express, for example, the action, saying *down*, coming down the stairs. The self is implied as agent but is not expressed. Finally, during *Level III*, in addition to expressing semantic functions of Level I and Level II, children were also able to communicate complex predicate-argument relations implying two arguments. For example, when expressing location, the child might say *chair* as the child places some object on a chair.

Operational Definition of Offers

The interactional unit chosen for analysis was an offer. Offers are defined as any one of four adult-initiated behaviors. On the sensorimotor level (1) the caregiver extends a hand to mediate a transfer of an object such as a pencil, or (2) the caregiver extends a hand to mediate the child's participation in an activity such as helping the child walk by extending the hand to serve as a support. Transfer and participatory offers can be initiated on the linguistic level as well. On the linguistic level (3) the caregiver asks, 'Do you want O (objects)?' or (4) the caregiver asks, 'Do you want to do A (activity)?' An offer can also be expressed simultaneously on both levels, yielding combinations of (1) and (3) or (2) and (4). In an offer, these may be followed by a pause, i.e. the caregiver waits until the child responds before realizing or completing the interaction. Without an intervening response by the child the interaction is ultimately interpreted as a command.

Organizational Framework of Offers

To elucidate the organization common to all offers we have developed an interactional model derived from viewing and re-viewing of the tapes. This framework reflects the offer's general structure comprised of two major components. Each component contains two constituents:

I. Offer establishment
    a. Offer presentation: Caregiver establishes the topic of the offer as well as the fact that an offer is imminent, i.e. the communicative force and propositional content are presented.
    b. Offer acknowledgement: The child's behavior is not only appropriate as a response to Ia but in the case of an acceptance elicits the offer realization, or in the case of a rejection, arrests it.
II. Offer consummation
    a. Offer realization: The caregiver proceeds to facilitate the consummation of the offer.
    b. Offer enactment: The child consummates the offer by taking the object, performing the activity, or refusing to do so.

The following example, Figure 1, will illustrate the framework. First, some very brief notes about our transcription system. Our transcription system was designed to give as much weight to nonverbal as verbal information. The transcript is organized into three components: attention as measured by eye gaze, action/state (nonverbal), and language (verbal). A brief description of the transcription conventions is included to aid in reading the examples. The caregiver's utterances are in standard English orthography. The child's utterances are written phonetically. The obliquely hatched column to the left of the mother's verbal column indicates the length of her utterance. Underlining indicates increased loudness. Punctuation marks (, : ?) are used for intonation, not as grammatical symbols. The end of an utterance is represented by an oblique (/). Contextual notes are enclosed in double parentheses, (( )). Uncertain transcriptions are enclosed in single parentheses, ( ). Colons (: :) indicate syllable lengthening. The direction of eye gaze is represented *vis-à-vis* the TV monitor screen horizontally as follows: facing right: >, facing left: <, facing away from the camera: △, facing toward the camera: ▽. Eye gaze direction on a vertical axis is represented in this way: , up; , down. Body orientation, in the upper left hand corner of the transcript, is schematized as follows: (, body facing to the right:), body facing to the left, and so on. The offer constituents, Ia, Ib, etc. are also entered to the left of the time code.

Figure 1: Level I: Immediately Successful Transfer Offer

Kitchen
L ⊂ ⊃ J
) Kitchen table

	TIME			MOTHER (Liz: L)			CHILD (Jeremy: J)		
	min	sec	frac	nonverbal	verbal	eye gaze	eye gaze	verbal	nonverbal
	11	00	30	seated in chair		↓ bananas in dish	<spoon		seated in high chair
		1	00	scooping up bananas					
Ia		2	04	extending spoon toward J		>J			
			70	pause					
Ib			80						mouth opening
IIa		3	04	food into J's mouth					
IIb			67						mouth closed over spoon
			85	extracts spoon from J's mouth					

This nonverbally initiated transfer offer is typical of many feeding sequences. According to information from the videotape that is recorded on the transcript in the upper left-hand corner, Jeremy is sitting in his high chair in the kitchen. His mother, Liz, is seated opposite him. Jeremy is looking at the spoon with which his mother scoops bananas from the dish. The mother presents the offer by lifting up the spoon, slowly approaching Jeremy with the food, and then pausing (1a). (The offer constituents can be found to the left of the time code; see 11:02:04 for Ia.) Jeremy's eye gaze follows the movement of the spoon from the bowl. When the spoon reaches the extended position, Jeremy opens his mouth as an acceptance of the offer at 11:02:80 (Ib). Opening his mouth is an acknowledgement of the offer as well as an appropriate response to elicit the offer's realization. Liz then realizes the offer by following through and lifting the spoon into Jeremy's mouth at 11:03:04 (IIa). Jeremy consummates the transfer of the food by closing his mouth over the spoon at 11:03:67 (IIb). Then the empty spoon is extracted from his mouth by the mother who resumes scooping from the bowl, and the process is repeated.

We want to emphasize that not just any behavior will be acceptable to the caregiver at Ib to bring off the offer. What Jeremy does is an appropriate response to the offering of food — that is, he opens his mouth. This also elicits the mother's next turn — putting the food in his mouth. She can't put food in his mouth when it's closed and have the interaction remain an offer. Shoving the food in his mouth certainly transforms the interpretation of this interaction from an offer to an imperative at the very least. Jeremy has many possible responses in his repertoire to an outstretched spoonful of food. Opening his mouth is not the only available response he has. He can vocalize — 'mm, mm', he can smile, touch the spoon, feel the food, knock the spoon from his mother's hand, and so on. An acceptable next, an appropriate response, is specific to the participant in an interaction, and is *not* some general response to objects. Furthermore, the specificity of the responses constituting the child's acknowledgement and consummation of offers constitutes the justification for using the term comprehension in talking of the child's responses.

Results

By making comparisons between successful and unsuccessful

offers in terms of semantic and linguistic background information, we discovered what makes an offer successfully communicative at each level of semantic development. We found that the caregivers use the sensorimotor structure of an offer to help children make the transition from sensorimotor to linguistic comprehension. Caregivers of Level I children initiated most offers solely on the sensorimotor level. By Level II, linguistically initiated offers had risen greatly in frequency, but a large proportion were presented on both the sensorimotor and linguistic levels. This cross-modal redundancy would provide the child with a sensorimotor translation of the linguistic message. Finally, at Level III, linguistically initiated offers continue to rise while cross-moral redundancy declines. Caregivers of Level III children sometimes act as though, when it comes to offers, the linguistic code has been cracked. The presentation, at Level II, of the same information both linguistically and extra-linguistically may be a key factor in helping the child make the transition from sensorimotor to linguistic communication in the comprehension offers. Successful offers at Level I had to present the entire offer on the sensorimotor level in an appropriate physical situation to a child who was paying attention. At Level II, fewer sensorimotor elements were required for successful transfer offers, most important, the offered object could be physically absent. The more complex participatory offers almost always required a more complete sensorimotor presentation, including a demonstration of the offered activity, for their successful communication. Finally, at Level III, even participatory offers could be comprehended without the presentation of all elements on the sensorimotor level; most important, participatory offers could be responded to without the mother first demonstrating the activity being offered. As the necessary sensorimotor cues decline in number, and the child's linguistic knowledge and representational capacities increase the child bears an ever greater share of responsibility for successful communication.

Qualitative Results

From a qualitative perspective it is helpful to describe the children's behavior at each level.

Level I. The background information that provides the sensorimotor structure of offers is of crucial importance to successful communication at Level I. During Level I, offers are *immediately successful* only when the child is attending, the location and spatial orientation of the co-participants is appropriate, and the entities and activity demonstration, when relevant, are available on the sensorimotor level (see Fig. 1). Figure 1 is a typical successful offer at this level. It is initiated entirely on the sensorimotor level. If we consider this feeding sequence with regard to those features which seem relevant to an interaction, it is not surprising that this sequence is so successful. This interaction has all the background elements present. The child is fed in this same location every morning, with the same general physical configuration, i.e. he is in the high chair and his mother is seated opposite. Further, his mouth is empty and ready to receive food. In summary, we can say that all of the related objects are present; the appropriate people are there in the appropriate configuration, and they are in the proper location for this activity to occur. In addition, Jeremy is looking at the spoon during the entire interaction.

This offer is categorized as immediately successful because each component of the offer framework follows in the adjacent or subsequent position. An eventually successful offer is one in which the acknowledgement does not occur in 'next' position but only after the caregiver provides additional linguistic or sensorimotor support. For example, if Jeremy had not been looking at the food in the spoon, his mother might have called his name to get his attention. If Jeremy does nothing that is taken as an acknowledgement, the offer is considered to be unsuccessful. He may just sit in the high chair looking dull or continue with a prior activity

In summary, we have found that at Level I, a child is capable of responding to a transfer offer when all the contextual and semantic information are presented and attended to on the sensorimotor level. The responsibility for providing these elements rests with the mother. A Level I child can respond to a participatory offer under the same conditions.

Level II. At Level II offers are often characterized by presentation on both the sensorimotor and linguistic levels. Further transfer offers are sometimes acknowledged when the sensorimotor structure of the offer is not quite complete. In addition, the children are beginning to actively provide elements of the sensorimotor structure.

Figure 2: Level II: Eventually Successful Participatory Offer

Living Room

A∩⊃
L   ◇ toybox

	TIME			MOTHER (Lila: L)			CHILD (Alice: A)		
	min	sec	frac	nonverbal	verbal	eye gaze	eye gaze	verbal	nonverbal
	2	21	56	seated, holding doll		< A	▷		seated
		22	58				> ↓ doll		
			90	counterclockwise turn, reaches into box		> ↓ box			
Ia		23	23		(Do ya) wanna comb the baby's hair?/				
			46	clockwise turn			> L's hand		stands up, holding hat
			90	holding out doll					
		24	00		Here's a co:mb/	< A	> (comb)		
			66	arm in box, pulls out comb					
			90						smiles

Figure 2 Continued

25			∇ comb					
26 50	26	smiling, combs doll's hair			> ı L			
12								
61 43	27		A:::h(m)/					
73				< ı A				arm extended, steps toward L: AC ⊃ L
93					> ı			
70	28	reaches up, combs A's hair						
73			Comb A:lice's hair/					
88							leans forward toward doll	
93 06	29 30						takes doll, drops hat	
16	Ib 2	sits up						

Figure 2 Continued

	TIME				MOTHER (Lila: L)			CHILD (Alice: A)		
	min	sec	frac		nonverbal	verbal	eye gaze	eye gaze	verbal	nonverbal
IIa Ia′			51		holds out comb					
IIa Ib′			70							reaches toward comb
IIa IIa′			90		extends hand closer to A					
		31	15	/////		(Here) comb Mommy's hair/				
IIa IIb′			20	/////						grasps comb
			40 / 80	/////				> ↓ doll		
			88		drops hand					
IIb			90							combs doll's hair

This offer is initiated on the linguistic level at 2:23:23 — *(Doya) wanna comb the baby's hair?* (la). Some of the background information is already present on the sensorimotor level, such as the doll at 2:21:56. What is not tangibly present is subsequently made present. At 2:24:66 Leeann, the mother, says, 'Here's a comb' as she pulls the comb out of the toy pot at 2:24:90. She provides a comb on both levels simultaneously. (The vertical column of obliques to the right of the time code indicates the duration of the utterance.) Leeann provides a demonstration of the activity at 2:26:12 by combing the doll's hair. Alice acknowledges the offer at 2:29:(93 (1b) by dropping what she had in hand and picking up the doll. She also supplies part of the appropriate configuration for combing the doll's hair by having the doll in hand. The caregiver facilitates the offer by initiating an embedded transfer offer of the comb from 2:30:51 to 2:31:20 so that Alice will have a comb with which to comb the doll's hair. (Ia', Ib', etc. indicates that the offer realization, IIa, is composed of an embedded offer.) At 11:31:90 Alice combs the doll's hair, thus consummating the offer (IIb).

This offer is complex; at the time of presentation, several referential elements were missing: the proper configuration, the objects, and the activity. Although one object was present, the doll, neither the comb nor the doll were in the child's possession. Without the necessary objects, no demonstration was possible. The mother provided the objects and a demonstration of the specific activity. However, it was Alice who took the initiative and helped herself to the doll. Alice was also responsible for supplying part of the proper configuration — she approached her mother who had the comb. Thus this example shows that Level II involves more linguistic input on the part of the caregiver. At Level II offers are typically run off with background information provided on both the sensorimotor and linguistic levels. Although the child provides a small portion of the sensorimotor structure, a great deal of interactive work on the part of the caregiver assures that the offer will be successful.

Level III. In addition to the abilities of a Level II child, at Level III, the caregiver and child can produce an immediately successful linguistically initiated participatory offer without a sensorimotor demonstration of the offered activity. This is the most advanced level of development in responding to offers. The Level III child is

Figure 3: Level III: Immediately Successful Participatory Offer

Bedroom

M ∩ ∩ J

TIME			MOTHER (Mitzi: M)			CHILD (Jeri: J)		
min	sec	frac	nonverbal	verbal	eye gaze	eye gaze	verbal	nonverbal
4	20	46	seated on the bed		< ( )	< ( )		seated on the bed
	21	26			< ⌐ doll			
		39				< ⌐ doll		
	22	00	reaches for doll					
		06			⌐ J			
		56				Δ (doll) (M)		leans toward M
	23	10	lifts up doll					
Ia		53		Wanna rock Nancy ta sleep?/				
	86		fixes doll's dress					
	24	49			> J			

Figure 3 Continued

	66			↓ doll				
25	34			> J				
	73	Ib	holds doll with both hands					vertical headshake
26	43					∨		
	50	IIa Ia′	extends doll to-ward J					
27	01	IIa Ib′						reaches for doll
	03			Si:ing Nancy a song?/				
	61	IIa IIa′	doll into J′s arms					
28	76	IIa IIb′						grasps doll
	04							

(continued)

Figure 3 Continued

TIME			MOTHER (Mitzi: M)			CHILD (Jeri: J)		
min	sec	frac	nonverbal	verbal	eye gaze	eye gaze	verbal	nonverbal
	28	90	inserted sequences: kissing doll, playing peek-a-boo, looking at doll's back					
5	1	61						puts doll in own lap
IIb	2	67					((singing))	rocks and sings to doll

capable of symbolizing not only referents for the various nominal expressions but also the relationship that holds between them, symbolized by an entire proposition, a verb and its arguments. Note that this offer is intiated on the linguistic level. At 4:23:53 the caregiver, Mitzi, says 'Wanna rock Nancy to sleep?' Although the doll, Nancy, is present, the mother is doing something quite different to Nancy. At 2:23:86 Mitzi fixes the doll's dress; she does not rock here. Jeri nods affirmatively at 4:26:43. In the midst of the transfer of the doll from 4:26:50 to 4:27:76 Mitzi includes at 4:27:03 'Si:ng Nancy a song?' After some inserted sequences Jeri, indeed, rocks and sings to Nancy at 5:2:67.

The mother gave no demonstration of the activity mentioned but, in fact, performed a totally different activity on the doll, i.e. fixed its dress. In this offer, we can conclude that Jeri knows what 'rocking Nancy' means, independent of some sensorimotor demonstration, since Jeri both provided the configuration for rocking and the activity. Jeri apparently has some internal representation of the meaning of 'singing to a doll' as well. Thus we can see that during the third level, a child can respond to any type of offer, transfer or participatory, when many elements are missing on the sensorimotor level. The child brings her/his own personal symbolic system to bear and is no longer dependent on the sensorimotor support that the mother previously needed to supply.

Conclusion

Our findings demonstrate that the sensorimotor structure of an event helps create a context in which the caregiver's communicative intent can be understood. Further, during the one-word period the responsibility for providing the sensorimotor structure of the event subtly shifts from the caregiver to the child, in tandem with the child's increasing ability to internally represent events with language. We have demonstrated a relationship between input and the development of comprehension abilities. We want to emphasize that to find these relationships we broadened the notion of caregiver input to include not only linguistic information but sensorimotor as well.

References

Bates, E. (1976) *Language and context: The Acquisition of Pragmatics*, Academic Press, New York

Bloom, L. (1973) *One Word at a Time: The Use of Single Word Utterances Before Syntax*, Mouton, The Hague

Braine, M. D. S. (1963) 'The Ontogeny of English Prose Structure: The First Phase', *Language*, *39*, 1-13

Braunwald, S. (1978) 'Context, Word, and Meaning: Toward a Communicational Analysis of Lexical Acquisition' in A. Lock (ed.), *Action, Gesture and Symbol: The Emergence of Language*, Academic Press, London

Braunwald, S. R. and Brislin, R. W. (1979) 'On Being Understood: The Listener's Contribution to the Toddler's Ability to Communicate' in P. French (ed.), *The Development of Meaning: Pedo-linguistic Series*, Bunka Hyoron Press, Japan

Brazelton, T. B., Koslowski, B. and Main, M. (1974) 'The Origins of Reciprocity: The Early Mother-infant Interaction' in Lewis, M. and Rosenblum, L. A. (eds.), *The Effect of the Infant on its Caregiver*, John Wiley, New York

Brown, R. (1973) *A First Language: The Early Stages*, Harvard University Press, Cambridge, Mass.

Brown, R. and Bellugi, U. (1964) 'Three Processes in the Child's Acquisition of Syntax', *Harvard Educational Review*, *34*, 133-51

Bruner, J. S. (1974/5) 'From Communication to Language — a Psychological Perspective', *Cognition*, *3*, 255-87

Bruner, J. S. (1975) 'The Ontogenesis of Speech Acts', *Journal of Child Language*, *2*, 1-19

Bruner, J. S. (1977) 'Early Social Interaction and Language Acquisition' in H. R. Schaffer (ed.), *Studies in Mother-infant Interaction*, Academic Press, London

Bruner, J. S. and Sherwood, V. (1976) 'Peekaboo and the Learning of Rule Structures' in J. S. Bruner, A. Jolly and K. Sylva (eds.), *Play: Its Role in Development and Evolution*, Basic Books, New York

Carter, A. (1975) 'The Transformation of Sensorimotor Morphemes into Words', *Papers and Reports on Child Language Development*, 10

Chomsky, N. (1965) *Aspects of the Theory of Syntax*, The MIT Press, Cambridge, Mass.

Cicourel, A. V. (1977) 'Language and Society: Cognitive, Cultural and Linguistic Aspects of Language Use', Address at the XIIth International Congress of Linguistics, Vienna, Austria

Dore, J. (1975) 'Holphrases, Speech Acts, and Language Universals', *Journal of Child Language*, *2*, 21-40

Garfinkel, H. (1967) *Studies in Ethnomethodology*, Prentice Hall, Englewood Cliffs

Garfinkel, H. (1972) 'Remarks on Ethnomethodology' in J. J. Gumperz and D. Hymes (eds.), *The Ethnography of Communication*, Holt, New York

Garfinkel, H. (1977, 1978) Lectures, University of California, Los Angeles

Garfinkel, H. and Sachs, H. (1969) 'On Formal Structures of Practical Actions' in J. C. McKinney and E. Tiryakian (eds.), *Theoretical Sociology: Perspectives and Developments*, Appleton-Century-Crofts, New York

Goffman, E. (1974) *Frame Analysis*, Harper Colophon Books, New York

Greenfield, P. M. (1972) 'Playing Peekaboo with a Four-month Old: A Study of the Role of Speech and Nonspeech Sounds in the Formation of a Visual Schema', *Journal of Psychology*, *32*, 287-98

Greenfield, P. M. and Smith, J. (1976) *The Structure of Communication in Early Language Development*, Academic Press, New York

130   *From Sensorimotor to Linguistic Communication*

Greenfield, P. M., Laufer, B. and Smith, J. (1972) 'Communication and the Beginnings of Language: The Development of Semantic Structure in One-word Speech and Beyond', unpublished MS, Harvard University

Grice, H. P. (1975) 'Logic and Conversation' in D. Davidson and G. Harman (eds.), *The Logic of Grammar*, Dickenson, Encino, California

Huttenlocher, J. (1974) 'The Origins of Language Comprehension' in R. L. Solso (ed.), *Theories in Cognitive Psychology*, Lawrence Erlbaum, NJ

Kaye, K. (1976) 'Infants' Effects upon Their Mothers' Teaching Strategies' in J. C. Glidewell (ed.), *The Social Context of Learning and Development*, Gardner Press, New York

Keenan, E. and Klein, E. (1975) 'Coherency in Children's Discourse', *Journal of Psycholinguistic Research*, 4, 365-79

Keenan, E. O., Schieffelin, B. and Platt, M. (1976) 'Propositions Across Utterances and Speakers', Paper presented at Stanford Child Language Research Forum, Stanford University

Ladefoged, P. (1975) *A course in phonetics*, Harcourt, Brace, Jovanovich, New York

Lieven, E. V. M. (1977) 'Turn-taking and Pragmatics: Two Issues in Early Child Language' in R. Campbell and P. T. Smith (eds.), *The Stirling Psychology of Language Conferences*, Plenum, New York

Macnamara, J. (1972) 'Cognitive Basis of Learning in Infants', *Psychological Review*, 79 (1), 1-13

Miller, W. and Ervin, S. (1964) 'The Development of Grammar in Child Language' in U. Bellugi and R. Brown (eds.), *The Acquisition of Language*, Monograph for the Society for Research in Child Development, 29

Minsky, M. (1975) 'A Framework for Representing Knowledge' in *The Psychology of Computer Vision*, McGraw-Hill

Moerck, E. L. (1978) 'Determiners and Consequences of Verbal Behaviors of Young Children and Their Mothers', *Developmental Psychology*, 14, 537-45

Newport, E. L., Gleitman, H. and Gleitman, L. R. (1977) 'Mother, I'd Rather do it Myself: Some Effects and Non-effects of Maternal Speech Style' in C. A. Ferguson and C. E. Snow (eds.), *Talking to Children: Language Input and Acquisition*, Cambridge University Press, Cambridge

Olson, D. E. (1970) 'Language and Thought: Aspects of Cognitive Theory of semantics', *Psychological Review*, 4, 257-73

Pomerantz, A. (1977) 'Agreeing and Disagreeing with Assessments: Some Features of Preferred/Dispreferred Turn Shapes', unpublished doctoral dissertation

Roberts, B. (1977) 'Elements of a Transfer', unpublished manuscript

Sachs, H., Schegloff, E. and Jefferson, G. (1974) 'A Simplest Systematics for the Organization of Turn-taking in Conversation', *Language*, 50, 696-735

Schaffer, H. R. (1977) 'Early Interactive Development' in H. R. Schaffer (ed.), *Studies in Mother-infant Interaction*, Academic Press, London

Schegloff, E. (1971) 'Notes on a Conversational Practice: Formulating Place' in D. Sudnow (ed.), *Studies in Social Interaction*, Free Press, Glencoe

Schegloff, E. (1976-78) Lectures, University of California, Los Angeles

Schlesinger, I. M. (1971) 'Production of Utterances and Language Acquisition' in D. I. Slobin (ed.), *The Ontogenesis of Grammar: A Theoretical Symposium*, Academic Press, New York

Schutz, A. (1971) *Collected Papers, Vol. I. The Problem of Social Reality*, Martinus Nijhoff, The Hague

Searle, J. R. (1969) *Speech Acts*, Cambridge University Press, London

Searle, J. R. (1975a) 'Indirect Speech Acts' in P. Cole and J. Morgan (eds.), *Syntax and Semantics III. Speech Acts*, Academic Press, New York

Searle, J. R. (1975b) 'A Taxonomy of Illocutionary Acts' in K. Gunderson (ed.), *Minnesota Studies in the Philosophy of Language*, University of Minnesota Press, Minneapolis

Snow, C. E. (1972) 'The Development of Conversation Between Mothers and Babies', *Journal of Child Language*, 4, 1-11

Stalnaker, R. (1974) 'Pragmatic Presuppositions' in Munitz and Unger (eds.), *Semantics and Philosophy*, New York University Press, New York

Stern, D. (1977) *The First Relationship: Infant and Mother*, Harvard University Press, Cambridge, Mass.

Trevarthen, C. (1977) 'Descriptive Analyses of Infant Communicative Behavior' in H. R. Schaffer (ed.), *Studies in Mother-infant Interaction*, Academic Press, London

Watson, J. S. (1977) 'Perception of Contingency as a Determinant of Social Responsiveness' in E. B. Thoman (ed.), *The Origins of the Infant's Social Responsiveness*, Lawrence Erlbaum Assoc., Hillsdale, NJ

Wikler (1976) unpublished doctoral dissertation, University of California

Wood, D., Bruner, J. S. and Ross, G. (1976) 'The Role of Tutoring in Problem Solving', *Journal of Child Psychology and Psychiatry, 17*, 89-100

10 MATERNAL STYLES AND COMMUNICATIVE DEVELOPMENT

Valerie Service

Source: specially written for this volume. Copyright © 1983 The Open University.

Despite the recent theoretical emphasis on the social nature of infant development, empirical research on the impact of the social environment on the development of language is not encouraging. In a recent review of the literature, Bates *et al.* (in press) are forced to conclude that, on present evidence, language is a developmental sphere that is unaffected by social factors. They are thus led to suggest that this sphere of development has a threshold of necessary social input for its activation, and that this threshold is very low, such that if an infant's basic needs are met by its caretaker, sufficient social input will have occurred to trigger language development, and any more interaction on top of this may be enjoyable to the infant, but will not have any noticeable effect on his language. This chapter reports research that, while not contradicting that conclusion, suggests that the presently available evidence may not be fine-grained enough for us to regard that conclusion as fact. The research being reported is not conclusive because its findings were not as expected at its outset: rather than answering the original question it was designed for, it found that life was a bit more complicated than anticipated, and so it generated a new set of unexpected questions. These questions are relevant to the effects of social interaction on language development, but are as yet unanswered.

The original question was this: Can one look at the pick-up gesture described by Lock (1978), and by making careful measurements of the relation between a mother's and her infant's activities, get an objective measure of the infant's social knowledge and its rate of development? That is, assuming the infant is motivated to want picking up, the length of time it takes him to act in a relevant way to his mother's offer to pick him up can be used as an index of how well he comprehends her efforts. Later, his ability to signal his desire to his mother before she has given him any cues that he is about to be picked up can similarly be taken as an index of his knowledge of his mother's social agency, and so on. What this question failed to take into account was that mothers are different, and pick up their infants in different ways. But interestingly, there only appear to be two different ways of doing it. These two differences turn out to relate to other differences in the ways mothers interact with their infants, and these differences may have important consequences for language development.

Ways of Picking Up

(1) Functional Style

What I will term here a functional pick-up generally occurs when the mother and infant are facing each other, but sometimes occurs from the side, or even behind. The mother simply moves her hands towards her infant's arm-pits, places them in position, and lifts.

(2) Symbolic Style

The symbolic style, by contrast, always occurs in the facing position. In this case the mother offers her outstretched arms to the infant, and holds them in that position until she has the infant's attention, only then proceeding to complete the intended pick-up.

The essential difference between these styles is the use of a gestural signal and the waiting for the child's attention. This occurs in those episodes termed symbolic, but not in the functional ones. The mothers who were studied showed a great consistency in their style: how they picked up did not vary from one situation to another. Mothers, as opposed to pick-ups, will be referred to as 'functional' or 'symbolic' from now on. It may seem faintly ridiculous to attribute a word with such far-reaching connotations to someone on the basis of such an insignificant act, but the style of pick-up adopted by a mother proved to be closely correlated with other differences in maternal behaviour. Further, this paper is intended as exploratory rather than gospel: thought-provoking rather than definitive. I will give a very brief account of the 'experimental' details and results.

Brief Details of the Study and its Results

The study was carried out with the assistance of 30 mothers and infants, who comprised 5 groups of 6, the groups being given by the infants' ages, respectively 6, 9, 12, 15 and 18 months. The mothers and infants came to the Child Laboratory at the University of Lancaster, with which they were familiar from a previous study. Toys and picture-books, etc., were scattered around the room, and the mothers were asked to 'amuse' their infants however they wished. When they heard a buzzer sound, they were to take their child to see a fixed toy or interesting object. This meant they had to pick the infant up. Having shown the child the toy, they would put him or her down, and carry on playing until the buzzer required them to pick the child up to go to see something else. Each session lasted for the same time, 20 minutes, so that meaningful comparisons of activities could be made between mothers and infants: i.e., Mother A did more of activity Y than mother B over the same period of time, and not because mother B didn't have as much opportunity as mother A. None of the mothers knew that picking-up was the activity of interest until the session was discussed with them afterwards. So what did the study find?

(1) As noted above, a mother consistently adopted one of 2 styles, functional or symbolic, when picking up her child. As would be expected, a functional pick-up occupies less time than a symbolic one.

(2) With respect to the mothers' activities:

(a) 19 of the 30 mothers were consistently 'symbolic', and they were evenly distributed over the different ages of the infants, suggesting that their style is not influenced by the infant's age.

(b) 'Symbolic' mothers used more pointing gestures than 'functional' mothers in showing things to their children ($p<0.01$), at all ages.

(c) Again for all ages, 'symbolic' mothers offer their infants fewer objects to play with than do 'functional' mothers ($p<0.001$). In general, a 'symbolic' mother would give the child a toy, point out bits of it, make up games to play with it, and hence interactively play with the toy, with the infant. By contrast, a 'functional' mother would give the child a toy, and sit back: the infant would look at the toy, play with it, put it down, and be given a new one by the mother.

(d) Maternal speech was analysed for one minute before each pick-up to one minute after. There turned out to be significant differences in speech between 'symbolic' and 'functional' mothers:

(i) 'Symbolic' mothers say more to their children ($p<0.001$), but do so in significantly shorter utterances ($p<0.05$).

(ii) The majority of both mothers' speech comprised questions, followed by imperatives. They differed in that 'symbolic' mothers used more first person singular and second person pronouns (e.g., for the 15 month group, 36% of symbolic utterances contained 'I' or 'You', compared to 11% of 'functional' utterances). By contrast, 'functional' mothers used far more first person plural pronouns (again, for the 15 month group, 47% of their utterances containing 'We' as compared to 14% of 'symbolics').

(iii) Finally, the two groups of mothers differed in what they said to their child at the pick-up time. In the same way that 'symbolic' mothers mark the act of picking-up non-verbally (gesture: pause, obtain child's attention: pick-up) they also do so verbally. A typical example of a 'symbolic' mother's speech would be: 'Jamie, Jamie, are you coming? Come on. Good boy. Up you come. Do you want to see the train?' A typical 'functional' mother would say: 'Shall we go and see the train set then?' Notice that the 'symbolic' mother breaks the interaction down into its two goals of picking up and going-to-see both verbally and non-verbally. The 'functional' mother does not do this in either channel: she stresses only the reason for picking up, and then only in her speech.

(3) If we look at the relation between some of these facets of the mothers' activities and those of their infants, we again find some clear relationships:

(i) there is a positive correlation between the amount of mothers' and infants' pointing ($p<0.001$);

(ii) there is an inverse correlation between the number of objects given and the amount of infant points ($p<0.05$). (And, as may be expected in the mothers' cases, there is an inverse correlation between the number of objects she offers her infant and the number of times she points ($p<0.05$).)

(4) Looking exclusively at the infants, we find that:

(i) Infants of 'symbolic' mothers begin to show *adjustive responses* to facilitate being picked up at 6 months of age, whereas 'functional' infants do not show evidence of this until 9 months.

(ii) By 9 months of age, 'symbolic' infants show marked *arm-*

raising responses to their mothers' pick-up gestures. 'Functionals' do not show this response at any age, presumably since their mothers do not provide them with the opportunity to do so.

(iii) 'Symbolic' infants can *initiate* pick-ups by using arm-raising from 12 months; 'functionals' only begin to do this at 15 months. (Drawing further conclusions from this study becomes difficult as the infants get older and appear to be able to decide that toy X is not worth being picked up to see, and so show no response to their mothers' efforts, not because they are unable to, but because they do not want to.)

What implications might these results have? A number of recent studies (Clark (1978) would be a paradigm case) have shown how one of Vygotsky's (1962) aphorisms — 'before being able to subject a function to deliberate volitional control, it must be possessed' (ibid) — applies in infant communicative development. A more restricted way of putting this point would be to say that before an infant can use an activity to *initiate* a communication, he must first be able to use it in *response* to one. If we place, say, giving and taking an object in its communicative context, as Clark does, we find that infants are able to take objects before they can reverse their interactive role and give them. Similarly here with pick-ups: in order to request being picked up the infant first needs to have developed an active response to his mother's requests.

Consequently, we can see the importance of the mother's activity in facilitating her child's development of these particular requests. The 'symbolic' mother makes her communicative intention very explicit to the child in the way in which she behaviourally structures the act of picking up. This is in contrast to the 'functional mother', who does little to allow her child the opportunity to decipher her intent. As a result, one group of infants comes to make requests before the other. It may well be that the two infant groups come to make the request by different routes: one via interaction, the other from their own later direct efforts to pull themselves up on to their feet, the direct action of stretching up the hands prior to pulling giving rise to the arm-raising gesture. Parenthetically, it is interesting to note that 20 years ago we would have been tempted to explain these findings by according the infant a much less social and less active role in his development. We would have focused our attention on how one style of mothering presented the child with a better observational model of the activities he had to acquire.

At this point I intend to be very speculative about the wider implications of these findings. Consequently, you should bear in mind in the following that none of it has empirical support. But if we allow ourselves a free rein, we start to uncover not only a number of suggestions for future work, but also the hazy outline of a larger story. We need first to gather our ideas from the literature:

(a) Wood and Middleton (1975) found on a problem-solving task that some mothers, those who were most able to monitor their child's level of ability and adjust their mode of teaching the child to solve the problem by offering him the information he both needed and could cope with, were more effective teachers than those who appeared less able to either break the task down into its components or pitch their level of instruction appropriately for the child. Remember that in picking up, one group of mothers differed from the other in breaking down the interaction into its components (the pick-up from its reason), and also indicated in their speech protocols a greater differentiation of themselves from their infants.

(b) Hess and Shipman (1965) found that the ability of mothers to teach their children to solve problems was dependent upon their ability to break the task down for the child and explicitly convey through language what the child's task was. This ability was also correlated with whether they related to others in terms of their individuality or their social roles. (See Robinson, Sect. V, for further details.) More recently, Light (1979) has empirically distinguished between positional and personal styles of caregiving, the former tending to produce children who score lower on measures of social sensitivity than do those of the latter.

(c) Bernstein (1972, again, see Robinson for details) has argued that the ability to explicitly code information in speech ultimately depends on the dominant nature of the social relations prevailing in the group the individual most often interacts with. Analytic concepts and articulated individuality are facilitated by the ability to code information explicitly (and vice versa).

(d) Cohen (1969), in a review of the literature, points to a relation between cognitive style (analytic thinking, characterised by breaking a problem down into its parts for solution, vs. synthetic thinking, characterised by relating disparate items in terms of their global similarities), problem-solving ability, explicitness of language coding, nature of social relations among schoolchildren's peer groups and home backgrounds, and level of achievement in school. This relation is in the direction that we may now anticipate.

(e) Kagan *et al.* (1963) reported a difference between 'reflective' and 'impulsive' children. An impulsive child tends to adopt a new technique very quickly without appearing to give it much analysis, whereas the reflective child is much more reticent, watching and considering before adopting.

(f) Another distinction in cognitive style has been termed 'field dependence' vs. 'field independence' (e.g., Witkin *et al.*, 1967). Field-dependent individuals, adult or child, are more controlled by the objective perceptual properties of a given situation, whereas field-independent individuals are more likely to impose internal constructions upon the same perceptual field.

(g) Nelson (1973) distinguished two styles of early language use, 'referential' and 'expressive', which Starr (1974) was able to extend into the two-word stage. Referential children tend to specialize in object names, whereas expressive children tend to pick up whole phrases (e.g., 'Don't do that') and words that function more to regulate interaction than to name or classify objects. None of these studies (e-g) have anything to say about social correlates of these styles.

(h) Bates (1979) summarizes these and a number of other relevant findings in tabular form, to reflect the overlap she perceives among them:

Table 1: Evidence for Individual Styles in Symbol Development

Style 1	Style 2
Referential (Nelson)	Expressive (Nelson)
— predominance of nouns in first 50 words	— heterogeneity of form class in first 50 words
— interest in labelling	— focus on social uses of language
— first-borns predominate	— later-borns predominate
— solitary play with objects (Rosenblatt)	— social orientation in play (Rosenblatt)
— consistency of style to two-word stage (Starr)	— consistency of style to two-word stage (Starr)
— typical of more advanced language learners (Ramber, Horgan)	— typical of later language learners (Ramer, Horgan)
Propositional Speech (van Lancker)	Formulaic Speech (van Lancker)
— associated with left hemisphere	— associated with right hemisphere
Word-Babies (Dore)	Intonation Babies (Dore)
— single word utterances	— contentless babbling with

	sentence contours
— oriented towards labelling	— oriented toward social functions of language
Elaboration of noun phrases in multiword speech (Bloom *et al.*)	Elaboration of verb phrases in multi-word speech (Bloom *et al.*)
High noun/pronoun ratio (Bloom *et al.*)	High pronoun/noun ratio (Bloom *et al.*)
Relatively low use of imitation (Bloom *et al.*; Leonard)	Relatively high use of imitation (Bloom *et al.*; Leonard)
First references to speaker and hearer by name	First references to speaker and hearer by pronoun
No use of empty 'Dummy' forms (Leonard)	Use of empty 'Dummy' forms (Leonard)
Patterners (Wolf and Gardner, 1979) — interest in rearranging and playing with component parts	Dramatists (Wolf and Gardner, in press) — interest in reproducing realistic patterns
Elaborated Code, middle class (Bernstein)	Restricted Code, working class (Bernstein)
Field Independence (Witkin)	Field Dependence (Witkin)
Reflective (Kagan)	Impulsive (Kagan)
	Formulaic approach to second language learning in older children (Fillmore)

Source: Bates (1979).

Bates interprets these different styles in the context of her views of language development (see Course Text for further details). Basically, she regards children exhibiting style 1 as good at analysing the relation between the signs they use and the referents they relate to, and at extracting the common characteristics of different objects and events: style 2 children as incorporating communicative strategies in their entirety as 'rules of thumb' without analysing them as to their components nor how they work. She makes no claims about why one child might tend towards one style and another towards another style.

I will not make any claims either, but will speculate. In everyday interaction, a mother functions to facilitate the child's solving of problems which, if successful, constitutes a major aspect of what we call development. A mother who marks both the constituents of the problem to be solved through the way she 'presents' the problem to the child, and draws an explicit distinction between herself and the individuality of her child, will facilitatively bias her child towards an analytic style of approaching problems and a later explicit verbal coding of his individuality. A mother who does the opposite will tend to bias her child in the other direction. Why a mother might tend to act consistently in one of these two ways is not a simple question. Given that all the mothers in my original sample would be classed as middle class, there is no simplistic answer to be found in 'class differences', and even if this answer were possible, it would still leave us with the problem of what was at the root of those differences. Further, we do not know if these differences are going to be reflected in other aspects of a mother's everyday life as a person who comes into contact with more social worlds than that of her and her child. My suspicion is that further research will show this consistency of 'being' if we have subtle enough concepts and methods to guide that research: that this microanalysis of an apparently insignificant interaction will lead us into a very sophisticated understanding of ourselves and what makes us that way. In the meantime, we must be careful how we pick up our children.

References

Bates, E. (1979)· *The Emergence of Symbols: Cognition and Communication in Infancy*, Academic Press, New York

Bates, R., Bretherton, I., Beeghly-Smith, M. and McNew, S. (in press) 'Social Bases of Language Development: A Reassessment' in H. W. Reese and L. P. Lipsitt (eds.), *Advances in Child Development and Behavior*, Vol. 16, Academic Press, New York

Bernstein, B. (1972) *Class, Codes and Control*, Vol. II, Routledge and Kegan Paul, London

Clark, R. (1978) 'The Transition from Action to Gesture' in A. J. Lock (ed.), *Action, Gesture and Symbol: The Emergence of Language*, Academic Press, London

Cohen, R. A. (1969) 'Conceptual Styles, Culture Conflict, and Non-verbal Tests of Intelligence', *American Anthropologist, 71*, 828-56

Hess, R. D. and Shipman, V. (1965) 'Early Experience and the Socialisation of Cognitive Modes in Children', *Child Development, 36*, 869-86

Kagan, J., Moss, H. A. and Siegel, I. E. (1963) 'Psychological Significance of Styles and Conceptualisation', *Society for Research in Child Development, 86*

Light, P. (1979) *The Development of Social Sensitivity*, Cambridge University Press, Cambridge

Lock, A. J. (1978) 'The Emergence of Language' in A. J. Lock (ed.), *Action, Gesture and Symbol: The Emergence of Language*,

Nelson, K. (1973) 'Structure and Strategy in Learning to Talk', *Monographs of the Society for Research in Child Development, 149*, 38 (1-2)

Starr, S. (1975) 'The Relationship of Single Words to Two-word Sentences', *Child Development, 46*, 701-8

Vygotsky, L. S. (1962) *Thought and Language*, MIT Press, Cambridge, Mass.

Witkin, H., Goodenough, D. and Karp, S. (1967) 'Stability of Cognitive Style from Childhood to Young Adulthood', *Journal of Personality and Social Psychology, 7*, 291-300

Wood, D. and Middleton, D. (1975) 'A Study of Assisted Problem-solving', *British Journal of Psychology, 66*, 181-92

11 THE DEVELOPMENT OF LANGUAGE-LIKE COMMUNICATION WITHOUT A LANGUAGE MODEL

Susan Goldin-Meadow and Heidi Feldman

Source: *Science, 197*, 1977, pp. 401-3.

Must a child experience language in order to learn language? Clearly some experience with language is necessary for the child to learn the established language of his particular community. The child of English-speaking parents learns English and not Hopi, while the child of Hopi-speaking parents learns Hopi, not English. But what if a child is exposed to no conventional language at all? Surely such a child, lacking a specific model to imitate, could not learn the conventional language of his culture. But might he elaborate a structured, albeit idiosyncratic, language nevertheless?

We have observed a group of children who lack specific linguistic input but who otherwise have normal home environments. Our subjects are deaf children of normal intelligence whose hearing losses prevent them from acquiring oral language naturally in the home. These children's hearing parents have decided against exposing them to a manual sign language in order to concentrate on oral education.[1] At the point at which we studied these subjects, their oral education program had not produced significant learning; they had acquired few, if any, spoken-language items that they could use regularly in their daily activities.

Six deaf children of hearing parents (two girls and four boys), ranging in age from 17 to 49 months at the first interview, were visited in their homes by two experimenters for 1 to 2 hours at intervals of approximately 6 to 8 weeks. The experimenters provided a standard set of toys for the child to play with during the interview and videotaped the informal interaction of mother, experimenter, child, and toys. Each videotaped session was coded by one of the experimenters or a research assistant. Selected samples were coded by both experimenters in order to calculate reliability scores on the coding categories.

The videotaped sessions were used to develop a coding system.[2]

141

(i) Instances of communicative gestures were designated in the stream of motor behavior.[3] In a randomly selected sample of videotape, 82 per cent of the gestures identified by either of two coders were identified and similarly described by both coders. (ii) On the basis of physical criteria, these gestures were broken down into single units analogous to words or signs and into multisign units analogous to phrases.[4] Of the gestures identified by both coders, there was 95 per cent agreement on sign boundary assignment and 85 per cent agreement on phrase boundary assignment. (iii) By the method of 'rich interpretation'[5], referential designates (such as Santa Claus or twist) were assigned to all word signs, and semantic elements, cases, and predicates (such as agent or act)[6] were assigned to the individual signs in all multisign phrases. Of the gestures identified by both coders, there was 98 per cent agreement on reference assignment and 96 per cent agreement on semantic element assignment.

Using these descriptive categories, we found that each of our deaf subjects developed a structured communication system that incorporates properties found in all child languages.[7] They developed a lexicon of signs to refer to objects, people, and actions, and they combined signs into phrases that express semantic relations in an ordered way.

Lexicon

The children developed two types of signs to refer to objects and actions.[8] First, they used deictic signs, typically pointing gestures which, like proforms in English (such as 'this' or 'there'), effectively allow the child to make reference to any object or person in the present. However, as is the case with proforms, context is necessary to interpret these signs. During the study, David, Donald, Dennis, Chris, Kathy, and Tracy produced, respectively, 4,854, 1,806, 309, 401, 1,218, and 366 deictic signs, representing 52, 62, 49, 41, 52, and 52 per cent of the signs each child produced.

The children produced a second type of sign, characterizing signs, which are motor-iconic signs that specify actions, objects, and, less frequently, attributes. The form of a characterizing sign is related to its referent by apparent physical similarity. For example, a closed fist bobbed in and out near the mouth referred to a banana or to the act of eating a banana. Two hands flapped up and down at shoulder height referred to a bird or the act of flying.

As a result of this motor-iconicity, the characterizing sign is less dependent on context for interpretation than is the deictic sign. David, Donald, Dennis, Chris, Kathy, and Tracy each produced, respectively, 210, 76, 25, 59, 35, and 95 different types of characterizing signs throughout the study.

Figure 1:

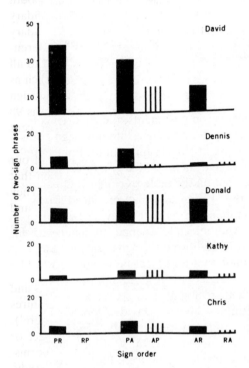

Number of two-sign phrases classified according to the order of each element in the phrase. Abbreviations: *P*, patient, the object or person acted upon; *A*, act, the action carried out to effect a change of either state or location; and *R*, recipient, the locus or person toward which someone or something moves. Patient signs tended to precede recipient sign ($\chi^2=36$, $P<.001$ for David; by the binomial test, $P<.03$ for Dennis, $P<.02$ for Donald). Patients tended to precede acts ($\chi^2=5.48$, $P<.02$ for David; $\chi^2=7.36$, $P<.01$ for Dennis). Acts tended to precede recipients ($\chi^2=13.00$, $P<.001$ for David; $\chi^2=10.28$, $P<.001$ for Donald). Subjects were observed over varying periods of time: David was seen from 2 years 10 months to 3 years 10 months for eight sessions; Dennis from 2 years 2 months to 2 years 6 months for four sessions; Donald from 2 years 5 months to 4 years 6½ months for 11 sessions; Kathy from 1 year 5 months to 2 years 8 months for nine sessions; and Chris from 3 years 2 months to 3 years 6 months for three sessions.

*Table 1: Comparison of Number of Characterizing Signs Produced during Sessions 1 to 4 by Mothers and Children (*Types *refers to number of different characterizing signs;* tokens *refers to number of occurrences across types)*

Subject	Types			Tokens			
	Child	Mother	In common	Child	Mother	In semantic relation phrases	
David	56	54	18	107	90	47	9
Dennis	25	23	5	50	58	18	3

Syntax and Semantics

In addition to these lexical accomplishments, the children concatenated their deictic and characterizing signs into multisign phrases that conveyed relations between objects and actions. For example, one child pointed at a shoe and then pointed at a table to request that the shoe (patient) be put on the table (recipient). On another occasion, the child pointed at a jar and then produced a twisting motion in the air to comment on mother's having twisted open (act) the jar (patient). Another child opened his hand with his palm facing upward and then followed this 'give' sign with a point toward his chest, to request that an object be given (act) to him (recipient). The children tended to produce phrases containing combinations of the patient, recipient, and act semantic elements represented in the examples above: David, Donald, Dennis, Chris, Kathy, and Tracy produced, respectively, 156, 64, 22, 23, 22, and 12 such phrases, representing 63, 76, 80, 79, 66, and 50 per cent of the action phrases each child produced. Phrases containing the agent or actor element were produced less frequently than phrases with the other three semantic elements, and phrases with place of action and instrument elements were rarely produced

Some of the children tended to produce their signs for the patient, recipient, and act semantic elements in consistent positions of their two-sign phrases. Specifically, as exemplified above, the children tended to produce phrases with patient-act, patient-recipient, and act-recipient orders (Fig. 1).[9] Not all children showed ordering tendencies for all pairs of the three elements; but if the children showed any ordering tendencies at all, those tendencies were ordered in the same direction. We can describe the children's two-sign phrases with the following element-ordering rule:[10]

Rule A: (choose any two maintaining order) Phrase → (patient) (act) (recipient)

Thus, it appears that some of the children expressed semantic relations in a systematic way, that is, by following a syntactic rule based on the semantic role of each of the sign units.

The children also produced longer phrases that expressed at least two semantic relations. David, Donald, Dennis, Chris, Kathy, and Tracy each produced, respectively, 240, 12, 4, 8, 11, and 10 multirelation phrases, representing 31, 7, 10, 14, 17, and 12 per cent of each child's semantic relation phrases. For example, David pointed at a picture of a shovel, pointed downstairs where a shovel was stored, produced a digging motion in the air with two fists, and finally pointed downstairs a second time. David had commented in one phrase on two aspects of the shovel, the act usually performed on the shovel and the habitual location of the shovel.

The Child Inventor

A crucial question is whether the deaf children rather than their caretakers first elaborated these signed communications. We observed that the children's mothers did use some gestures. To determine who invented the system, we transcribed the gestures produced by the mothers of two of our subjects during the first four interviews. Our impression was that these mothers did not alter their behavior in front of the camera and that our samples were representative of the mothers' communication efforts.

A comparison of the mothers' and the children's signs suggests that indeed it was the children who first produced the system. The children showed that they could invent characterizing signs by creating motor-iconic gestures for new stimulus toys they had not previously encountered. Although the mothers produced as many different types of characterizing signs as did their children, only about 25 per cent of these signs were common to both mother and child (Table 1, column 1). There is thus some suggestion that the mothers' lexical vocabularies differed from their children's and that each of the children could invent characterizing signs on his own.

Furthermore, the children produced multisign phrases that conveyed semantic relations earlier than their mothers. Both children produced a number of these phrases in session 1. David's mother produced only three such phrases in session 1 (compared to Daivd's 27 during session 1), and Dennis' mother did not start production at all until session 2. In addition, the children produced many more multisign phrases conveying semantic relations than did their mothers. Over the course of the four interviews, David and Dennis produced 127 and 42 such phrases, respectively, while their mothers produced only 41 and 13, respectively. There is thus no evidence that the children learned to concatenate signs to express semantic relations by imitating their mothers' gestures.

Finally, the children were far more likely than were their mothers to use characterizing signs in their multisign phrases. The mothers produced as many characterizing signs in single-unit phrases as their children but far fewer characterizing signs in multisign phrases (Table 1, columns 2 and 3). Consequently, there is no indication that the children learned to integrate their characterizing signs into an ordered system by imitating their mothers' productions.[11]

We have shown that a child can develop a structured communication system in a manual mode without the benefit of an explicit, conventional language model. This achievement is cast into bold relief by comparison with the meager linguistic achievements of chimpanzees. While chimpanzees seem to learn from manual language training,[12] they have never been shown to spontaneously develop a language-like communication system without such training — even when that chimp is lovingly raised at a human mother's knee.[13] On the other hand, even under difficult circumstances, the human child reveals a natural inclination to develop a structured communication system.[14]

Notes

1. Deaf children who are orally trained are instructed in lipreading and in speech production with no audio feedback. These children have been observed to spontaneously gesture to one another 'behind the teacher's back.' L. Fant, *Ameslan* (National Association of the Deaf, Silver Spring, Md., 1972); B. T. Tervoort, *Am. Ann. Deaf*, *106*, 436 (1961).

2. A rationale and justification of our coding methods and a more detailed discussion of results are given by H. Feldman, S. Goldin-Meadow, and L.

Gleitman, *Action, Gesture, and Symbol*, A. Lock (ed.), Academic Press, New York, 1978.

3. Communicative signs were motor behaviors, directed to a person, which served no direct function in the setting. The physical form of the signs was described by a system similar to the one used to describe American Sign Language. The dimensions used in the descriptions are described by W. C. Stokoe, Jr., *Stud. Linguist. Occas. Pap. 8* (1960).

4. A detailed account of the criteria for single signs and an account of the lexical data are given by H. Feldman (thesis, University of Pennsylvania 1975); the criteria for sign phrases and for the data on syntactic and semantic relations are described by S. Goldin-Meadow, *Stud. Neurolinguist*, 1979.

5. A description of the method of rich interpretation is given by L. Bloom, *Language Development* (MIT Press, Cambridge, Mass., 1970); *One Word at a Time* (Mouton, The Hague, 1973).

6. The system we use to describe the deaf child's phrases is an adaptation of the case system presented by C. J. Fillmore in *Universals in Linguistic Theory*, E. Bach and R. T. Harms (eds.) (Holt, Rinehart & Winston, New York, 1968), pp. 1-88.

7. R. Brown, *A First Language* (Harvard Univ. Press, Cambridge, Mass., 1973); D. I. Slobin in *Studies of Child Language Development*, C. A. Ferguson and D. I. Slobin (eds.), Holt, Rinehart & Winston, New York (1973), pp. 175-208.

8. The children produced a third type of sign, the marker, which did not refer to things and events but rather served modulation functions. Sign markers were head nods and side-to-side head shakes and were reminiscent of words such as 'yes' and 'no' in English; for instance, in the sentence 'There are no trucks,' the 'no' modulates, in particular negates, the existence of trucks.

9 The data in Fig. 1 include only two-sign phrases. We exclude phrases containing three elements (such as point at book, 'give' sign, point at self, to request that the book be given to the child) and also exclude phrases containing either repeated elements or simultaneously sign elements (such as point at book, 'give,' point at book; or point at book signed simultaneously with 'give'). In addition, we exclude all phrases containing points at pictures because the children tended to point at pictures before producing other signs. The pictures pointed at were often facsimiles of objects playing the patient role; thus, we would have, perhaps artifactually, inflated our patient-first orderings if we had included these phrases. As a result, Tracy (observed for two sessions at 4 years 1 month and 4 years 3 months) was not included in this analysis because she produced very few action phrases which did not contain points at pictures. The data that appear in Fig. 1 represent 64, 83, 92, 70, and 86 per cent of all the two-sign, pictureless action phrases produced by David, Dennis, Donald, Kathy, and Chris, respectively.

10. The following conventions are used in describing the order rule: (i) → indicates that the symbol on the left can be rewritten as the symbol or symbols on the right. The order of the symbols on the right must be maintained in the rewriting process. (ii) ( ) indicates that the symbol in the parentheses is optional, that is, it either can or cannot be chosen in the rewriting process.

11. S. Goldin-Meadow and H. Feldman, *Sign Lang. Stud, 8*, 225 (1975).

12. R. A. Gardner and B. T. Gardner, *Science, 165*, 664 (1969); B. T. Gardner and R. A. Gardner, *Behav. Non-Hum. Primates, 4*, 117 (1971); A. J. Premack and D, Premack, *Sci. Am., 227*, 92 (Oct. 1972). Gardner and Gardner report that Washoe has invented signs for certain objects; although striking, this accomplishment does not address the issue of whether or not Washoe would invent such signs if she had not been exposed to a standard manual language model.

13. C. Hayes, *The Ape in Our House* (Harper, New York, 1951); W. N. Kellogg, *Science, 162*, 423 (1968). Although the Kellogg chimpanzee Gua

148 *The Development of Language-like Communication*

occasionally did gesture (such as protruding lips toward a cup to mean 'drink'), her gestures appeared to be far less explicit than our deaf children's signs (such as tilting a C-shaped palm toward the mouth several times without the cup in the hand, which was David's signs for 'drink'); moreover, Gua did not combine signs into phrases as did our deaf children.

14. We thank D. Burke, J. Huttenlocher, K. Kaye, J. McClelland, and B. Meadow for reading earlier versions of this paper; E. Newport for helpful suggestions; L. Tefo and B. Gray for help in coding videotapes; our subjects and their families for continued cooperation throughout the study; and L. Gleitman for contributions to both our thoughts and language. Supported by a Spencer Foundation grant to S.G.-M. and H.F. while they were students at the University of Pennsylvania, an NSF graduate fellowship to H.F., an American Association of University Women predoctoral fellowship to S.G.-M., NIH training grant HD 00337 under the direction of J. Aronfreed, and NIH research grant HD 52744 to R. Gelman.

SECTION V: LATER DEVELOPMENT OF LANGUAGE

Some readers may be wondering why so many of the previous chapters in this collection have, firstly, been devoted to the very early stages of language development, and secondly, said so little about grammar. There are a number of reasons behind our selection strategy. Studies of grammar and its development have formed the bedrock of most recent research, but have lead to an increasing emphasis on questions whose concern has been in a different direction. To some extent, the field of child language has lost sight of grammar in the last few years, and only at the time of writing is it beginning to realise this. We suspect that a review of the field at the end of the century might say that the 1960s was a decade of grammatical studies, the 1970s one in which the problems posed by those studies were pursued, and in the 1980s a return was made to reconfront the problems of grammar, armed with a new perspective. Our aim, then, has been to try and balance recent concerns against what many preconceive to be the traditional approach of the field. We have been able to pursue that goal in the way we have because of the excellent review of language development recently published by Atkinson, Kilby and Roca. They have managed in a very short space to cover nearly all the salient points that would otherwise have required the great deal more space we expected to devote to these topics. Because their chapter is so clear, we need say no more about it.

Slobin's paper returns to a perspective that has lain almost dormant since the time of Romanes' writings (see Chapter three). At the outset he notes: 'the development of language is, of course, part of the general development of consciousness and self-consciousness'. He presents a very clear picture of the way that what at one time is a means for reflecting and acting on the world becomes itself part of the world to be reflected and acted on. Slobin's paper provides us with a context for those that follow: a clear example of Vygotsky's dictum that 'consciousness and control appear only at a late stage in the development of a function, after it has been used and practiced unconsciously and spontaneously. In order to subject a function to intellectual and volitional control, we must first posses it' (1962, p. 909). We also see how this transition has a sequential order to it. Comments on the speech of others come before those on one's own speech, since the speech of others is to the child *a part of the world* whilst her own, at least initially, seems to her *a part of herself*. Development is clearly a case of making explicit what is already implicit in one's existing abilities.

This characterisation of development, previously apparent in Lock's paper (Chapter 4), is also one of the lessons to emerge from Robinson's review. The differences in speech coding that Robinson discusses are differences of explicitness. When two speakers know each other and the subject under discussion, there is no need for either of them to explicitly state everything they want to communicate. As Vygotsky (1962) points out, Tolstoy gives us a dramatic example in this interchange between Kitty and Levin in *Anna Karenina*:

'I have long wished to ask you something.'

'Please do.'

'This,' he said, and wrote the initial letters: *w y a: i c n b, d y m t o n*. These letters meant: 'When you answered: it can not be, did you mean then or never?' It seemed impossible that she would be able to understand the complicated sentence.

'I understand', she said, blushing.

'What word is that?' he asked, pointing to the *n* which stood for 'never.'

'The word is "never",' she said, 'but that is not true.' He quickly erased what he had written, handed her the chalk, and rose. She wrote: *I c n a o t*.

His face brightened suddenly: he had understood. It meant 'I could not answer otherwise then.'

She wrote the initial letters: *s t y m f a f w h*. This meant: 'So that you might forget and forgive what happened.'

He seized the chalk with tense, trembling fingers, broke it, and wrote the initial letters of the following: 'I have nothing to forget and forgive. I never ceased loving you.'

'I understand,' she whispered.

The essence of the work Robinson reviews is that the structure of social relationships puts different pressures upon a speaker to state his intended message in an explicit form. When this is looked at in an historical context, the argument is that social structures are enduring, and thus facilitate the elaboration of language for this purpose within them to differing degrees. Thus an individual born into some social groups will find both less need and less resources in it to enable him to code fully explicit messages into speech. This does not mean that he is a less efficient communicator, just that the resources he uses for communication are different. Even so, it may prove that these resources do not facilitate his use of language in both talking and other spheres to the same extent as someone using the communicative resources of a different social tradition. Further, the articulation of the self may be less verbally marked, following the line put forward in Slobin's paper. (This is a point made explicitly by Bernstein, see table in Robinson, Sect. V.)

This approach is directly relevant in a more global developmental context. The mother-child relationship can be thought of as a very close one. Consequently, it is not surprising that an infant begins talking with all the characteristics of Bernstein's 'restricted code': it is a language of implicit meaning. Language development can then be characterised as a progression to a more elaborated mode, in which meaning is made more and more explicit at the verbal level. In this way we begin to see how the nature of the social relationships that the child is growing among can lead to differences in his mode of language development, and the elaboration or articulation of his sense of self.

References

Vygotsky, L. S. (1962) *Thought and Language*, Harvard University Press, Cambridge, Mass.

Suggested Further Reading

Relevant linguistic background can be found in the appendix to D. MacNeill (1970) *The Acquisition of Language*, Harper and Row, New York. Anyone who wishes to know more will find M. Atkinson, D. Kilby and I. Roca (1982) *Foundations of General Linguistics*, George Allen and Unwin, London, a mine of digestible information. Two useful texts on the more traditional aspects of child language research are P. Dale (1976) *Language Development: Structure and Function*, Holt, Rinehart and Winston, London; A. Elliot (1981) *Child Language*, Cambridge University Press, London; V. Lee (1979) *Language Development*, Croom Helm, London, contains a number of papers on the social themes summarised here in Robinson's (Ch. 14).

12 LANGUAGE DEVELOPMENT IN CHILDREN

Martin Atkinson, David Kilby and Iggy Roca

Source: Atkinson, M., Kilby, D. and Roca, I., *Foundations of General Linguistics*, (George Allen & Unwin, London, 1982), pp. 292-308

Early Syntactic Development

Small children usually begin to combine words when they are about 18 months old and most studies of syntactic development have treated this as a natural starting-point. There has been an enormous amount of work done on these earliest steps in syntax and, at the outset, it is important to distinguish two distinct approaches to the area.

The first, popular in the 1960s, owes most, in its methodology, to the school of American structuralism, attempting to define grammatical classes and produce statements governing the co-occurrences of such classes on the basis of a distributional analysis of a corpus of utterances collected from the child. The child is treated as if he were a speaker of an 'exotic' language and no attempt is made to incorporate features of context or guesses as to what the child might mean into the analysis; the approach is known as the *lean* approach. Opposed to it is the *rich* approach, aligning itself, to some extent, with the transformational school of syntax and taking seriously the problem of representing what the child knows about the syntactic structure of the language he is learning. This approach *does* take account of context in an effort to get at what the child is meaning, the belief being that, without this sort of information, it will be difficult to avoid seriously underestimating his structural knowledge.

The lean approach led to the formulation of a number of distributional regularities based on early two-word speech. Thus, it appeared that there was, for each child, a small number of words which occurred particuarly frequently in two-word utterances. Furthermore, such words appeared to have strong positional preferences. To take a typical example, the following utterances might well crop up in a corpus collected from a child at this stage.

(1) a *more milk, more shoe, more baby, more outside, more train*

   b *mummy gone, mummy chair, mummy coat, mummy up, mummy house*

   c *shoe off, coat off, socks off, this off, fall off*

In (1)*a* and (1)*b* we find *more* and *mummy* appearing in first position, in (1)*c*, *off* in second position. The terminology that was introduced to describe these regularities involved referring to the fixed-position words as *pivots*, with remaining positionally mobile words belonging to an *open* class. Additional suggestions which had some initial support were that pivots did not appear as one-word utterances, whereas open-class words did, and that pivots did not combine with each other to form two-word utterances, whereas open-class words did. This added up to a sound distributional basis for the distinction and some workers went so far as to suggest that the child's first grammar should be constructed so as to represent these regularities and nothing more. Such a grammar would have the phrase-structure rule of (2) where P_1 refers to the class of first-position pivots, P_2 to the class of second-position pivots and O to the open class.

$$
(2) \quad S \rightarrow \quad
\begin{matrix}
P_1 & + & O \\
O & + & P_2 \\
(O) & + & O
\end{matrix}
$$

There are some difficult problems arising from this suggestion, not least of which concerns how the child moves from a grammar employing the grammatical categories, P_1, P_2, and O to one using a more standard set (N, V, Adj, etc.). This was tackled in an ingenious way by the suggestion that, although the child's primitive categories do not correspond to any adult category (note, for example, that in (1) both *more* and *mummy* would be assigned to P_1), nevertheless, they honour the adult categories *generically*. That is to say that the child initially puts together a number of adult grammatical categories as one of his primitive categories, not making distinctions which are necessary in the adult language. However, the fact that he does this indicates that he is not innocent of the adult categories — if he were we would anticipate a situation in which different members of the same adult category were assigned to different child categories — and the development of grammatical categories can then be seen as a gradual unfolding of this set of implicit distinctions. Of course, the problem of where the implicit knowledge of the grammatical categories comes from is a real one and the answer that it is innate was the obvious one for proponents of this view to adopt.

Unfortunately, it was not long before the evidence necessary to refute this speculation appeared. In the speech of some children it was necessary to assign some adjectives to a pivot class and others to the open class. This should not happen if the pivot and open classes were honouring adult categories generically.

From a different perspective, work was starting using the rich approach and supporters of this technique were eager to point to phenomena which they believed could not be adequately analysed distributionally. The classic example was put forward at the end of the 1960s by Lois Bloom[1] who, having classified *mummy* as a first-position pivot on distributional grounds, drew attention to the two utterances of (3) produced by one child.

(3) mummy sock

In itself (3) tells us little, but attention to context of utterance revealed that the two tokens of (3) required quite different interpretations. On one occasion it was uttered as the child was picking up her mother's sock; on the other, as the mother was putting the sock on the child. The moral is clear: the first situation reveals that the child is attempting to encode a genitive relation (*mummy's sock*) but is not inflecting *mummy*, and the second suggests that she is concerned with mummy being the instigator of some action on the sock (*mummy is doing something to the sock*) but there is no explicit marking of the action. But this argues that, at some level, the child knows about genitives, about subjects of sentences and about objects of sentences, and representing both tokens of (3) as instances of the grammatical structure $P_1 + O$ fails totally to represent this knowledge.

If this sort of data analysis is permitted, the way is open to postulate other grammatical relations at the two-word stage, and this is exactly what Bloom and many other workers did. The results of these activities were taxonomies of two-word utterances and, while correspondences between different studies were rarely exact, the list in (4) is a fairly representative sample.

(4)   *a*   subject-verb (*mummy go*)
      b   verb-object (*wash baby*)
      c   subject-object (*mummy sock* (second interpretation))
      d   possessor-possessed or genitive (*mummy sock* (first interpretation))
      e   adjective-noun (*big dolly*)
      f   subject-locative (*sweater chair*)
      g   verb-locative (*jump chair*)

Focusing briefly, now, on (4)*a-c*, we can raise one of the problems that the rich approach faced. These three syntactic relations suggest that the child has all the syntactic machinery to produce subject-verb-object strings. In a standard transformational grammar this sort of competence would be captured by crediting the child with phrase-structure rules along the lines of (5).

(5)   S   →   NP + VP
      VP   →   V + NP

However, this set of rules would enable the child to deal with three-term strings and this he does not do. The solution proposed for this was to postulate a 'transformation' which, given a three-term string, deletes one of the components. But this is uncomfortable for at least two reasons: (i) it is *ad hoc*, i.e. has no application outside the immediate problem context (it is also formally incorrect in that transformational rules are not permitted to delete arbitrary material); (ii) it has all the appearances of a constraint on the child's linguistic productions (i.e. one aspect of his performance) being represented in a theory of his syntactic knowledge (his competence).

This second problem raises a more general and fundamental one for the investigator intent on producing a grammar to represent the child's linguistic knowledge. It is generally accepted that a speaker's utterances only provide one sort of evidence in this enterprise, and the methodology of grammar-writing for adult languages relies crucially on the availability of native speaker intuitions. For small children, however, we do not have access to such intuitions and, correspondingly, our grammar construction is less constrained. This sort of consideration eventually led to a reduction in interest in grammar-writing for early child speech, the focus of interest switching to semantics. Before we pursue this shift, however, we would like to briefly mention some evidence which suggests that the small child is struggling with something like transformational rules in his acquisition of syntax.

Transformational Rules in Language Development

One type of evidence which is consistent with children acquiring transformational rules comes from an attempt to interpret the Derivational Theory of Complexity in a developmental context. Very simply, this interpretation says that the more complex a sentence-type is in the grammatical description, the *later* it will be acquired by the child. This was discovered to be the case for a number of simple sentence-types including affirmative declaratives, negative declaratives, affirmative interrogatives, negative interrogatives and truncated versions of each of these. These sentence-types are illustrated in (6) and the ordering predictions of (7) were made on the basis of a transformational analysis of the sentences.

(6)   *John hit the ball* (affirmative declarative — AD)
      John didn't hit the ball (negative declarative — ND)
      Did John hit the ball? (affirmative interrogative — AI)
      Didn't John hit the ball? (negative interrogative — NI)
      John did (truncated affirmative declarative — TrAD)
      John didn't (truncated negative declarative — TrND)
      Did John? (truncated affirmative interrogative — TrAI)
      Didn't John? (truncated negative interrogative — TrNI)
(7)   AD before each of the others
      ND before NI, TrND, TrNI
      AI before NI, TrAI, TrNI
      NI before TrNI
      TrAD before TrND, TrAI, TrNI
      TrND before TrNI
      TrAI before TrNI

In a study of three children and their acquisition of these sentence-types, as revealed by their spontaneous speech, a high proportion of these predictions were confirmed. Against this, however, it is necessary to point out that a number of predictions that would be made for other sentence-types, using a standard transformational analysis, have been shown to be incorrect. To mention just one example, small children begin to use short passives before they use full passives; in the grammar a short passive will be derivationally more complex than a full passive.

Evidence of a different sort comes from the child's acquisition of *Wh*-questions, in which the identity of a particular constituent is queried. A number of *Wh*-questions appear in (8).

(8) *a* What did John hit?
    b Who hit John?
    c Where did John find the ball?
    d How did John hit the ball?

Standardly, these have been derived in transformational grammars by generating the *Wh*-word in the position which makes its relationship with the verb clear. For example, (8)*a* will be derived from a source along the lines of (9).

(9) John did hit what?

In (9) *what* is positioned immediately after the verb indicating its direct object function. Two rules operate on (9) to give (8)*a*: the first of these, *Wh*-movement, takes the *Wh*-word and moves it to the front of the sentence, yielding (10).

(10) What John did hit?

The second inverts the subject of the sentence (*John*) and the auxiliary verb (*did*), giving us (8)*a*. Now, the interesting thing is that some children produce intermediate forms like (10) as they develop *Wh*-questions, i.e. they get the *Wh*-word in the right position, but fail to invert. Such evidence points strongly towards the fact that inversion is something that children have to learn and obviously argues against *Wh*-questions being learned by imitation.

Finally, there is some evidence that children go wrong in interesting ways with some rules that are traditionally analysed as involving movement and deletion. *Wh*-movement is such a rule but, interestingly, the sort of error we are concerned with does not appear in connection with this rule. Consider the simple rule of particle movement. This is usually introduced as deriving a sentence like (11) from structures of sentences like (12).

(11)   The barber cut my hair off
(12)   The barber cut off my hair

What the rule does is copy the particle (*off*) immediately behind the following NP and delete the original occurrence of *off*. Some children appear to get the copying part of a rule like this right withot deleting, thus producing utterances like (13).

(13)   The barber cut off my hair off

There is currently a good deal of controversy as to why this phenomenon appears to occur with some movement rules and not others, but, again, it indicates that children do not passively imitate the structures they learn and suggest that they entertain structural hypotheses of an abstract kind.

Semantic Development: Relational Meanings

There are two aspects of semantic development that have been extensively studied. One of these concerns the range of application of single words and will concern us in the next section; the other examines the relational meanings which are encoded in children's early utterances and, since this is not an immediately obvious distinction, we can begin by considering a particular example.

Suppose that a small child says *chair* as he places an object in a chair. We might be interested in the fact that here he uses *chair* to refer to a certain chair and we might inquire as to whether he will refer to other chairs in the same way or whether he will refer to some things we would not regard as chairs using this same word. Such queries are the concern of the next section. Alternatively, we might note that *chair* appears to be playing the role of a location for an object which is not itself represented linguistically in the utterance. Contrast this with a situation in which the child requests that an adult move a chair towards him, again using *chair*. Once more we can wonder about the range of objects to which *chair* might be applied but here, in contrast to our earlier situation, it seems more appropriate to regard the word as representing an object of an action or desire ('You move chair' or 'I want chair'). When we focus our attention on such noting as 'location of an object' or 'object of an action' in such examples, we are paying attention to relational meanings — they are 'relational' because there is some additional entity implicit in the interpretation, an object in the first case and an action in the second.

This way of talking proved attractive to workers in child language for a number of reasons. First, it seemed reasonable to suggest that there might be a relatively small number of such relational meanings in early child speech and it would be interesting to study their development. Secondly, it could be extended naturally to one-word utterances as the above examples demonstrate, thereby establishing some sort of continuity between one-word utterances and later stages of development (recall that studies of syntactic development usually begin with two-word utterances and ignore earlier stages). Finally, in not committing us to grammatical notions like subject and direct object, it avoided the question of where these notions came from — the standard answer to this had been, not surprisingly, that they are innately supplied. Of course, this leaves open two questions. (i) If we provide a semantic characterisation of early child speech in these terms, at the expense of the sort of syntactic approach briefly discussed (. . .) above, where are we to locate the beginnings of syntax? (ii) Where do the relational meanings themselves come from? The first of these questions has not received any cogent discussion but there has been speculation regarding the second (see below).

Initially, when these ideas were first put forward, their application was restricted to an analysis of two-word utterances. In his monumental work *A First Language*, Roger Brown,[2] one of the foremost scholars of child language, having painstakingly surveyed the difficulties confronting a syntactic approach to two-word utterances, provides a taxonomy of what he calls 'basic semantic relationships'. These 'relationships', listed in (14), account for over 70 per cent of the utterances in which he was interested.

(14) *a*   Agent and action (*Daddy throw*)
     b   Action and object (*throw ball*)
     c   Agent and object (*Daddy ball*, as Daddy throws a ball)
     d   Action and locative (*sit chair*)
     e   Entity and locative (*teddy chair*)
     f   Possessor and possession (*my shoe*)
     g   Entity and attributive (*big teddy*)
     h   Demonstrative and entity (*that teddy*)

First, note the almost total overlap between (4) and (14), making it clear that they are applicable to the same sets of data. The important difference, however, is that (14) is a *semantic* taxonomy. Accordingly, it is not necessary to postulate abstract unrealised grammatical elements for the relations in (14); as they are not syntactic they do not take on their significance from syntactic relations. Thus, in the case of (14)*c*, we are not forced into recognising the existence of an underlying *verb* as we were in the case of (4)*c*. The (14)*c* schema requires that, at some level, the child has a representation of an action which is not linguistically encoded, but this does not demand crediting him with an abstract and elaborate syntactic system — we merely have to assume that he is capable of representing events and their components.

Secondly, (14) answers an objection to (4) which points out that the subjects recognised as occurring in syntactically oriented studies are, at the two-word stage, almost without exception animate instigators of action, i.e. agents. English subjects fulfil a variety of semantic roles, including agent (15)*a*, experiencer (15)*b* and instrument (15)*c*, but only agents appear at this early stage of child speech.

(15) *a* John opened the door
      b John heard the sound
      c The key opened the door

Therefore, the argument goes, the syntactic notion of *subject* is too abstract for characterising what children of this age know about the language and what is required to represent this knowledge is a more concrete semantic notion. Similar arguments have been put forward for other grammatical relations deemed necessary by (4).

Thirdly, since (14) is a semantic taxonomy, we can investigate its cross-linguistic validity without being concerned about how particular relations are expressed in different languages. There are difficulties in identifying grammatical relations across languages and this will make the generality of (4) dubious. However, there is no reason to believe that the notional categories of (14) cannot be found in all languages, and such cross-linguistic comparisons as have been carried out tend to converge on such a notional set. Languages investigated in this connection include German, Finnish, Turkish, Samoan, and Ludo (a tribal language of Kenya) in addition to English, and this has prompted some investigators to suggest that the relations in (14) constitute a developmental universal; all children, no matter what language they are learning, express just these relations first in their two-word utterances.

At this point it makes sense to ask about the source of these relations. Brown resists the inference from universality to innateness by citing some of Piaget's views on early cognitive development, arguing that if Piaget[3] is correct, then the child is equipped with the relevant cognitive categories before he begins language development. Therefore, Brown is attempting to explain the *fact* of these early relations by discovering their source in cognitive development and also their *early appearance* by locating this course in *early* cognitive development.

Piaget's views on cognitive development are, of course, extremely complex and we cannot attempt to summarise them here. However, one of the achievements of the *sensori-motor period* (which, in Piaget's framework, extends from birth to about 18 months — approximately the onset of two-word speech) is what Piaget calls a 'mature object concept'. Before the end of the sensori-motor period, the child is claimed not to distinguish clearly between objects and actions which are performed on them or locations in which they appear. This is illustrated, for example, by occasions when the child, having successfully located an object hidden at a particular location, fails to find it when it is taken to that location again and then, in full view of the child, moved from that location and hidden at a second one; the child, at a certain stage of cognitive development, will search unsuccessfully at the first location. On the basis of this, we might conclude that such a child does not clearly distinguish object from location.

Now, one could argue, clearly if the child is to express an entity-locative relation, he must distinguish the two elements being related. Accordingly, the mature object concept is seen as a prerequisite for the expression of this relation. Although no author has gone into great detail on this issue, there is a general feeling among people working in the field that this sort of argument could be constructed for each of the relations in (14).

Similar arguments have recently been offered for one-word speech, where again a taxonomy of semantic relations has been suggested and attempts have been made to relate these to the child's non-linguistic cognitive development. We shall not pursue this analysis here (. . .), and we wish to close this section by considering a different, though equally important question.

If Brown's analysis of the relationship between cognitive development and basic semantic relations is correct, it demonstrates that cognitive development of a certain sort is a *necessary* condition for a certain aspect of linguistic development. However, it does not demonstrate that such cognitive development is a *sufficient* condition for the appropriate expression of the basic semantic relations according to the rules of the language the child is acquiring. This is straightforwardly illustrated by the fact that initially entity-locative utterances lack a preposition where the adult language requires one (i.e. the child says *dolly chair* and not *dolly in chair*). The possibility is therefore raised that there is something specifically linguistic about the *expression* of the basic semantic relations, although the relations themselves are characteristic of general cognition. This has been pursued, in a most interesting argument, by Dan Slobin.[4]

Slobin cites data from the development of children being brought up bilingually in Hungarian and Serbo-Croat, paying particular attention to their expression of the entity-locative relation. What he discovered was that the *same* children were expressing this relation appropriately in Hungarian at a time when they were not doing so in Serbo-Croat (i.e. they said the equivalent of *dolly in chair* when speaking Hungarian but only *dolly chair* when speaking Serbo-Croat). Why should this be?

An examination of the ways in which each language expresses locative notions reveals that they differ in a number of important ways.

(*a*)   Hungarian expresses its locative notions only with suffixes whereas Serbo-Croat uses both suffixes and prepositions.

(*b*)   All Hungarian suffixes are unambiguous whereas some Serbo-Croat propositions have the same ambiguity as, for example, *in* in English (*He jumped in the water* can mean either that he jumped when he was in the water or that he jumped into the water).

(*c*)   Some Serbo-Croat prepositions 'take' particular suffixes thus rendering the suffix semantically redundant; others allow a choice of suffix.

(*d*)   Serbo-Croat suffixes are phonologically conditioned by the stem to which they are attached; Hungarian suffixes are invariable.

It should be clear from this that there is an obvious intuitive sense in which the expression of locative notions in Serbo-Croat is *more complex* than it is in Hungarian. This is independent of the notions which are being expressed and, Slobin suggests, represents a contribution of purely linguistic complexity to the developmental process.

Semantic Development: Referential Meanings

It is common observation that, when small children begin to use language, they often use words in a way which is inappropriate from the adult perspective. Thus, stories of children referring to all four-legged animals as *dog* or to all men as *daddy* are well known and the source of much amusement. They do, however, lead to a serious and important question concerning the nature of the child's semantic representation of words.

Concerning the child's first attempts to label aspects of his world, there have been three distinct attempts to approach this question.

The first, put forward by Eve Clark,[5] emphasises the importance of *perceptual* information in the semantic representation of a word. The view assumes that a word's meaning consists of a set of semantic features and that, initially, these features encode perceptual information about references of the word. So, the child perceives a ball and hears the word *ball*, notes that the ball has certain perceptual characteristics (e.g. roundness, redness, squashiness) and establishes a meaning for *ball* on this basis. Now, Clark's claim is that the child might only attend to a subset of the total set of perceptual parameters associated with the ball and, subsequently, establish a meaning for the word which is too general (in the case in question we can imagine that the child only attends to roundness and is thus in a position where he will refer to all round things as *ball*). She predicts, on this basis, that instances of *overextension*, examples of which opened this section, will be explicable in perceptual terms and she herself has cited data indicating the importance of a number of perceptual dimensions in this regard. A small sample of these appears in Table 1.

Clark has not been content to cite data which support her position but has also attempted to give that position some explanatory status. On the one hand, it is possible to refer to studies of perceptual development which suggest that the relevant abilities to analyse objects perceptually are present before the child begins to use language — this can be seen as an attempt to explain part of the fact of lexical development by identifying perceptual prerequisites — and, on the other, it has been claimed that the course of lexical development can be predicted if we assume that the child learns the most general features first. Unfortunately, this latter suggestion suffers from a lack of explicitness in the notion 'general feature', although it does display a healthy awareness of the problem of explanation.

In contrast to Clark's emphasis on perceptual features, Katherine Nelson[6] has suggested that it is *functional* criteria which determine initial word use. These functional criteria are seen as emerging from the child's interaction with objects and people and it is indeed the case that the child's first words tend to refer to aspects of his environment with which he actively interacts rather than to objects which are constantly and invariably present. Two sorts of evidence might be cited in support of this position. First, there are instances of overextension which readily admit a functional explanation but which are difficult to accommodate on a perceptual hypothesis; one of the best examples with which we are familiar is offered by the child who refers to a clothes-brush as *brush* and to a comb and a hair-brush as *comb*. Secondly, in an experimental study, Nelson herself showed that, when confronted with a set of more or less ball-like objects and asked to identify the ball, children of 9 months would initially base their choice on either shape (a ball fixed to a stand) or function (a rubber cylinder free to move). After having been allowed to play with the objects, however, a large number of children changed their choice in the direction of function.

It now seems clear that both perceptual and functional criteria are going to be important in understanding early lexical reference, but in a recent study Melissa Bowerman[7] has questioned one of the basic assumptions of both Clark's and Nelson's positions. Both of these theories hold that a set of criteria (perceptual or functional) constitute necessary and sufficient conditions for the applicability of a word to a referent (in this sense, they are standard semantic feature theories) (. . .). But now consider the following data cited by Bowerman.

A child initially uses *kick* in circumstances where she is kicking a ball with her foot so that it moves forwards. Subsequently, she

Table 1: Some Examples of Overextension

Perceptual Dimension	Language Being Learned	Child's Form	First Referent	Overextensions
shape	English	bird	sparrows	cows, dogs, cats, any animal moving
shape	English	kotibaiz	bars of cot	large toy abacus, toast-rack with parallel bars, picture of building with columns
sound	Russian	dany	sound of bell	clock, telephone, door-bells
taste	French	cola	chocolate	sugar, tarts, grapes, figs, peaches
touch	Russian	va	white plush dog	muffler, cat, father's fur coat

Source: Adapted from Eve V. Clark, 'What's in a word? On the child's acquisition of semantics in his first language' in T. E. Moore (ed.), *Cognitive Development and the Acquisition of Language* (Academic Press, New York, 1973), pp. 65-111.

uses *kick* when she kicks a floor fan which does not move, when she sees a moth fluttering over a table, when she makes a ball roll by bumping it with the wheel of a car and when she pushes her stomach against a mirror. The suggestion is that these events do not share a criterial set of features determining the applicability of *kick*. Rather, the initial usage determines a *stereotype* and subsequent uses are determined on the basis of resemblance to the prototype. Thus, we could regard the initial usage of *kick* as involving three 'features': waving limb, sudden sharp contact and object propelled, with subsequent uses being determined by the presence of *any one* (or more) of these; no single feature or set of features is criterial.

Bowerman provides additional data which point to the same conclusion but it is more interesting at this point to speculate on the source or sources of such prototypes. One obvious source could be the child's linguistic environment, with the child's mother (unconsciously) directing the child's attention to prototypical instances of categories and attaching linguistic labels to them. To our knowledge no research has been undertaken to investigate this possibility. As an alternative, however, we could investigate the child's non-linguistic cognitive development in an attempt to establish that certain prototypes are cognitively salient for the child before he learns the associated linguistic labels. Research in this area is still in a poorly developed state (. . .).

First, there is evidence to suggest that some colour categories exist in very young infants. This is relatively easy to show by adapting infants' attention to light of a particular wavelength. This technique involves projecting the light on to a screen above the horizontal infant and recording eye-movements; after a certain amount of time the infant will cease to be interested in the light and this will be reflected in a sharp drop in the amount of time he spends looking at it. At this point we can either increase or decrease the wavelength of projected light by a fixed amount and, if we have chosen our initial stimulus carefully, one of these transformations will leave us within the same colour category (from the perspective of adult colour categories) and the other will take us across a boundary into a distinct colour category. Of course, from the point of view of the infant we cannot assume that these categories have any reality but it transpires that his attention is immediately recaptured by the wavelength change which involves crossing a boundary whereas this is not so for the change which leaves him within the same category. Recall that this happens despite the fact that the *physical* changes are of the same extent in each case. This, then, would seem to establish the psychological reality of some colour categories long before the onset of speech.

Secondly, using children who have begun to develop language but who do not yet control full colour lexicons, it has been possible to demonstrate that the focal colours of Berlin and Kay[8] (. . .) control such children's attention more readily than non-focal colours. This would be consistent with the colour categories being structured around focal colours for children who have not yet mastered the relevant vocabulary. Whether similar sorts of demonstration will appear for other areas of vocabulary must await the outcome of ongoing research but it seems likely to be a dominant question during the next few years.

The Development of Speech-acts

One aspect of language development which has been completely ignored so far in this chapter is that which pays attention to the *functions* which the small child's language serves (NB it is important to distinguish this sense of 'function' from that used in the previous section where we were briefly concerned with the functions that various *objects* served. Here we discuss the communicative functions of *language*). The basic terminology of speech-act theory (. . .) has been applied by some authors to the child's developing system.[9] Probably the most influential approach to functional development, however, is that of Michael Halliday,[10] and it is this approach that we shall pay particular attention to here. Halliday does not present his ideas in terms of speech-act theory but in terms of his own functional framework. Nevertheless, most of his terminology can easily be translated into that used by more standard approaches and, although we shall not indulge in a detailed comparison of this sort here, the reader is referred to the Course Text for alternative approaches to functional development.

Halliday suggests that it is possible to identify communicative function in the child's utterances before the child has any recognisable conventional language — he refers to this period of the child's development as that in which the child has a *proto-language* and, in the case of his own son on whom his ideas are based, this extended from about 9 months to 18 months of age. What communicative functions can be identified in this period?

Six functions are postulated by Halliday, with a seventh being added later after the child has made some progress in learning the conventional language system around him. These six functions are:

1 *Instrumental* — involved in the child obtaining objects and satisfying his material needs (e.g. between 9 and $10\frac{1}{2}$ months the child says [nā] when requesting an object). This is the 'I want' function of language.
2 *Regulatory* — involved with controlling the behaviour of others (e.g. between 9 and $10\frac{1}{2}$ months old the child says [ē] with the 'meaning' of 'do that again'). This is the 'do as I tell you' function of language.
3 *Interactional* — involved with using language to interact with others (e.g. between 9 and $10\frac{1}{2}$ months the child says [ø], or several variants of this, to initiate an interaction). This is the 'me and you' function of language.
4 *Personal* — involved in expressing the child's own identity (e.g.

expressions of pleasure and interest such as [a] with the 'meaning' of 'that's nice' between 9 and $10\frac{1}{2}$ months). This is the 'here I come' function of language.

5 *Heuristic* — involved in the child using language to explore his environment (e.g. various forms produced by the child between 15 and $16\frac{1}{2}$ months which are interpreted as requesting the name of an object). This is the 'tell me why' function of language.

6 *Imaginative* — involved in using language to create an environment (e.g. various sounds used by the child between 12 and $13\frac{1}{2}$ months to accompany his pretending to go to sleep). This is the 'let's pretend' function of language.

The seventh function, which only appears later, is the *Informative* function, whereby the child seeks to inform an addressee of some fact of which he is previously ignorant. We must now inquire into the strengths and weaknesses of this sort of approach.

Halliday sees one major virtue in his work in establishing continuity between a primitive system of communication — the proto-language — and later conventional linguistic development; both systems can be characterised using the same functional framework. Furthermore, he sees a source for the functions he wishes to identify in his treatment of the adult language in his six primitive functions. Thus, he can be seen as attempting to establish attempts at communication to the fully fledged grammatical system of the adult.

From a different perspective, some of his functions have a good deal of intuitive content and, as already remarked, can be readily identified with functions postulated by other authors working within more standard frameworks. Thus, to mention just two examples, it seems reasonable to identify Halliday's Instrumental and Regulatory functions with the categories of Request Object and Request Action in a taxonomy of communicative functions worked out by the American psychologist Ann Carter.[11] Additionally, Halliday offers an explanation for why the Informative function is late to appear.

His claim is that the six functions listed above are all defined in the social system in which the child is immersed quite independently of language. However, in the case of the Informative function, this can only be understood in the context of language. It will, therefore, follow that the Informative function cannot appear until language exists in some form, whereas the other six functions can all be seen as grounded in the child's social milieu and available to him independently of language.

Our view on this argument is that, while it may be correct, it is extremely difficult to evaluate because of a good deal of vagueness in the crucial theoretical concepts. It is fairly easy to accept that, say, the Regulatory function is implicit in the child's social situation; after all it is well known that there are clearly defined power hierarchies in various non-human species which are sustained without the intervention of language. In contrast to this, however, we find it more difficult to see the Heuristic function as originating in some non-linguistic social reality. If we are to take seriously its informal characterisation as the 'tell me why' function, it would seem, no less than the Informative function, to presuppose language. There is another source of worry concerning this argument: if we accept Halliday's claim that the Informative function appears late because it requires language we might be concerned about *how much* language it requires, i.e. all six primitive functions or only some of them. Note that this is not to say that Halliday is incorrect in claiming that the Informative function does appear late; it is his explanation of this fact which is at issue.

One notable omission from Halliday's set of functions, recognised by several other writers on the topic, is the function of directing an addressee's attention to some aspect of the environment in which the child is interested. Many children have, among their earliest words, *see* or *look* or some variant of *that, this, here,* or *there*. These words are often accompanied by a pointing gesture and appear to have the function in question. A moment's reflection will indicate that it is an extremely important function as, in a sense, to be in a position to say anything about anything a speaker must have routines available for making sure that his addressee can identify what he is talking about. Routines involving the manipulation of attention are exactly what is called for here, and so it should come as no surprise that such routines are relatively easy to identify in the early communicative behaviour of the child.

Overall, theorising within functional frameworks is not highly developed and what we have in the literature is a set of taxonomies with isolated attempts to establish developmental relations between members of the taxonomies of the sort we have just mentioned.

Notes

1. L. Bloom, *Language Development: Form and Function in Emerging Grammars* (MIT Press, Cambridge, Mass., 1970).
2. R. Brown, *A First Language* (George Allen & Unwin, London, 1973). Also published by Penguin.
3. J. Piaget, *The Child's Construction of Reality* (Basic Books, New York, 1954).
4. D. I. Slobin, 'Cognitive Prerequisites for the Development of Grammar' in C. A. Ferguson and D. I. Slobin (eds.), *Studies of Child Language Development* (Holt, Rinehart & Winston, New York, 1973).
5. E. V. Clark, 'What's in a Word?' in T. E. Moore (ed.), *Cognitive Development and the Acquisition of Language* (Academic Press, New York, 1973).
6. K. Nelson, 'Concept, Word and Sentence', *Psychological Review*, *81*, 267-85 (1974).
7. M. Bowerman, 'The Acquisition of Word Meanings: An Investigation of Some Current Conflicts' in N. Waterson and C. Snow (eds.), *The Development of Communication* (Wiley, Chichester, 1978).
8. B. Berlin and P. Kay, *Basic Color Terms: Their Universality and Evolution* (University of California Press, Berkeley, Calif., 1969). Berlin and Kay's study of colour terminology across different cultures revealed that while there was little argument over the boundaries of different colours, if people were asked to select the best example of a colour term from a set of colour cards, there were significant clusterings of choices around a small number of colours. Thus, while a particular language may have no colour term that has the same boundaries as the English *Red*, it is likely to have a colour term whose best exemplar (termed focal colour by Berlin and Kay), as judged by native speakers, corresponds to the best exemplar of *Red*, as judged by English speakers.
9 For further details see Course Text.
10. M. A. K. Halliday, *Learning How to Mean — Explorations in the Development of Language* (Edward Arnold, London, 1975).
11. A. Carter, 'From Sensori-motor Vocalizations to Words: A Case Study of the Evolution of Attention-directing Communication in the Second Year' in A. Lock (ed.), *Action, Gesture and Symbol* (Academic Press, New York, 1978).

13 A CASE STUDY OF EARLY LANGUAGE AWARENESS

Dan I. Slobin

Source: Sinclair, A., Jarvella, R. J., Levelt, W. J. M., (eds.), *The Child's Conception of Language* (Springer–Verlag, Heidelberg, 1978), *2*, pp. 45-54.

Along with the development of language itself, there emerges a capacity to attend to language and speech as objects of reflection. The development of language awareness is, of course, part of the general development of consciousness and self-consciousness. One can distinguish levels of metalinguistic capacity, from the dimly conscious or preconscious speech monitoring which underlies self-correction, to the concentrated, analytic work of the linguist. Much of this route is traversed in the preschool years. The following aspects of language awareness appear, between the ages of two and six:

(1) self-corrections and re-phrasings in the course of ongoing speech;
(2) comments on the speech of others (pronunciation, dialect, language, meaning, appropriateness, style, volume, etc.);
(3) explicit questions about speech and language;
(4) comments on own speech and language;
(5) response to direct questions about language.

This paper is a discussion of the development of language awareness in my daughter, Heida, between the ages of 2;9 and 5;7. Examples are drawn from my diary observations of her linguistic development, reflecting the range of metalinguistic phenomena observable in one preschool child. Heida lived abroad between the ages of 2;9 and 3;11 — chiefly in Turkey, but with travel through a number of other countries. The resulting contact with a series of foreign languages makes this case different both from normal monolingual and bilingual development, and may have stimulated particularly early attention to linguistic phenomena. I discuss several aspects of this attention below.

Metalinguistic Vocabulary

It would be valuable to study the language available to children for the discussion of language and speech. Heida used the verb *mean* at an early age, due to contact with foreign languages; however, it was also used to request definitions of English words. By 3;4 the following metalinguistic vocabulary items were attested: *mean*, *name*, *word*, *say*, *speak*, *voice*, and *look like* (meaning *sound like*).

Mean

The use of *mean* was present from the second day in Europe, at age 2;9. At first it was used to elicit pairings of English and foreign words, in either direction. After having been in Czechoslovakia, Germany, Austria, and Yugoslavia, she would initiate a series of questions, such as: 'What does *bread* mean in German? What does *bread* mean in Yugoslavian?' and so forth. This question frame was later replaced by frames using *say*, *call*, and *word*: 'How say X?', 'What do you call X?', 'What is X called?', and 'What the word for X?' Apparently she understood that naming a language (*German*, *Turkish*) in one of these question frames would elicit a strange-sounding word which could be used with practical effect in a communicative setting (ordering food, buying things, etc.). (Dictionaries, being the frequent source of such verbal counters, became prized possessions.)

She did not understand, however, that her own speech could be part of such a language game. English words could not be distinguished from the concepts to which they make reference. This is most clearly revealed in an observation from age 3;4, after she had been in Turkey for over four months:

> 1. (3;4) She doesn't accept her English words as a language, but apparently treats them as something like pure word meaning. She asks: 'How a say *red* in English?' she doesn't accept *red* as an answer, but insists on something else to be called an English word, along with words in other languages. Later in the day she asks: 'What is spoon called in English?'

In response to questions of the form, 'What does X mean?', I would sometimes provide an English definition rather than a foreign word. Heida readily accepted both translations and definitions as responses, and came to use *mean* for both functions in her own speech:

> 2. (3;3) She offered the following spontaneous translations, which are correct: '*Gel* means *come* and *koş* means *run*.'
> 3. (3;3) She has been confused for some time about the meaning of *before* and *after*, and today asked explicitly: 'What does *before* mean?' (Note that the same question is used both to request definitions and foreign equivalents.)

At the same time she was able to discuss the meanings of her own statements, accepting and rejecting paraphrases as 'meaning' what she was trying to say. Somewhat later, when almost 3;6, she was able to offer her own paraphrases:

> 4. (3;5) She explains her own idiosyncratic usage, 'Even I want some milk.' She accepts a paraphrase with *really*, and says it means: '*I* want some milk — very much I want some milk.'

It is evident that part of Heida's understanding of *mean* related to the appropriate usage of words, either English or foreign. The requests for definitions and discussions of paraphrases indicate that she was not applying *mean* solely to elicit pairs of English and foreign words. It was not always clear, however, what kind of answer she expected to a 'What does X mean' question. Beginning at 3;1 she began to take English words apart, expecting each part to have a 'meaning,' as if unwilling to accept the existence of duality of patterning:

> 5. (3;1) Heida asks: '*Cookie*. What does *cook* mean?' When given an answer, she went on to ask: 'What does *ku* mean?' She did this with several other words, e.g., '*Tiger*. What does *ti* mean?' She even dissected *č* into *t* and *š*: 'Wit — what does wit mean — wit — witch?' She also broke down *w*: 'What does *oo* mean? Wall — *oo . . . all*.'
> 6. (3;1) She attempts to break an utterance down into phrases, words, and parts of words: 'Are these little petal things? What's *are these*? What's *are*? What's *are* mean? What's *me* mean?'

It was not until 4;7 that she offered a spontaneous definition: 'Today I learned what *super* means. It means *really, really, really* something.'

Say

Say first appeared in reference to writing, at 3;1. Looking at signs, she would ask, 'What does it says?' *Say* was also used as another way of asking for translations: 'How say X?' These uses seem tied to the immediate speech situation, but the following example may indicate a generic use of *say* as habitual speech behavior. At 3;1 she was learning to count in Turkish, and seemed to be struck by the arbitrariness of ordering of number words: 'Why cause you don't say first *beş, iki, dört (five, two, four)*?'

At 3;4 *say* was used to refer to inner speech: 'I said to myself, "I want my mama and my papa to play with me".'

Use of Other Metalinguistic Terms

Speak was used only in the context of specific language names:

> 7. (3;3) She asks: 'Do we speak English because we're from Engly?' I explain, and then ask: 'Where's German from?' She answers: 'Germany . . . Germy.' I go on: 'Russian?' 'Rushy.' 'Turkish?' 'Turkey.' 'Italian?' 'Talmy.'

From the first month in Europe, at 2;10, she noted that some foreign words 'sound funny.' On one occasion, at 3;3, she created terms to characterize foreign accent (also indicating memory for accent):

> 8. (3;3) I was telling a joke in a Yiddish accent and Heida said: 'That looks like Great-Grandma' (who speaks with a Yiddish accent). There was no one on the street who looked like her great-grandmother. Heida added: 'That's like Great-Grandma's voice.' Eight days earlier she had heard a five minute tape recording of her great-grandmother's voice. Apparently this was sufficient for her to recognize the foreign accent.

Metalinguistic Comprehension

In the context of various informal tests, Heida showed ability to comprehend instructions to attend to features of language or aspects of language use. At 3;5 she was able to play a game with the instruction, 'Give me a word that sounds like X.' At 4;3 she was able to answer questions about 'Which is right to say' in reference to past tense forms (discussed below). At 4;4, with limited reading ability, she could play a category game using first letters as cues, as in, 'Give me a food starting with A.' At 4;5 she understood *backwards* as an instruction both to spell and to pronounce words backwards. At the same age she was easily trained to understand *opposite* as an instruction to provide antonym responses.

Spontaneous Attention to Adult Speech

The examples discussed above of attention to foreign speech and accent indicate that Heida was actively monitoring adult speech. Furthermore, there were many examples of explicit discussion of things which puzzled her, including metaphor, anomaly, synonymy, asking: 'Why cause you have two names, *orange* and *tangerine*?', apparently thinking that the two names apply to the same fruit. An observation from 4;2 shows attention to new words:

9. (4;2) She monitors adult speech closely for unfamiliar words and asks for their meanings — both in speech addressed to her and in overheard conversations. For example, I say: 'She's really tired. Maybe she'll sleep really soundly, and then she won't have any dreams.' She asks: 'What does *soundly* mean?'

At 4;5 she was struck by an apparent anomaly:

10. (4;4) While drawing, she overhears an adult conversation in which someone says, 'Klee says . . .' Heida interjects: 'Clay doesn't have mouths!'

And at 4;9:

11. (4;9) She picks up one usage which violates her sense of grammaticality. On the TV news she hears the word *persons* and mulls over it for some time, since she had recently discovered that *people* is the normal plural of *person*.

Spontaneous Attention to Own Speech

The lowest level of attention to own speech comes from

spontaneous corrections and re-phrasings. An obvservation from 3;1 suggests that self-monitoring was relatively late to develop:

> 12. (3;1) If her verbal formulations are not at once understood, she lies on the floor and cries or screams — but doesn't attempt to reformulate her statement.

This suggestion is supported by a diary note from 3;2:

> 13. (3;2) Self-corrections are still rare, but note: 'It's watching we cutting . . . our cutting . . . we cutting . . . It's watching our's cutting.'

This level of attention is well established by 3;4; for example:

> 14. (3;4) Successive reformulations: 'Some friend of mine gave it to me. A girl friend gave it to me. A girl of my friend gave it to me. A girl my friend gave it to me.' Self-correction: 'You didn't give me a fork. You didn't gave me a fork.'

Attention to the sound qualities of words seemed to appear earlier than attention to meaning or grammar. I have already noted spontaneous analysis of words into syllables and sounds, beginning at 3;1. At the same age she engaged in rhyming play, noticing sound similarities in words in her own speech:

> 15. (3;1) 'Eggs are beggs. Enough — duff. More — bore.' Other attention to word details: 'It's just the same — *tuna tune*.' She made up the name *hokadin* and broke it into syllables: *hoke–a–din*.

Similar attention to word and sound segmentation appeared about a year later, in connection with acquisition of reading.

At 4;3 she was aware of her own speech articulation skills, noting progress:

> 16. (4;3) She clearly repeated 'Look at *that*,' trying to draw my attention to something, but really trying to draw attention to her first clear pronunciation of *th*.

Degree of Personal Control Over Language

The immediate impact of the foreign language experience on Heida was the introduction of non-English vocabulary. From the second day in Europe, at age 2;9, she invented a new word for milk, insisting that it be called [bap]. She frequently babbled in foreign sounds, and continued to invent words of her own. She clearly had no difficulty in accepting alternate sound patterns as names of things in different languages, and could play the game of asking for translation equivalents from 2;9 on. At the same time, as indicated in the discussion of *mean* above (1.), English words seemed to be exempt from this flexibility of usage. *Bread* really is 'bread,' though it can be called *Brot* or *hleb* or *ekmek* in certain special languages games. In similar fashion, Heida was troubled by synonymy (orange and tangerine example, above) and rejected metaphor, insisting on literal meanings.

Yet, at the same age (3;4-3;5) she began to take a pretend attitude toward name changes, tentatively willing to unhook word and referent, at least in play:

17. (3;4) She plays with the idea of changing names with her best friend, Jess: 'I wanna be called *Jess*. Sometimes Jess can be called *Jess* and I can be called *Jess*. I will have two names: Heida and Jess.'
18. (3;5) She is wearing pants but wants to be wearing a dress so that she can dance. She says to me: 'Call it a dress, please.' I reply, 'It's not a dress.' She says, 'Pretend.'

It is impossible to know to what extent these uncertain attitudes about the fixed or variable nature of word-referent relationships were due to her multilingual exposure. She actively reflected on this problem, showing a concern with justification for word usage, both within and between languages. Her questions suggest a nascent awareness of the separability of sound vehicle and concept. At 3;2 she questioned both the use of a proper name ('Why cause he name was George?') and a compound noun ('Why cause it's called *Thanksgiving*?'); and at 3;3 she questioned Turkish usage ('Why in Turkish *kaka* is BM?'). Although the data are scanty, these and other observations (specially those on word segmentation) at least suggest that a child of this age is able to reflect on the sound-meaning relationship.

Organization Below the Level of Awareness

All regularities of speech, of course, reflect underlying structures. Heida's oriented strategies for acquiring foreign vocabulary, however, reflect semantic structures on the level of the lexicon rather than the individual sentence. Two examples are suggestive, one very early, and one much later:

19. (2;10) [In Prague] She became fascinated with a little dictionary, which she seemed to see as the key to foreign language. She easily got the idea of asking me to give Czech words from the dictionary in response to English words, and spent a half hour of concentration asking for words which I gave her. (After playing the game with Czech words, she then wanted German words, indicating some awareness of different languages.) She first asked only for nouns, giving me one English object name after another. Then I suggested 'another kind of word, like *walk* or *eat*.' She easily switched to verbs, but soon fell into verb phrases (e.g., 'eat some meat'). She could not pick up on adjectives, though.
20. (3;6) [In Istanbul] Great increase of interest in Turkish. Asks how to say things. Very systematic — e.g., wanted to know how to say: 'It's mine, it's yours, it's not mine, it's not yours.' She asked for a variety of locative expressions, placing her finger in a cup, in a hole, on the table, under a plate, etc. Then asked for pairs of affirmative and negative sentences, e.g., 'You spilled your water — You didn't spill your water.'

An Emerging Sense of Grammaticality

A sense of grammaticality is implicit in self-corrections, and perhaps in puzzlements over unassimilable aspects of adult speech. In the case of Heida's developing awareness of the English past tense, however, one can trace a path from initial awareness, to a sense of correctness accompanied by uncertainty in regard to particular words, to an explicit normative sense.

The story begins at 4;2, when Heida's speech was rich in overgeneralizations. (Presumably these forms had been used unselfconsciously for some time.) An observation at 4;2 notes: 'She adamantly refuses to accept irregular past tense — i.e., the

correct forms — insisting on her own, long-term overregularizations.' A sense of appropriateness is already present — but for *her*
forms, rather than the adult forms.

A few weeks later, at 4;3, she judges adult forms as correct in a
test situation, though she does not use all of these forms herself:

21. (4;3) I ask Heida a series of questions of the following form:
'Suppose you were eating something yesterday. Which is right to
say: "Yesterday I ate something" or "Yesterday I eated something"?' The order of correct and incorrect verb forms varied. The
sentences frames varied, but all avoided mention of the verb in the
past tense. She accepted the task at once, and almost always gave
me one word answers — confidently supplying the correct form of
the verb (with two exceptions). That is, her response to the
example was *ate*. This is unusual, in that she rarely uses some of
these verbs correctly in her own speech; yet she is clearly aware of
the correct forms. Note that about a month ago she was adamant
in defending her overregularizations (e.g., *camed*). Also, in
dictating a letter today, she corrected herself twice: '. . . comed
. . . came . . . comed . . . came.'

Informal testing of this sort continued, with no feedback, but
probably drew her attention to discrepancies between her forms
and adult forms. At 4;4 she would change judgements in conflicts:

22. (4;4) In the past tense test she accepts correct alternatives
and rejects incorrect alternatives, even if she doesn't use the
correct forms in her speech. For example, she offers *knowed*
but accepts *knew*; she offers *winned*, rejects *won*. She will
occasionally change her initial form when challenged ('Are you
sure?' 'Is there another way?'). Thus she has a sense of
grammaticality which is not regularly reflected in her use of past
tense forms.

By 4;5 she began to judge both her forms and the standard forms
as correct:

23. (4;5) She now accepts several past tense forms as correct for
irregular verbs. For example, she says *stringed*; I offer *strung*;
she concludes: '*Strung* is OK too.' Apparently she has decided,
for now, that some verbs have equally correct alternate past
tense forms.

24. (4;5) Her sense of past tenses is becoming more open. For example, on the past tense today, she accepts both *finded* and *found*. I ask 'How come there are two ways, like *finded* and *found*? Are they both right?' She replies: 'I don't know. I *think* they are.' For many verbs, now, she accepts both forms on the test.

This is a curious intermediate stage in forming an explicit sense of grammaticality. It continued for several months, at least until 4;9. During this period of concerted attention to the past tense — both spontaneously and in periodic testing — apparently both forms sounded correct to her. It is as if she had a good statistical sense that both standard and overgeneralized forms occurred frequently, but had failed to note that the overgeneralizations came from her own speech and the standard forms from the speech of adults. Perhaps a sense of familiarity with both forms led her to judge both as grammatical (that is, as 'right'), suggesting that judgements of acceptability may be based as much on familiarity as on consistency with norms. A charming and rather amazing example from 4;7 graphically reveals the flickering nature of the sense of grammaticality at this stage. Overgeneralizations planted in adult speech elicited protest from Heida only if the standard form happened to be momentarily present in her consciousness:

25. (4;7) If she has just used the correct past tense of an irregular verb, she is annoyed with me if I respond to her with the overregularization; but if she has used the overregularization, she does not object to my following suit. If I follow her incorrect form with the correct form, she will often switch to the correct form. The following dialogue is a good example of how the two forms flit in and out of consciousness in the course of natural conversation:

Dan: Hey, what happened last night after we left? Did Barbara [the baby sitter] read you that whole story? Remember you were reading *Babar*?

Heida: Yeah . . . and, um, he . . . she also . . . you know . . . mama, mama, uh, this morning after breakfast, read[1] the whole, um, book of the three little pigs and that, you know that book, that . . .
[digression of about one minute]

Heida: I don't know when she readed . . .

Dan: You don't know when she what?
Heida: . . . she readed the book. But you know that book
— that green book — that has the gold goose, and
the three little pigs, and the three little bears, and the
story about the king?
Dan: M-hm.
Heida: That's the book she read. She read the whole, the
whole book.
Dan: That's the book she *readed* huh?
Heida: Yeah . . . *read*! [annoyed].
Dan: Oh.
Heida: Dum-dum!
[brief interlude about dressing]
Dan: Barbara readed you *Babar*?
Heida: *Babar*, yeah. You know, cause *you* readed some of it
too.
Dan: Well I just started it.
Heida: Yeah. She readed all the rest.
Dan: She read the whole thing to you, huh?
Heida: Yeah . . . nu-uh — *you* read some.
Dan: Oh, that's right; yeah, I readed the beginning of it.
Heida: *Readed*?! [annoyed surprise] *Read*! [insisting on the
obvious].
Dan: Oh yeah — read.
Heida: Will you stop that, papa?
Dan: Sure.

Beyond 4;9, she began to accept a single standard of correctness, recognizing her own overgeneralizations as errors. Perhaps these examples represent a general phenomenon of the emergence of linguistic norms in various domains.

Language Awareness and Reading

Learning to read requires awareness to several levels of language. Early attempts to segment words into syllables and small units of sound preceded the acquisition of reading and writing. Detailed phonetic analysis was reflected in early spelling. I will not explore these issues here, as they are similar to the phenomena reported in detail by Charles Read (1971). A few examples indicate this sort of metalinguistic attention:

> 26. (4;4) She 'tries to spell *pee* and insists that it should be spelled PHEE, emphasizing the aspiration on P, but also the end-glide on the vowel, which she shades off into H. She spells *pad* as PD, not feeling a need for a vowel, but following the tongue as it comes to rest. She begins to sound out *ice cream* as /a/, and tries to spell it with initial A; begins to sound out *angel* as /e/.
>
> 27. (4;4) She can play a category game using first letters as cues, e.g., 'Give me a food starting with A.' In playing this game, she offered *chair* as a response to, 'Give me the name of a piece of furniture starting with T.'

Conclusion

These observations are only suggestive of the nature and extent of early language awareness. The capacity to reflect on the form, meanings, and uses of language is clearly present at a very early age. More detailed investigation is needed to establish the generality and sequencing of the metalinguistic abilities reflected in this case study.

Acknowledgements

This research was supported, in part, by grants from NIMH to the Language-Behavior Research Laboratory and from the Grant Foundation to the Institute of Human Learning, University of California at Berkeley. Special thanks to Heida Slobin, for originally providing the data at an early age, and agreeing to their publication at age ten.

Note

1. 'Read' represents /red/ throughout.

Reference

Read, C., 'Pre-school Children's Knowledge of English Phonology', *Harvard Educational Review*, *41*, 1-34 (1971)

14(i) SOCIAL CLASS AND LANGUAGE

W. Peter Robinson

Source: Robinson, P., *Language and Social Behaviour* (Penguin, Harmondsworth, 1972), pp. 148-85. Reprinted by permission of Penguin Books Ltd.

Introduction

Why treat social class as a variable that merits special consideration in a general review of relationships between language and social behaviour? A weak reason is that there is empirical work to report about the subject. Like Mount Everest, it is there. Better reasons can be given. The majority of problems and studies mentioned so far have been of a social psychological nature, concerned as they are with functions and patterns of speech in face-to-face interaction: how encounters are regulated, role relationships expressed or defined, how individuals do or can draw inferences about the states and conditions of others. These and other problems can also be investigated at a sociological level of analysis (or of course a social anthropological level). It seems appropriate to include at least one area of study at a level beyond social psychology, at the same time illustrating how the two disciplines are connected.

It is also true that work already mentioned has concentrated upon descriptions and explanations of the performance of adults: we have not asked how people come to learn what they know. In fact, since we know little about this as yet, the omission is unavoidable. By contrast we can adopt a developmental perspective with social class and language, this policy having a double advantage. To describe and explain the developmental processes has an intrinsic value; it also helps to exemplify the relation between sociology and social psychology. For example, the sociological specification that life chances differ according to differences in starting position defined by social class may be partly explicated when one begins to examine the differences between the child-rearing practices of LWC and MC[1] mothers. This is an example of how the sociological is translated into the social

1. LWC refers to *Lower Working Class* and MC refers to *Middle class*.

psychological. Later we concentrate upon socialization, while here we attend to social class differences in language behaviour *per se*.

We must briefly mention problems of the definition of social class. Sociologists have not been as helpful as they should have been. On the one hand, there are philosophical theories of class with definitions based on the differential distributions of power over a variety of environmental features; on the other, classes are defined pragmatically by measurable indices of income or prestige. The links between the two are not immediately obvious. The operational indices themselves are varied. The seven basic category scale of Hall and Jones (1950) is derived from the prestige status of occupations as judged by a sample of the adult population of Great Britain. The four category A-D system preferred by market research organizations is based on income and patterns of consumption. The Registrar General's 1961 Census (General Register Office, 1960) used five social class groupings, but these can be contracted down to manual or non-manual or expanded into seventeen or more socio-economic groups. The categories and their ordering are derived presumably from the judgements of experts who have taken into account income, prestige, type and degree of skill, length of training, as well as rural/urban distinctions. In fact, indices of occupational prestige, income, amount and quality of education, place and type of domicile are highly correlated (see, for example, Brandis, 1970). It is as well to remember that, given this complexity, it may be an improper question to ask to what social class a person belongs when the normally associated criteria are found to diverge. It may also be more useful to use one index than another in particular inquiries. For example, if we were interested in what the patterns of beer consumption were likely to be, the occupation of husband might be more useful than education of wife. However, the gap remains between such indices and a Marxist or Weberian analysis of class, and neither is likely to be of immediate use if we are interested in family life styles, for instance. In fact, investigations making comparisons most frequently rely on the indices most easily obtained and are not really concerned with higher level theories of social stratification. Unfortunately this can lead to a misleading degree of over-simplification. Bernstein's analysis provides a case in point. When writing about the working class and codes of language use, he has insisted that he is contrasting the *lower working class* (semi-skilled and unskilled) with the middle class, yet in writing about his ideas, other people frequently drop the term *lower*. This can make a substantial difference.[2]

But there are social class differences in language use and if so what are they, what do they mean and why should they occur?

Fries and Schatzman and Strauss

A truly scholarly approach to the problem of social class differences in language use and usage would require us to trace a long history of anecdotes, observations and ideas. Such an enterprise is well beyond the present frame of reference, but there are two studies conducted before the 1960s that are worth more than a brief mention. Fries (1940), in an almost totally neglected book, set out to specify grammatical differences in letters written by professional and lower class correspondents. Schatzman and Strauss (1955) successfully anticipated many of the semantic and pragmatic features of lower working class speech, later mentioned by Bernstein, in the analysis they made of interviewees' accounts of a tornado in Arkansas. Both investigations are of methodological interest in that they exemplify in different ways investigations at the initial stages of scientific inquiry.

Fries is explicit about his criteria of social class, except in one respect. To be in the working class group, the respondents had to have left school before ninth grade (basic secondary); certain formal non-linguistic features of the letters had to indicate more than semi-literacy (spelling, capitalization and punctuation); and their occupations had to be 'manual and unskilled', paying them less than ninety dollars a month. The tag 'manual and unskilled' is ambiguous. The sample was also biased to the extent that those LWC persons who were illiterate or semi-literate were excluded directly — or of course did not even write in. Three hundred such letters were used; the number of 'professional' letters is not mentioned. Here, the criteria for inclusion amounted to three years college education, membership of a generally recognized profession and non-linguistic literacy. Following these descriptions, the elaborate analyses of these samples of 'vulgar' and 'standard' English are then presented as total counts or

2. Where investigators have clearly used lower working class subjects, LWC is used; where it is either ambiguous or skilled workers have been included, WC is used.

percentages. No statistical analyses were conducted, nor are they possible on the data as given. Strictly speaking, no reliable inferences about differential usage can be made, in spite of a meticulous attention to the provision of information about the scoring of the linguistic categories. Schatzman and Strauss, on the other hand, offer little information about procedure, no description of scoring, no descriptive or analytic statistics, but plunge quite happily into statements about the social class differences 'found'. What is even more irritating is that, having broken one of the more binding rules of the scientific game — that the steps between hypotheses and conclusions should be publicly available — they come up with results that later workers have arrived at only after rigorous and painstaking adherence to the rules.

While some later studies of social class differences in language use have unfortunately not taken the linguistic notion of register into account, both these investigations did. Precise information is lacking, but Fries's letters were all apparently sent to an administrative department of the armed forces that dealt with exemptions from service, payments to dependents, compassionate leave, etc. Hence there was an experimental control for topic, and possibly for problem within topic, i.e. letters were generally requests for action backed up with supporting arguments (a personal inference from the examples!). They were all formal in that the recipient was an unknown bureaucrat and, of course, they were written rather than spoken. Similarly, all the speech analysed by Schatzman and Strauss had been orally related to an unknown interviewer who might be assumed to be unfamiliar with the events which were to be described, and this speech was also about a single topic — the tornado.

With slight hesitation a number of results are offered in Table 1 as a summary of Fries's data. They represent a number of morphological and lexical differences that would probably have emerged as significant if they had been properly analysed. Syntactic differences also occurred.

What can be extracted? WC letters differ from MC letters in several respects that might reasonably be attributed to dialect; the WC usage of 'My son James, he . . .' does not result in ambiguity or indefiniteness. On the other hand, their more frequent usage of the verbs 'do' and 'get' suggests a preference for leaving information less precise than it might be, while the more frequent

Table 1: Some Morphological and Lexical Differences between Standard and Vulgar English (from Fries, 1940)

More common in standard		More common in vulgar
Nominal group		
Head:	plural zero form	s-less form for time and distance when deviant
Modifier:	nouns, double	–
Intensifier:	more, most	-er, -est
	suffix -ly	all, awful, bad, but, mighty, pretty, real, right
Pronouns		
Plural form:	–	youse, you all, you people
Verbs		
Lexis:	–	get, do as full verbs
Modals:	should, might	would, can
Tense:	have+been+past participle	has been
Prepositions		
Location:	–	with pronouns
Lexis:	by, during, of, until, upon, with, within	for, about, at, under, without, till, off, onto, double prepositions (off from)
Function Words		
Lexis:	that, which, while, who	and, but, as, if

usage by MC writers of certain prepositions and compound nominal groups may signify a greater concern on their part for precision. There seems to be a greater concern to make meanings unambiguous and organized.

Although the validity of their categorizations is not that obvious, Schatzman and Strauss report their results under four headings: perspective, correspondence of imagery in speaker and listener, classifications used, and framework and style of ordering in the description.

WC speakers are reported as retailing events from their own perspective only. They did not accommodate to the fact that the listener had not been present. 'We', 'they' and persons' names were used with no explicit reference or further identification. There was no qualification or elaboration, and phrases such as 'and stuff like that' were substituted for more detailed exposition. Information given was concrete, referring to particular individuals rather than to roles, groups or organizations. Finally, stories were basically straight narratives, but digressive, one observation triggering off a second, which triggered a third sometimes unconnected with the first, except by verbal devices such as 'and', 'then' and 'so'. The authors employ the analogy of a cine-camera moving around from place to place with the speech being a loose commentary predicated upon the assumption that the listener is watching the same film.

By contrast, the MC accounts sifted perspective from self, to other individuals, groups or organizations; the listener was supplied with context to set the stage for events to be related; possible disbelief and misunderstanding were anticipated; and meanings were qualified to take into account the listener's absence from the events. Classifications transcended the particular and attempted to order the total action. The narratives themselves were tightly organized with considerable cohesion, digressions occurring but only as sub-plots followed by a return to the main theme.

The results are explained in terms of life styles and the likely needs of the speakers to relay information. It is suggested that the WC speaker normally deals with 'listeners with whom he shares a great deal of experience and symbolism' where 'motives are implicit and terminal requiring neither elaboration nor explanation' (Schatzman and Strauss, 1955, p. 337). The authors did not notice the possibilities of comparison with Piaget's work showing that children take their own point of view prior to realizing that other people have different ones, that they learn as they grow older to handle longer and longer sequences, and can handle the particular before the general, the concrete before the abstract. One suspects that investigators are loath to infer that some sub-cultures of a society may be more child-like than others.

These studies contrast in one further important way. While Schatzman and Strauss ignore grammar and lexis, except where they can use such units as indices of one of the categories in which they are interested, Fries meticulously sweats through the grammatical indices with no obvious concern for the significance that these might have in communication situations. While Fries is all structure and unit, Schatzman and Strauss are implicitly function orientated. The difficulty is to integrate the two.

Bernstein

A hiatus of several years was followed by Bernstein's entry into the field from a different tack. Why do LWC children not do better in the educational system? Almost any index of 'better' will suffice to show up social class differences, from entry into higher education to attainment within stream of school. Bernstein (1958) argues that a major neglected determinant of these differences is likely to reside in a differential use of language: the lower working class use language mainly to define role relationships (public), whereas the middle class use language for other functions as well (formal). He later listed likely structural characteristics of 'public' and 'formal' languages (see Table 2) in an attempt to integrate the functional codes and their structural realizations. The subsequent evolution of these ideas is charted by Lawton (1968).

Table 2: Characteristics of Public and Formal Languages (after Bernstein, 1961, p. 169)

Public language
1. Short, grammatically simple, often unfinished sentences with a poor syntactical form stressing the active voice.
2. Simple and repetitive use of conjunctions (so, then, because).
3. Little use of subordinate clauses to break down the initial categories of the dominant subject.
4. Inability to hold a formal subject through a speech sequence; thus, a dislocated informational content is facilitated.
5. Rigid and limited use of adjectives and adverbs.
6. Infrequent use of impersonal pronouns as subjects of conditional clauses.
7. Frequent use of statements where the reason and conclusion are confounded to produce a categoric statement.
8. A large number of statements/phrases which signal a requirement for the previous speech sequence to be reinforced: 'Wouldn't it? You see? You know?', etc. This process is termed 'sympathetic circularity'.
9. Individual selection from a group of idiomatic phrases or sequences will frequently occur.
10. The individual qualification is implicit in the sentence organization; it is a language of implicit meaning.

Formal language
1. Accurate grammatical order and syntax regulate what is said.
2. Logical modifications and stress are mediated through a grammatically complex sentence construction, especially through the use of a range of conjunctions and subordinate clauses.
3. Frequent use of prepositions which indicate logical relationships as well as prepositions which indicate temporal and spatial contiguity.
4. Frequent use of the personal pronoun 'I'.

5. A discriminative selection from a range of adjectives and adverbs.
6. Individual qualification is verbally mediated through the structure and relationships within and between sentences.
7. Expressive symbolism discriminates between meanings within speech sequences rather than reinforcing dominant words or phrases, or accompanying the sequence in a diffuse, generalized manner.
8. It is a language use which points to the possibilities inherent in a complex conceptual hierarchy for the organizing of experience.

A Small Misunderstanding?

Subsequent empirical work has generally been directed towards the establishment of the facts about grammatical, lexical, semantic and pragmatic features distinguishing LWC and MC usage, but while the results have been confirmatory, it is still possible to raise certain criticisms. One type of attack at least needs a short digressive comment. About the Bernstein work, Labov has written:

> There is little connection between the general statements made and the quantitative data offered on the use of language. It is said that middle class speakers show more verbal planning, more abstract arguments, more objective viewpoint, show more logical connections, and so on. But one does not uncover the logical complexity of a body of speech by counting the number of subordinate clauses. The cognitive style of a speaker has no fixed relation to the number of unusual adjectives or conjunctions that he uses. . . . When we can say *what* is being done with a sentence, then we will be able to observe how often speakers do it. (1970, p. 84)

Coulthard has suggested that code differences are simply quantitative,

> The figures [Bernstein, 1962b] suggest that the linguistic performance of the working class boys, as a group, is depressed in relation to that of the middle class boys; they certainly do not show two distinct groups 'differently oriented in their structural selections'. (1969, p. 45)

If we concede that Labov's stricture about the lack of connection between the theoretical statements made and the predicted linguistic differences has a measure of validity, and that the *logical* force of his later remarks has power, this does not prevent us from posing questions about the significance of the quantitative differences found. Labov argues that 'when we can say *what* is being done with a sentence, then we will be able to observe how often speakers do it' (1970, p. 84), but is it not also the case that if we observe how often speakers use certain forms in certain contexts, we may be able to hazard some guesses as to what they are doing with their sentences?

Similarly Coulthard's worry may carry logical force, but be empirically empty. Take for example the set of objects labelled 'ships and boats'. Are the differences among them quantitative or qualitative? We could use a fleet of coracles as platforms from which to throw stones at an offending galleon, but a suitably equipped twentieth-century guided missile delivering destroyer would solve the problem with greater ease. Ships differ in function, and within economic and engineering limits their structures are related to these functions. Particular ships can be refitted or adapted to improve their efficiency or change their use. To use certain basic similarities as an argument for ease of conversion would not impress a marine engineer who was asked to run up an aircraft carrier out of a Roman galley. If we were to take this large set of objects labelled 'ships and boats', group its members into sub-sets, and then count or measure the structural variables, only quantitative differences could be found — by defined parameters of the investigation. As with one technological innovation, so with another. Given that we analyse two sets of speech corpuses in terms of a *single list* of linguistic categories, we can only arrive at quantitative differences, even if certain categories have a null entry in one set. Both Labov and Coulthard are making a fairly deep error. Similarities and differences can always be found between any sets of elements, and these can be expressed quantitatively. This logical point does not have significance *in vacuo*, but might have in particular cases. We may, however, pause to sympathize with the possibility that Labov and Coulthard are posing a serious objection, namely, that we cannot argue from a set of quantitative differences *back* to a qualitative distinction. What they have failed to see is that this was not the direction of the original argument — which was from function to structure. While Bernstein's argument takes the form 'If A, then B' and the data show up features relevant to B, all empirical science has this characteristic.

A similar problem arises with differences in the use of lexical items. Bernstein states:

> The restriction on the use of adjectives, uncommon adjectives, uncommon adverbs, the simplicity of the verbal form, and the low proportion of subordinations supports the thesis that the working class subjects relative to the middle class do not explicate intent verbally. (1962b, p. 234)

That lexical differences occur, and these have been reported with fair frequency (Bernstein, 1962b; Lawton, 1968; Robinson, 1965b), indicates something and is probably not irrelevant. Bernstein's argument is that the code differences are likely to result in lexical differences, although the existence of these differences does not necessarily imply differences in code.

Bernstein's Theoretical Framework

There are a number of difficulties associated with an exposition of Bernstein's theoretical framework, and it may be helpful to distinguish some of the distinguishable levels of analysis.

As a *sociologist*, Bernstein is concerned to specify sociological conditions conducive to the development of different communication systems. He has chosen to focus attention on the differences in the positions and life styles of the lower working class and the middle class in twentieth-century Britain — a complex urban industrialized society with a class structure that allows some mobility. His observations obviously have a potential relevance both to other class and caste-based societies. Retaining a sociological perspective, Bernstein is also interested to explain how 'special' forms of communication are retained from generation to generation, especially in the circumstances prevailing in Britain where the existence of a universally available primary and secondary education might be expected to remove such differences. An analysis of these sociological problems might well enable a specification of language codes which are likely to maintain a *status quo*. As one example, we should expect that the codes of the under-privileged groups would not facilitate the verbal expression of an accurate analysis of their situation — working class consciousness may require a command of an elaborated code of language use before the condition can be articulated and communicated.

One common idea in the background of many explanations is the 'least effort' principle: organisms are not likely to proliferate and develop many capacities beyond their needs. The work roles of low social status groups currently and previously have involved relatively unskilled repetitive tasks. Verbal instruction will not have been particularly significant for the learning of the skills and verbal interaction on a job that involves no more than brief commands or requests will not be necessary (and conditions of noise, etc., may well discourage anything more than the brief exchanges of repartee). Neither subsistence farming nor unskilled factory work require great mastery over the referential function of language and the associated structures and lexis.

As Bernstein writes more generally:

> If a social group, by virtue of its class relation, that is, as a result of its communal function and social status, has developed strong communal bonds; if the work relations of this group offer little variety; little exercise in decision making; if assertion, if it is to be successful, must be a collective rather than an individual act; if the work task requires physical manipulation and control rather than symbolic organization and control; if the diminished authority of the man at work is transformed into an authority of power at home; if the home is over-crowded and limits the variety of situations it can offer; if the children socialize each other in an environment offering little intellectual stimuli; if all these attributes are found in one setting, then it is plausible to assume that such a social setting will generate a particular form of communication which will shape the intellectual social and affective orientation of the children.
>
> Such a code will emphasize verbally the communal rather than the individual, the concrete rather than the abstract, substance rather than the elaboration of processes, the here and now rather than the exploration of motives and intentions, and positional rather than personalized forms of social control. (1970, p. 28)

While this list has persuasive appeal, it does not yet have the orderliness that will eventually be required. Eventually it will be necessary to disentangle those attributes of low social status that are functionally related to particular codes and those which are incidental to these. It will be necessary to investigate which attributes of class determinants of code, which consequences and which are interdependent. This last form of relationship is one which sometimes presents conceptual difficulty for people who hold beliefs based on only a simple cause/effect model. 'Does A cause B or B cause A?' can be an improper question in several respects. First, it presupposes that a single variable analysis can be applied rather than a complex interactional one. Secondly, it presupposes a single direction of causation rather than a two-way relationship; and thirdly, it confers a discreteness upon that event rather than viewing it for example as a (dis)continuously operating servo-mechanism. The class/language code problem is probably best construed as a servo-mechanism — with negative feed-back loops. The lower working class status and particular language codes are locked together. Any potential change in role definition is constrained by conceptual categories linked to a code of language usage. Any potential change in conceptual categories and associated verbal representation is constrained by role definitions. If this is so, we may have to rest content with an explication of the facts of life style and language use — and point out how they mesh. To ask how they came to fit is to ask historical questions. To begin to answer why they continue to do so from generation to generation is taken up in Chapter 14 ii. And this will involve a shift from sociology to social psychology and to psychology, and back again.

It is not difficult to see how certain aspects of life style will relate to language use. If the work situation requires no speech, either in learning or execution of the work task, there is no need for a learner or operator to have a language available for this. Many unskilled, semi-skilled and even skilled jobs come close to this. If the work situation requires fast, unambiguous verbal instructions to be decoded, a specialized and efficient jargon is likely to develop, as in aircraft control, deck behaviour on yachts, trawlers or warships. If the work situation involves a heavy proportion of reception, transmission and production of verbally encoded information (as in bureaucratic positions), only minor adaptations to the forms of everyday general language code may be necessary. For specialized activities in the law or science, distinguishable and different language codes are necessary. There will also be demands in bureaucratic, business and scientific posts for a considerable degree of correspondence between what is said or written and the non-verbal world, that is, a premium will be placed on effective use of the referential function. Crudely speaking, one can see what type of relationships are likely to exist between work and use of language.

It is not so likely perhaps that leisure pursuits of brass bands or bingo rather than Bach or badminton will be functions of language codes. We shall then need some much closer specification of those aspects of lower working class life style that are causally linked to language usage and those which can be attributed to other factors such as tradition, aesthetic preference or lack of material resources.

In the meantime it may be useful to offer a summary of some of the empirical evidence obtained. Features particularly associated with language development and socialization are treated separately [. . .]. Here a brief review of other differences is given. This is complicated by the fact that the subjects of investigation differ in age from young children to near adults. It might have been appropriate to present results systematically separating phonology, grammar, lexis, semantics and pragmatics for encoding and decoding of both speech and writing, if the primary interest had been linguistic. In time it may be possible to start at the pragmatic end and show how differences at that level are realized semantically, how they are achieved by a differential use of grammar and lexis. At present this can not be done. Studies are reported by authors, with an attempt at a final interpretation. This gives rise to some confusion. Some workers have collected speech, some writing, while others have used the written medium for collecting information about speech. Conditions of collection vary from free discussions to controlled filling in of gaps in sentences and identifying grammatical roles of nonsense words. Studies have varied in the level of linguistic analysis attempted. The order of presentation is as far as possible: grammar and lexis within speech, then in writing and in mixtures, followed by semantic and pragmatic studies.

Empirical Evidence

Speech

While Schatzman and Strauss (1955) and Fries (1940) cited their undocumented differences at various levels of linguistic analysis with no controls for possible differences in intelligence, both Bernstein (1962a, 1962b) and Lawton (1968) controlled for verbal and/or non-verbal intelligence test scores. Using tape recordings of small group discussions about the abolition of capital punishment by sixteen-year-old boys, Bernstein (1962a) found that LWC subjects used a longer mean phrase length, a shorter word length and spent less time pausing than MC subjects. In line with Goldman-Eisler's (1968) interpretation of pauses as indications of verbal planning time, Bernstein argued that LWC subjects were spending less time planning because the sequences they were producing were heavily precoded 'chunks' and hence highly predictable for the speaker. These same oral materials were subsequently analysed for grammatical, lexical and other differences. Extent of subordination and complexity of verb stem (including passives) were greater in MC speech. 'I' was more common in MC speech, but 'you' and 'they' less so. Lexically, 'uncommon' adjectives (and all adjectives), adverbs and conjunctions were less frequent in LWC speech. Sociocentric sequences such as 'wouldn't it?', 'isn't it?', and 'you know', were more frequently used by LWC, and 'I think' was more frequently used by MC speakers.

Lawton (1968) repeated Bernstein's design, increasing the standardization of the procedure and using more generally accepted linguistic indices. He also included twelve-year-olds in the investigation. Very similar results were obtained with sociocentric sequences and the use of 'I think', structural complexity with the verb group, personal pronouns, and the range of adjectives and adverbs used, especially with the fifteen-year-old boys. The way in which use of subordinate clauses is related to class is shown up by Lawton's employment of the Loban Index (Loban, 1963, p. 6) which measures the 'depth' of a clause. Using this index he found that the deeper the clause, the greater the social class differences. Lawton also examined the semantic quality of utterances, with a four-fold distinction between (i) abstract, (ii) category (class of events), (iii) concrete, and (iv) clichés and anecdotes. Abstract arguments and categorial examples were more common in MC speech, concrete and particular examples in LWC speech. This was true in both age groups. Anecdotes and clichés did not give a significant discrimination, although younger boys were more likely to use them.

Similar differences were found with the fifteen-year-old boys in individual interviews where subjects were required to narrate a story about a series of pictures, describe features of their previous school, say what they thought about the purposes of education, say what they thought a 'good' teacher would be like, and justify commonly accepted solutions to some moral problems (Lawton, 1968). Lawton additionally examined whether there were shifts in style from description to abstraction. Nine indices, of which all were grammatical except the ratio of egocentric to sociocentric sequences, showed shifts in a consistent direction overall. Twelve-year-old MC subjects shifted more than LWC subjects on all nine measures, fifteen-year-old MC boys showed a greater shift on seven. Interestingly enough, Lawton did not find significant differences in a content analysis of the moral judgement answers. His conclusion was:

> . . . in an 'open' situation the working class boys tend to move towards concrete narrative/descriptive language, but in a structured situation where they have little or no choice about making an abstract response, they will respond to the demand made upon them. They may have found the task extremely difficult, but it was not impossible for them. (Lawton, 1958, p. 138)

Not impossible perhaps, but the examples of their performance offered by Lawton (1968, pp. 134-8) show little systematic organization.

Evidence for differential tendencies to switch styles has also been put forward by Henderson (1970b) for five-year-old children. MC children changed the proportions of form classes used more than LWC children as task demands switched from description to narration. As part of the same study, she found considerable differences in type/token ratios for adjectives and nouns, with MC children being higher. With a related sample of children, Hawkins (1969) found that LWC in narrative stories and descriptions were less likely to specify referents of pronouns (this, that, here and there). They also used fewer epithets at head, fewer modifiers other than 'big' or 'little', fewer ordinatives, intensifiers or rank-shifted clauses at head. In both cases, however, materials discussed were visible to both child and interviewer.

Two recent failures to find class differences in the United States have unfortunately to be written off for methodological reasons.

Shriner and Miner (1968) found no differences in the ability of young children to apply certain morphological rules to nonsense syllables; but although their two social class groups were matched on age and Peabody Picture Vocabulary Test scores, these were on mean scores only. The age range was two-and-a-quarter years, and since age was a relevant source of variance, a matched-pairs design at least would have been necessary to provide a sensible test. LaCivita, Kean and Yamamoto (1966) also reported no class differences in the use of morphological and syntactic cues to identify parts of speech; but since their analysis was in fact by school and the MC schools had only 58 per cent MC pupils and the WC school 76 per cent WC pupils, their conclusion is hardly warranted. Both studies have been reported (Cazden, 1970) as though they provide evidence relevant to the issues of the relationship between language and social class.

Using elicited imitations of sentences involving six instances of verb inflexions, three in MC and three in their LWC forms, Jordan (1972) found no differences with nursery school children in their ability to imitate, but both groups showed strong tendencies to change presented forms to those appropriate to their class norm. While this is clear evidence for grammatical differences in use at an early age, the investigation seems to pose the further problem that *both* groups must have been able to *recognize* the form from the other social class in order to make the appropriate changes.

Writing

Lawton's (1968) results with four essays the boys wrote and with the sentence completion tasks they performed yielded similar grammatical, lexical and semantic differences to those found in speech. The semantic features examined were two estimates of the proportion of abstract and general content in essays on 'Home' and 'My life in ten years' time', both having a higher incidence of occurrence in the writings of older and middle class boys — and within the range of the sample, class was more relevant than the age gap. This contrast is illustrated with two examples:

Working class fifteen-year-old boy's essay on:

My life in ten years' time
I hope to be a carpenter just about married and like to live in a modern house and do a ton on the Sidcup by-pass with a motor-bike and also drinking in the Local pub.

My hobby will be breeding dogs and spare time running a pet shop. And I will be wearing the latest styles of clothes.

I hope my in ten years time will be a happy life without a worry and I have a good blance behide me. I am going to have a gay and happy life. I am going to work hard to get somewhere in the world.

One thing I will not do in my life is to bring disgrace and unhappiness to my family. (In Lawton, 1968, p. 112)

Middle class fifteen-year-old boy's essay on:

My life in ten years' time
As I look around me and see the wonders of modern science and all the fantastic new developments I feel a slight feeling of despondency. This is because I am beginning to wonder who will be in control of the world in ten years time, the machine or man. Already men are being shot around earth in rockets and already machines are being built that will travel faster and faster than the one before. I wonder if the world will be a gigantic nut-house by the time I'm ten years older. We are told we will be driving supersonic cars at fantastic speeds, with televisions, beds, and even automatic driving controls. Do we want this, do we want to be ruled by machinery. Gone will be the time when the family go out for a picnic on a Sunday Afternoon, we will be whisked along wide flat autoroads we will press a button in a way and out will come a plate of sandwiches ready prepared. You may think that this is a bit far fetched but if things keep on improving men will not have to think for themselves and we will become a race of bos-eyed mawrons. There is, if this is going to happen, no way to stop it. Men say we will have just one or two more luxuries and it never stops. I enjoy the luxuries of today, but in my opinion there is a limit. But who decides what the limit will be. No one knows its just a lot of men all relaying on someone to stop this happening, but non-one is going to. We're doomed. No prayers can save us now, we'll become slaves to great walking monstrosities. Powerless in the hands of something we helped to create. I'm worried about 'my life in ten years time'. (In Lawton, 1968, p. 113)

Lawton points out that the differences found can be said to reflect only choice and not capacity, but this is a hypothesis that can be tested.

For twelve-year-old children writing informal and formal

letters, Robinson (1965b) found significant social class differences, mainly in the informal letters for both boys and girls. The formal letter was to be addressed to a school governor explaining why the child should be given a prize to go on a visit or holiday. The informal letter was to a friend sick in hospital describing what had been going on in the last fortnight. Grammatical differences, apart from errors, were few in number and not systematically consistent with Lawton's results or Bernstein's theory. Lexical differences in the informal letters were consistent with both. There is some worry that the working class in this investigation were not purely lower working class, a fair proportion being children of fathers in skilled manual occupations. In addition, the grammatical indices were not linguistically respectable.

Cloze Procedure

Cloze procedure is a technique devised by Taylor (1953) in which a corpus of speech or writing has artificially created deletions made in it and subjects have to guess what has been omitted. Successful decoders (gap fillers) are presumably familiar with the language habits of the encoders. By varying encoders, decoders, messages and types of deletions, a range of possible questions can be posed. In this context we can ask about the ways in which WC and MC decoders fill in gaps created in speech and writing of WC and MC encoders.

Robinson (1965a) collected sentences obtained from the samples of the speech and writing of thirteen-year-old WC and MC boys and deleted one item (noun, adjective, verb, adverb, preposition, pronoun, conjunction) from each. MC and WC subjects, controlled for verbal and non-verbal intelligence test scores and a measure of vocabulary in use, were required to write in words that might fit in the gap in the order in which they thought of them. For twenty-five out of thirty items MC boys gave a wider variety of responses than WC boys. The most common word chosen by one social class group was unlikely to be the most common response of the other. Finally, measures of conformity were calculated for each item. The most common first response of WC boys was used by more of them than the most common response of MC boys. A measure which took into account the frequency of occurrence of all first response words also gave differences between the groups. The greater conformity — and hence predictability — of WC responses was confined to the written items. Unfortunately this type of approach has not been developed, either in terms of giving oral presentations with oral replies or in terms of using a greater variety of language samples to see to what extent members of different classes are better at predicting gaps from speech of their social peers.

Deutsch, Levinson, Brown and Peisach (Deutsch *et al.*, 1967; Peisach, 1965) explored the relations of age, sex, intelligence test scores, race and social class to filling gaps created in both teacher and child speech. They used criteria of correctness of responses rather than conformity — correctness defined absolutely, contextually (semantic sense preserved), and grammatically (in term of form class). For teacher speech, the superior performance of MC children was eliminated when statistical controls for intelligence test scores were introduced. For eleven- to twelve-year-old children's speech, the more efficient guessing of MC children survived partialling out of intelligence test scores. While MC and WC children were equally effective at guessing gaps in WC speech, MC children were more efficient than WC children on MC speech. Similar results were obtained with race, Negroes having relatively more difficulty than whites with the speech of white children, rather than vice versa. The investigators used auditory as well as visual presentation in their design.

Williams and Wood (1970) deleted every fifth word from four-person group discussion sessions involving MC and WC Negro junior high school girls talking about students' problems and attitudes to school. A research student attempted to manipulate the style of the discussion by adopting standard English for a formal discussion and what is referred to as 'home-talk' for an informal one. MC girls were more efficient than WC girls at prediction overall, this being particularly true for predicting MC speech. It was true of absolute and form class measures, and for omissions of both lexical and function words. The omissions from WC speech were more accurately filled than those from MC speech. However, the manipulation of formal and informal was not very successful. WC girls apparently switched styles more than MC girls, although what this means cannot be inferred from the journal article since the authors confine themselves to noting, that '. . . WC encoders were markedly reticent in the formal condition'.

These three studies give a consistent picture of the greater redundancy of WC speech and writing for both MC and WC decoders, but the attempts to vary the other scales of register (mode, style and topic) have not given useful information. There are clearly opportunities for manipulating these aspects, as well as participants.

At least two technical difficulties need to be overcome. Robinson's decision to use written presentation of oral utterances can be criticized on the grounds that it would be more appropriate to use oral administration. However, Deutsch *et al.* (1967) report much lower scores with oral presentation, arguing that this technique places a heavy memory load on the subjects. With first-grade children they were forced to delete the last words of sentences to make the administration feasible. It might be instructive to contrast the two methods empirically with comparable samples of subjects.

A second difficulty consists in the decisions as to what are to constitute 'correct' answers. Taylor (1953), Deutsch *et al.* (1967), and Williams and Wood (1970) all used the deleted word as a criterion of correctness. Robinson argued that this could be construed as only one response for that location and that degree of agreement among subject was of more relevance for estimates of predictability. While this argument has some merit, high agreement on the part of WC children as to what a teacher has said when they are all wrong is clearly not satisfactory. The dilemma may be a false one. Each calculation may have a utility contingent upon the purpose of the investigation.

Relationships Between Function and Structure

The structural and lexical differences so far mentioned are most likely to have semantic and pragmatic significance. The LWC use of a less complex grammar, a less diversified lexis, and the relative lack of change in proportions of various structures and items as the task definitions are changed suggest a lack of adaptability with changing circumstances — a lower degree of efficiency of communication, if by efficiency we mean unambiguous reception by a mythical generalized listener or reader with a minimum of effort. But such summary statements are by no means inconsistent with Labov's criticisms which, although couched in terms of the misleading quantitative/qualitative issue, also raised the question of what people are doing with the utterances they make.

If we accept Bernstein's original thesis that the restricted code of the lower working class is primarily geared to direct control of behaviour and role definition in face-to-face situations, are the empirical studies cited strictly relevant to this? Or are they more relevant to demonstrating that when the language used is geared to the referential function, LWC respondents are less efficient than MC ones? In fact, in all the studies reported, the referential function was of prime significance as far as the task requirements were defined. In many, the communication was to be received by a MC person, e.g. Lawton's interviews and essays, Robinson's letters to a school governor, Fries's letters to government officials, Schatzman and Strauss's interviewers. In some studies the written medium was used. But is the LWC restricted code ever in written form in its natural state? It is, of course, quite appropriate to examine the adequacy of the language used to transmit meanings in such settings and report structural and lexical indicators of difference that may be relevant to probable sources of inefficiency. But even this has only been done at a general level. Schatzman and Strauss write about failures to organize material or to take the ignorance and possible different imagery of the listener into account, but they do not instantiate with any precision how these failures are realized structurally and lexically. The other studies report these differences, but tend not to show how they relate to failures in efficiency of communication. Generally the lesser syntactical complexity and narrower lexis of LWC subjects more than suggest a lesser capacity for the efficient transmission of a variety of referential messages. Even with the indicators of sympathetic circularity, there is no independent evidence brought forward to show that these are social psychological checks upon agreement — a reasonable hypothesis but needing stronger evidence in the long run.

There are a few investigations that have tried to relate structure to function in situations where the referential use of language has been at a premium. Rackstraw and Robinson (1967) looked at answers of five-year-old children to questions about how a toy elephant worked, what titles they would suggest for some pictures and how 'Hide and Seek' is played. The speech of MC children was both more general and more precise and displayed more signs of an objective rather than a self-centred perspective. These attributes were exemplified in their lexical choices, grammatical constructions and use of pronouns, i.e. the differences in communicative efficiency can be exposed by a linguistic analysis.

Explicitly dissatisfied with the idea of the pursuit of grammatical and lexical differences exemplified by the Bernstein, Lawton and Robinson studies, Williams and Naremore (1969) have contrasted functions of speech used by some 200 ten- to thirteen-year-old children interviewed about three topics: games played, TV, and vocational aspirations. Adopting extensions and giving operational definitions to some of the features of speech examined by Schatzman and Strauss (1955), Williams and Naremore found a number of class differences: LWC speech contained a higher proportion of incomplete sentences (fragments), and LWC replies to initial questions were more likely to be minimally acceptable simple responses without elaboration. This was mainly in response to questions about TV, where the LWC replies to 'Do you watch TV?' were often a plain 'Yes!'; MC children were often more prone to begin mentioning programmes and their contents. When the LWC children were pressed to elaborate, these class differences disappeared. For perspective, they found LWC more likely to use a generalized 'You' in describing the game (previously found with five-year-olds by Rackstraw and Robinson, 1967) but otherwise a self-singular stance was preferred. This contrast with the MC third person perspective. MC answers were more highly organized while LWC children were more likely to use request interjections (e.g. What do you want?) and phrases of sympathetic circularity. This work begins to tie up structures with function in a limited set of situations.

But is there a more positive side? What is it that the LWC do with language? Do they write less? When they write letters, to whom do they write and for what purposes? What linguistic features characterize their letters? What are the functions and structures used in telephone conversations? Similar questions might be asked about the role of speech in everyday situations at work and home. We have no observational studies that begin to answer these questions. How much role definition and direct control of behaviour is there? And what about other functions and their associated linguistic features? Are the rules governing the forms of speech in encounter regulations peculiar to a sub-culture? What are the rules relevant to effective instrumental activities? Clearly the opportunities for research work in these areas are many, and we have hardly begun to make even naturalistic observations of the ethnography of communication and the relevance of language to this. Such activities have not been prosecuted with any social group for any comparative purpose as yet.

By way of consolation we can begin to see the emergence of a pattern in social class differences in mother-child interaction and the studies reported in the next section do begin to show what LWC mothers do, as well as what they do not do.

14(ii) SOCIAL CLASS, LANGUAGE AND SOCIALIZATION

Introduction

The agglomeration of social class differences in child-rearing beliefs, attitudes and practices enforce the use of some selective principle here, even though our interest is already confined to the development of verbal skills only. While we might properly be concerned about each of the four activities of speaking, listening, reading and writing at all levels of linguistic analysis and could cover development from birth to maturity, we shall not. If we assert that essentially what we wish to know here is whether or not we can establish a *prima facie* case for the existence of functional differences in the use of language, with the lower working class emphasizing direct control of behaviour and role definition, we can answer this most readily by making a mainly patriotic survey of the work of Bernstein and his colleagues.

We could start with the presumption of social class differences in interactions of mothers with their children along the theoretical lines suggested. It is their behaviour that we would expect most generally to be relevant to what young children acquire, purely on the basis of time spent together. The simplest principle of transmission would claim that the children's learning is a direct and simple function of what is made available for them to learn. The actual mechanisms might be specified in terms of Skinnerian and/or Piagetian concepts. What the children learn will guide their behaviour.

In the other direction, the mother's behaviour will be determined by a combination of her knowledge, beliefs, attitudes and relevant constraints in the total context: one would expect her 'ideal strategies' to be modified by such constraints, whether these be acute, e.g. very busy and tired, or chronic, e.g. seven children in the family. The attitudes of the mother herself have no direct relevance to the child's behaviour for they are at two stages removed from it. More distal still, the mother's basic capacities and dispositions will be related back to social class. Why members of particular social classes should have the capacities and dispositions they do is a sociological and historical problem.

These different features of the problems are mentioned here because some odd thinking can result if the distinctions are not preserved between what used to be called immediate and final causes on the one hand and between social psychology and sociology on the other. Social class of mother does not cause children to answer questions in peculiar ways, mothers' beliefs that children should answer interviewers' questions does not cause them to do so. As we have already mentioned, this type of mistake is not discouraged by the design of the many investigations that do directly relate mother's social class to child's behaviour in terms of the statistical analyses conducted. The intermediary links are often assumed rather than made explicit.

In what follows three levels are separated out: mothers' attitudes; mothers' actual and reported behaviour; children's behaviour. All of these are related back to social class. The inter-relationships of the three are not explored both because it is social class which is of direct relevance to the theoretical framework and because so few studies have tried to descend to social psychology for both sets of the variables believed to be related.

Mothers' Attitudes Towards Language and Language Development

Henderson (1970a) analysed data relevant to mothers' reported frequency of speaking for each of a listed variety of reasons. A set of items labelled 'social chit chat' did not differentiate between MC and LWC mothers, but LWC mothers claimed to speak more often than MC mothers for affective (e.g. to show my feelings to others) and role defining (e.g. to decide what is right and wrong) reasons, while the reverse was true for what were labelled cognitive reasons (e.g. to exchange ideas). These preliminary results pose the problem of how far even self-report inventories might shed light on what people do with language.

More directly related to child-rearing, Bernstein and Henderson (1969) asked mothers how much more difficult it would be for a dumb mother to teach her child a number of things. Items were grouped into 'general cognitive', 'affective' and 'specific skills'. MC mothers saw greatest difficulties overall, but this was particularly pronounced in the general cognitive area. LWC mothers reported that the teaching of specific skills like learning to dress would be most affected and emphasized difficulties in this area more than MC mothers. (Work on complex sensori-motor skills in fact stresses the desirability of actual practice with knowledge of results for efficient learning of these.) MC mothers also expressed a readiness to talk with their children across a wider variety of situations and a greater willingness to answer difficult questions than LWC mothers (Bernstein and Brandis, 1970).

Mothers' beliefs about language development in children, how they think it comes about, and what relevance they consider their own behaviour has for this remain unknown. From more general evidence, it might well be expected that MC mothers believe that children have to be taught how to speak and that it is part of their role to encourage such development in a systematic way. As we shall see below they also use language as a means of communicating information of a referential nature. On the other hand, LWC mothers are probably more likely to adopt a passive view believing that children learn to speak 'naturally' or 'automatically'. This *laissez faire* policy is supplemented by beliefs in boundaries being maintained between school and home — teachers teach children school topics and the mother teaches the child role-appropriate behaviour. These possibilities have not been systematically examined.

Reported Behaviour of Mothers

J. Cook (1971) has analysed mothers' responses to questions about controlling their child's behaviour, namely, discipline problems. A distinction was made between 'imperative techniques', 'positional appeals' and 'personal appeals'. *Imperative* techniques included brief commands such as 'Shut up!' as well as non-verbal intervention like smacking and forcible removal from situations. Of the other two verbally based strategies, *positional appeals* comprised those reasons given for behaviour in which membership of a general status category was invoked, often age, sex, or family, e.g. 'Only little boys pull their sister's hair!' What are given here are prescriptions for behaviour appropriate to a given role, e.g. 'five-year-old boys'. By contrast, *personal appeals* invoke the consequences, affective and/or behavioural, for specified individuals such as self, mother, sister, e.g. 'Now you've broken that cup and I am very angry. You will not take advice. You have to learn the hard way, upsetting everybody'. These appeals tend to combine specificity and generality, specific acts being related to general consequences for specific people. There is also in the example an implicit higher level principle 'You should not make people angry.'

There were no social class differences in the incidence of positional appeals, but MC mothers used more personal appeals specifying consequences for the child than LWC mothers, while the exact reverse was true for imperative techniques. Comparable results have been obtained with slightly younger children in Nottingham (Newson and Newson, 1970) and with Negro children in Chicago (Hess and Shipman, 1965).

What do these results imply? In the first place LWC mothers are less likely to use language in discipline situations except in the form of direct commands. Their greater use of simple commands or non-verbal strategies leaves the child to work out for himself the connections between other events and the maternal intervention. On a classical conditioning paradigm, avoidance learning, mediated or not by anxiety, should associate contiguous events with the maternal behaviour, e.g. looking at the clock, day-dreaming about sweets, as well as spilt tea. Repeated trials with consistent reinforcement should render the learning more specific to 'offences', but the other associations might well remain unextinguished. On cognitive developmental theory, the child should seek to accommodate such experiences and derive working rules to apply to them, but the representation of this knowledge at five is likely to be mainly enactive and ikonic, neither of which permits higher order abstraction. There is the further possibility that maternal interventions are not perceptibly rule-following with sufficient consistency for successful accommodation to be possible. Newson and Newson (1970) remark upon the relatively high incidence of threats used by WC mothers, often involving outside authority figures such as policemen. Since policemen seldom come in to carry out maternal threats Newson and Newson ask how far such tactics encourage both a fear and ultimately a contempt (at the impotency) of authorities.

Given that the child can learn the positional appeals, these do afford definitions of role-appropriate behaviour. Where the appeal is based on sex or age relation, such rules have potential durability, but where they are based on age they do not. A caricature might offer a picture of a child spending his sixth birthday checking which rules for five-year-olds continue to apply — and perhaps sadly finding that many still do. It may also be noted that positional appeals define only a small number of roles and that these are ascribed and hence inescapable.

Personal appeals have rather different possibilities as opportunities for learning. They are in fact used to make referential statements about the material and social environment. Emotional states are defined verbally, and actions leading to their occurrence specified; they are made specific to individuals, hence allowing that differences between persons may exist. But children may also acquire information about more general social matters: where one buys teacups to replace broken ones; that lemon juice removes tea stains from tablecloths. It has already been mentioned that such appeals often invoke rather general moral principles, like not hurting other people. Such principles give explanations for behaviour — whereas positional appeals only assert what is allowed or proper — and hence the child has the opportunity of applying them to new situations. He can pose problems in terms of who will be hurt. 'I give you a new commandment: love one another . . .' is used to transcend eight of the Ten Commandments. Cook also found that MC mothers were more likely to take the child's intention into account, and we may note in passing that this is referring to an unobservable variable less easily inferred than emotional states.

To summarize briefly, LWC children are exposed either to conditions similar to those that a rat in a maze enjoys when learning to avoid electric shocks, or to prescriptions for role-appropriate behaviour. Language is used as a medium for the direct control of behaviour by commands or to define roles. MC children also receive such prescriptions, but in addition are given verbally expressed reasons for certain behaviours and information about the material and social environment in general. For the LWC child to contest the validity of a positional appeal or an imperative is to challenge the authority of the mother. A MC child can question the empirical basis of personal appeals without necessarily evoking such a confrontation.

Robinson and Rackstraw (1967) analysed answers that mothers said they would give to a variety of 'wh' questions supposedly posed by their five-year-old children. In this situation MC mothers were more likely to answer the questions, gave more factual information when they did, the information was more accurate and the types of explanations to 'why' questions differed. MC mothers were more likely than LWC mothers to mention causes, consequences, analogies, and class (not social for once) membership as reasons; LWC mothers were more likely than MC mothers to answer by reorganizing the question as a statement — 'Because they do', or by making an appeal simply to the regularity of the event — 'They always do'. These LWC replies make it tempting to argue that, as in the discipline situations, LWC mothers are more prone than MC mothers to control the child directly than to extend his general knowledge. Rackstraw (Robinson and Rackstraw, 1972, p. 244) argues for a grouping of certain types of reply to 'why' questions which she calls answers that 'focus on the proposition'. To use these a person need have no empirical knowledge relevant to the question, but only a small set of sentence frames, e.g. '. . . always . . .' What are called appeals to essence, denials of a need for an explanation, and appeals to unspecified authority or tradition for moral and social questions are combined with repetitions of questions as statements and appeals to simple regularity to form the total set. In a subsequent analysis of similar data, Robinson (1972) found LWC mothers used 'focus on proposition' modes of reply more often than MC mothers. This study also found that MC mothers were more likely than LWC mothers to use more than one mode of explanation and more likely to point to similarities and differences in their answers.

What is made available for children to learn in this situation? The fact that LWC children are more likely to receive no answers or to receive only 'focus on proposition' modes to 'why' questions might be expected to discourage them from asking questions. Curiosity is neither satisfied nor encouraged. LWC children are receiving less information of a referential nature and what they do receive is less accurate. The relative absence of analogies, or specifications of similarities and differences, or appeals to categorization for 'why' questions reduces the changes of knowledge becoming organized — co-ordinate, super-ordinate and sub-ordinate groupings are less likely to develop. The relative shortage of appeals to cause and consequence reduces the extent to which knowledge acquired is ordered sequentially and meaningfully. Language is the medium by which these differences are made explicit.

A Methodological Critique

It might be argued that what mothers report does not relate in any systematic way to what they in fact do. Perhaps LWC mothers are nervous talking to interviewers, and this anxiety affects their verbal behaviour in interviews. If this were so we might expect to find a higher refusal rate among the working class, in what was after all a voluntary situation, and we might expect to detect some signs of anxiety. The first was not true. The second was not systematically investigated, but superficial impressions of the tape recordings do not support this idea. Alternatively, MC mothers may be operating under the influence of a 'social desirability' response set, the tendency to give some type of ideal rather than true answers (Edwards, 1957). Investigations into social desirability as a factor influencing replies normally exploit overtly obvious statements of opinion to which it is relatively easy to distort replies, whereas in this investigation no easy opportunities for distortion were available; mothers had to construct their replies from their own resources and had no foreknowledge of how their answers were likely to be scored. It is possible that the maternal replies provided would not in fact be employed with their children; especially perhaps when domestic situations become fraught with many simultaneous demands, informative causal answers to 'Why are you so red in the face, Mummy?' may not have a high frequency of occurrence. On the other hand, when moods are good and pressing problems few, we might reasonably expect MC mothers to offer more. One way of looking at the problem would be to suggest that, while almost all mothers may well use non-verbal means of control and not reply to questions under some conditions, some mothers are less likely to start in this way under favourable conditions, conditions describable in terms of numbers, types and strength of pressures to do other things.

While these worries about the validity of maternal reports should be exposed and their force investigated, it is also possible to check what the children are like. If the children's behaviour relates to the maternal reports, and we can generate reasonable explanations for such associations, the likely validity of these reports is enhanced.

Behaviour of Children

Robinson and Rackstraw (1972) interviewed fifty-six children whose mothers' answers had been collected two years earlier. These children answered some of the same questions as their mothers, but the number of questions was made up to thirty, covering the full range of common interrogative words as well as different content areas for 'why' questions. In reply to these, MC children gave more information, the information was more accurate and their answers were less likely to be irrelevant to the question asked. For 'when' and 'where' questions, distinctions of convenience were made between absolute (e.g. on 17 October 1941) and relative (e.g. when my sister got married; when the bell goes) answers. In contexts where absolute answers were more likely to be useful, MC children gave more of them. In answer to 'why' questions LWC children used more appeals to simple regularity (e.g. always) and unspecified authority (e.g. it's naughty), while MC children made more appeals to classification, cause and consequence, more to wants of individuals, and mentioned effects upon other people more often. Among appeals to consequences, LWC children were more likely to mention avoidance of punishment as a reason for not doing things, the reality-based wisdom of this being complemented by Cook's data.

The parallels between the social class differences of both mothers and children have been developed in an extended re-analysis of these data in mother-child pairs within social class (Robinson, 1972). Although the sample size was small and there had been a two year gap between the collection of mothers' and children's answers, in which children had been exposed to the influence of their schools, mother-child similarities could still be found — although some strange findings emerged as well. The simplest interpretation remains: that the learning opportunities offered by the mother are determinants of the verbal behaviours of the children.

Turner (1972) has also used the factorial sample of five-year-old children whose mothers were included in the Robinson and Rackstraw study (1972), as well as a sub-sample of the same children at seven, for analysis of control directed speech. These children had to tell a story to a series of questions asked about a four picture cartoon strip in which some boys appear to kick a football through a window, and subsequently interact with a man and possibly with a woman as well. In summary, he found that LWC children were more likely to cite tellings off and use abrupt imperative commands and context-specific threats, while MC children were more likely to use positional appeals focused upon the affective state of the controller. MC children made more explicit reference to attributes of offenders and the effects on controllers; used intensifiers (e.g. very) to make more specific reference to states; and they offered fewer examples of implicit reference marked by exophoric pronouns.

As with the question-answering, so with the control situation: if we make allowance for the difference in level of cognitive development between mothers and their five-year-old children, the social class differences among the children echo their mothers.

Observed Mother-child Interaction in a Teaching Situation

Hess has conducted a series of investigations examining relationships between maternal attitudes and behaviour and children's cognitive development. Of immediate interest are those studies which show social class differences in maternal control procedures and in maternal teaching styles (Hess and Shipman, 1965). With Negro mothers of four social class groups equivalent to upper middle ($n = 40$), upper working ($n = 42$), lower working ($n = 40$), and a fatherless public assistance group ($n = 41$), they found control differences similar to those reported by Cook (1971). The categorizations of control were different in that non-verbal strategies and positional appeals were combined into an imperative-normative category, but personal appeals were divided into those with an affective basis and those with a cognitive-rational one. The results were like Cook's. Social class differences appeared on all three categories in the expected directions. These results are mentioned not so much to demonstrate cross-cultural similarities, but to suggest that Hess's subsequent results on maternal teaching styles and children's behaviour are likely to have been found with the London sample as well.

As a warm-up task a preliminary teaching problem was set to each mother with her four-year-old child as pupil. This was followed by a block-sorting problem requiring simultaneous categorization on two attributes (each two valued). The mother was given as long as she wanted to teach her child and was told to continue until she was satisfied with her child's performance on the task. The child was then tested both for the accuracy of his performance and for his ability to verbalize the basis of his sorting. The mother-child interaction was recorded. The higher social class children made more correct sortings and verbalized these more accurately, although no co-variance analysis appears to have been used to ascertain whether the more effective verbalizations were not simply a direct function of having more correct solutions to verbalize. In their teaching, MC mothers were more likely to seek to motivate the child, establish an appropriate set, give positive verbal reinforcement, give specific instructions and seek verbal responses from their children. They were less likely to give negative verbal reinforcement or seek non-verbal feedback, i.e. to get the child to move the blocks around.

The second task, Etch-A-Sketch, utilized a commercial toy which consists of a rectangular white screen with two control knobs that can be turned to produce black vertical and horizontal lines respectively. The toy was explained to the mother and it seems to have been established that she knew how to work it effectively. The child was brought into the situation and the instructions given: the mother was told she was to operate one knob, the child the other; she could say or do anything except actually turn the child's knob (or his hand on the knob), and after three minute's practice, they were to copy five patterns. The interaction was observed, tape-recorded and accuracy scores computed. The three-minute practice session was rated for preciseness and specificity of instructions given; a sample of twenty-five instructions in the test sessions was scored for specificity of instructions; and a count was made of the number of designs to be copied shown to the child. A combination of these scores gave a multiple correlation of 0·64 with a measure of task performance. The class differences were considerable; the middle class performed better, but spent less time on the task. MC mothers gave more specific instructions and showed their children more of the designs and were rated more highly in the practice sessions. Some of the differences were extraordinary. The 'highest' level of instruction given by any working class mother was 'Turn your knob'. The mean number of designs shown to working class children by their mothers was only 1·2 out of the five possible.

References

Bernstein, B. B. (1958) 'Some Sociological Determinants of Perception', *Brit. J. Sociol.*, *9*, 159-74

Bernstein, B. B. (1961) 'Social Structure, Language and Learning', *Educ. Res.*, *3*, pp. 163-76

Bernstein, B. B. (1962a) 'Linguistic Codes, Hesitation Phenomena and Intelligence', *Language and Speech*, *5*, 31-47

Bernstein, B. B. (1962b) 'Social Class, Linguistic Codes, and Grammatical Elements', *Language and Speech*, *5*, 221-40

Bernstein, B. B. (1970) 'A Socio-linguistic Approach to Social Learning' in F. Williams (ed.), *Language and Poverty*, Markham

Bernstein, B. B., and Brandis, W. (1970) 'Social Class Differences in Communication and Control' in W. Brandis and D. Henderson, *Social Class, Language and Communication*, Routledge & Kegan Paul, London

Bernstein, B. B., and Henderson, D. (1969) 'Social Class Differences in the Relevance of Language of Socialization', *Sociology*, *3*, pp. 1-20

Brandis, W. (1970) 'An Index of Social Class' in W. Brandis and D. Henderson, *Social Class, Language and Communication*, Appendix 1, Routledge & Kegan Paul, London

Cazden, C. B. (1970) 'The Neglected Situation in Child Language Research and Education' in F. Williams (ed.), *Language and Poverty*, Markham

Cook, J. (1971) 'An Inquiry into Patterns of Communication and Control between Mothers and Their Children in Different Social Classes', PhD thesis, University of London

Coulthard, M. C. (1969) 'A Discussion of Restricted and Elaborated Codes', *Educ. Rev.*, *22*, 38-51

Deutsch, M., Levinson, A., Brown, B. R., and Peisach, E. C. (1967) 'Communication of Information in the Elementary School Classroom' in M. Deutsch (ed.), *The Disadvantaged Child*, Basic Books, New York

Edwards, A. L. (1957) *The Social Desirability Variable in Personality Assessment and Research*, Holt, Rinehart & Winston, New York

Fries, C. C. (1940), *American English Grammar*, Appleton-Century-Crofts, New York

General Register Office (1960) *Classification of Occupations*, HMSO, London

Goldman-Eisler, F. (1968) *Psycholinguistics*, Academic Press, New York

Hall, J., and Caradog Jones, D. (1950) 'Social Grading of Occupation', *Brit. J. Sociol.*, *1*, pp. 31-55

Hawkins, P. R. (1969) 'Social Class, the Nominal Group and Reference', *Language and Speech*, *12*, pp. 125-35

Henderson, D. (1970a) 'Contextual Specificity, Discretion and Cognitive Specialization: With Special Reference to Language', *Sociology*, 4, pp. 311-37

Henderson, D. (1970b) 'Social Class Differences in Form Class Usage among Five-year-old Children' in W. Brandis and D. Henderson, *Social Class, Language and Communication*, Routledge & Kegan Paul, London

Hess, R. D., and Shipman, V. C. (1965) 'Early Experience and the Socialization of Cognitive Modes in Children', *Child Develop.*, *36*, pp. 860-86

Hess, R. D., and Shipman, V. C. (1967) 'Cognitive Elements in Maternal Behavior' in J. P. Hill (ed.), *Minnesota Symposium on Child Psychology*, vol. 1, University of Minnesota Press

Jordan, C. (1972) 'The Grammar of Working and Middle Class Children using Elicited Imitation', *Language and Speech*, vol. 15

Labov, W. (1970) 'The Study of Language in Its Social Context', *Studium Generale*, *23*, pp. 30-87

LaCivita, A. F., Kean, J. M., and Yamamoto, K. (1966) 'Socio-economic Status of Children and Acquisition of Grammar', *J. Educ. Res.*, *60*, pp. 71-4

Lawton, D. (1968) *Social Class, Language and Education*, Routledge & Kegan Paul, London

Loban, W. D. (1963) *The Language of Elementary School Children*, Research Report 1, National Council of Teachers of English, Champaign, Ill.

Newson, J., and Newson, E. (1970) *Four Years Old in an Urban Community*, Penguin Books, Harmondsworth

Peisach, E. C. (1965) 'Children's Comprehension of Teacher and Peer Speech', *Child Develop.*, *36*, pp. 467-80

Rackstraw, S. J., and Robinson, W. P. (1967) 'Social and Psychological Factors Related to Variability of Answering Behaviour in Five-year-old Children', *Language and Speech*, *10*, pp. 88-106

Robinson, W. P. (1965a) 'Cloze Procedure as a Technique for the Investigation of Social Class Differences in Language Usage', *Language and Speech*, *8*, pp. 42-55

Robinson, W. P. (1965b) 'The Elaborated Code in Working Class', *Language and Speech*, *8*, pp. 243-52

Robinson, W. P. (1972) 'Where Do Children's Answers Come From?' in B. Bernstein (ed.), *Class, Codes and Control*, vol. 2, Routledge & Kegan Paul, London (in preparation)

Robinson, W. P., and Rackstraw, S. J. (1967) 'Variations in Mothers' Answers to Children's Questions', *Sociology*, *1*, pp. 259-79

Robinson, W. P. and Rackstraw, S. J. (1972) *A Question of Answers*, Routledge & Kegan Paul, London

Schatzman, L., and Strauss, A. (1955) 'Social Class and Modes of Communication', *Amer. J. Sociol.*, 60, pp. 329-38

Shriner, T. H., and Miner, L. (1968) 'Morphological Structures in the Language of Disadvantaged and Advantaged Children', *J. speech and hearing Res.*, *11*, pp. 605-10

Taylor, W. L. (1953) ' "Cloze Procedure": A New Tool for Measuring Readability', *Journalism Quarterly*, *30*, pp. 415-33

Turner, G. J. (1972) 'Social Class and Children's Language of Control at Ages Five and Seven' in B. Bernstein (ed.), *Class, Codes and Control*, vol. 2, Routledge & Kegan Paul, London

Williams, F., and Naremore, R. C. (1969) 'On the Functional Analysis of Social Class Differences in Modes of Speech', *Speech Monogr.*, *36*, pp. 77-102

Williams, F., and Wood, B. S. (1970) 'Negro Children's Speech: Some Social Class Differences in Word Predictability', *Language and Speech*, *13*, pp. 141-50

SECTION VI: LANGUAGE AND THOUGHT

The relation between language and thought is not a topic that can be dealt with in a summary introduction such as this. It has been a perennial question in Western thought, and has, as one time or another, generated the full range of possible answers. Here we present just two readings. Olson discusses the relationship between the different modes of language, spoken versus written, and the cognitive processes of children. The effects of literacy are difficult to investigate, and we must beware of extravagent claims that have an intuitive plausibility yet little empirical support. As Shweder writes in a sober review: 'The idea that literacy causes changes in basic cognitive processes is one of those seductive ideas that deserves to be true, but probably is not' (1982, p. 360) Whilst we might agree with Schweder's conclusion that literacy probably does not affect the basic repertoire of cognitive processes an individual has at his or her disposal, we might still argue that it has a marked effect on which procedures are selected for use, and the speed and efficiency with which they are employed. If this were the case, then a literate person might appear to think differently from an illiterate one, through choosing to use different procedures in the contexts in which they are assessed, and not because one of them possesses skills that the other one lacks.

Further, literacy is not a possession that can be divorced from other aspects of a person's life: and neither, in all likelihood, can the nature of those other aspects be divorced from literacy. For example, supposing a study were to show that a crucial factor in the way people approached problem-solving was not literacy, but whether they were formally schooled. We might be tempted to conclude that it was the manner in which literacy was taught, or even the process of teaching, that was responsible for any subsequent differences found. Hence, literacy would not be a significant factor. However, it could well be that the very forms of teaching we adopt that lead to these differences are themselves historically embedded in practices of literacy, and are outcomes of the possibilities that literacy has created. So literacy might still be the important factor, but be acting at second remove. In sum, literacy appears to be one of those abilities for which we have a poorly developed vocabulary. A literate system may have all sorts of potentialities, and these may or may not be available to any individual user of the system at any particular point in time. The big question then becomes 'What is responsible for allowing a person to tap and use the potentials of a system he already possesses?' Neither psychologists nor linguists have yet developed theories that adequately deal with the topics of potentiality and its realisation. There are, therefore, a number of possible interpretations of Olson's chapter. It thus needs to be read with care.

Bloom's chapter requires similar qualifications. It is obvious from his results that while the grammatical structures of English could be said to facilitate the solving of certain problems, speakers of a language that lacks these facilitating structures are not prevented from finding the solutions. Chinese speakers obviously find some problems more difficult, but not impossible: the structure of their language does not determine their thought processes, it merely fails to make the articulation of certain problems easy for them. Some interesting speculations arise from Bloom's chapter with regard to some of the other themes in this collection. Bloom characterises the specific grammatical constructions he is concerned with as devices for describing the world 'in terms of theoretical entities that have been conceptually extracted from the speaker's baseline model of reality and granted, psychologically speaking, a measure of reality of their own.' Perhaps, then, they would be high in the ordering of metalinguistic abilities that Slobin discussed; likely to remain implicit in communication, and only be given a form for marking them quite late, both in development and history. Whether the time of their marking is related to changes in literacy, the form of writing (pictographic vs. alphabetic), or changes in social structure (Chinese social structure has been much more stable historically than Western), are all speculative questions that other views expressed in this collection would lead us to entertain.

References

Shweder, R. A. (1982) 'On Savages and Other Children', *American Anthropologist. 84*, 354-66

Suggested Further Reading

The classic statements in this area stem from the work of Scribner, Cole and their associates. We would recommend M. Cole and S. Scribner (1974) *Culture and Thought: A Psychological Introduction*, Wiley, New York and S. Scribner and M. Cole (1981) *The Psychology of Literacy*, Harvard University Press, Cambridge, Mass.

15 ORAL AND WRITTEN LANGUAGE AND THE COGNITIVE PROCESSES OF CHILDREN

David R. Olson

Source: Olson, D., *Journal of Communication, 27*, Pt 3, 1977, pp. 10-26

*The bias and structure of the
two modes of discourse define two
types of knowledge and competence.*

It is widely agreed that direct, personal experience results in the acquisition of knowledge which may, in turn, be represented in language. I shall consider the possibility that the knowledge that children acquire bears a direct relation to several different 'languages of experience,' each of which has a biasing effect on the cultures that use them and on the cognitive processes of the children who master them. Two of these languages are considered in detail: the oral language of ordinary commonsense experience and the written language of objective knowledge and formal schooling.

Oral language, the 'mother tongue,' is a universal human device for representing, communicating, formulating, and exploring the knowledge appropriate to the regulation of practical actions directed to the achievement of personally and socially valued ends. Oral language is a flexible, unspecialized, all-purpose instrument with a low degree of conventionalization in which the meanings of sentences must be 'negotiated' in terms of the social relations, the context and the prior world knowledge of the participants. The coding of knowledge in a form compatible with oral language and practical action may be called 'commonsense.' It is the picture of reality and the use of language which the child brings to school.

Written language, on the other hand, is a specialized tool of a literate, schooled culture. The significance of written language is often overlooked by the mistaken assumption that writing is merely speech 'put down.' Written language, by virtue of its demands for explicitness of meaning, its permanence as a visible artifact compatible with repeated scrutiny and reflection, and its realignment of social and logical functions, serves the intellect in several ways. It is an essential means for the formulation of the abstract true statements that constitute objective knowledge; it is critical to the particular mental achievements we designate as conceptual intelligence; and it is the predominant instrument of formal schooling. The bias of written language could account both for the difficulties young children frequently have when they first encounter the formalized languages of group instruction and printed texts, and also for the significant role that formal language of schooling plays in the development of certain forms of intellectual competence.

The gulf between the language of the child, the
'mother tongue,' and the language of literate prose of the
adult, and the alternative conceptions of reality that
those languages sustain will be our central concerns.

In his lectures on *Pragmatism*, William James (1907) described what he took to be the basic, irreducible mode of knowing as 'commonsense' knowledge and contrasted it with its more 'educated sisters,' scientific knowledge and philosophical knowledge. Although scientific knowledge, he admits, puts the control of nature into our hands, it is commonsense that is more universal in that it has 'turned all of ordinary language into its ally.'

Unlike his successors, James never attempted to reduce all legitimate knowledge into a single form. He was, we may say, the original cognitive pluralist. But while for John Dewey and William James these 'modes' of knowing consisted of the major achievements of mankind — science, religion, law — for me it is the forms of the languages in which the knowledge is represented, that is the structure of action and symbols, that give knowledge and the cognitive processes their distinctive properties. While there are, obviously, a large number of such *languages*, I shall confine my attention to only two: oral conversational language and written statements, which for economy we may call 'utterances' and 'texts'; the pictures of reality these languages map onto we may call 'commonsense' reality and 'scientific' reality.

While my concern is with the nature and *bias* of these *languages*, we may profitably begin by considering the structures of knowledge with which the languages are associated. Let us consider the relation between science and commonsense and then return to consider oral 'utterances' and written 'text.'

Historically, Western culture has had an extremely low regard for commonsense knowledge. The Greeks were thoroughly 'intellectualist,' trusting only what they could prove and not the variable appearance of things (1962, p. 3). Since Descarte's time, modern science has depended upon mathematical proofs 'which start from propositions artificially divorced from the actual experience of living' (i.e., from commonsense). For Bacon, commonsense beliefs were 'the idols of the tribe'; for the Enlightenment, commonsense was the collection of irrational superstition and cliché to which unreasonable people appeal when they are stuck for a logical argument.

The advance of science is usually described as a process of discarding commonsense knowledge, myth and superstition. The greatest block to Galileo was the commonsense view that the world stood still while the sun rose and set each day; the block to Newton was the commonsense view that motion and at rest were different and not both exemplars of inertia; to Darwin, that men were not animals; to Freud, that people were not doing what they said and even thought they were doing.

While men of science have low regard for commonsense, men of action, so-called practical men, have an equivalent low regard for theory. The first question to confront any new theory is 'What is the good (use) of that?' If it cannot be shown to have immediate practical usefulness, it is discarded as 'so much theory.' Practical men advocate some 'experience' as an alternative to study and they accuse the universities of producing graduates who consider work as ignoble.

In literature these orientations were contrasted by Cervantes in the characters of Don Quixote, the literate, theoretical man of ideals and Sancho Panza, the good-hearted man of commonsense. While Don Quixote will summon his best scientific knowledge of Ptolemy's celestial mechanics to determine how many thousand miles they have drifted downstream in their small, oar-less boat, Sancho Panza knows it cannot be too far because he can still see and hear his donkey braying on the shore (Schutz and Luckman, 1973).

Let us, then, contrast the structure of commonsense
knowledge with that of theoretical, scientific knowledge.

The picture of reality that sustains practical, goal-seeking activity which is socially valued we may call commonsense knowledge, along with Dewey (1938), Lonergan (1957), Shutz and Luckman (1973). This practical, socially valued knowledge has some general characteristics. First, it specializes in the particular and concrete. As each situation we encounter is to some extent unique, commonsense is tuned to that uniqueness. It is therefore extremely context sensitive.

Second, commonsense generalizations reflecting the variability of events are frequently coded as proverbs or aphorisms — tips worth bearing in mind, not exhaustive truths.

Third, commonsense experience results in elements of knowledge which are not in complete agreement with each other. This inconsistency is a consequence of the fact that this knowledge is acquired in a large variety of situations and retrieved only if it is relevant to the mastery of some current situation. The contradictions are not usually noted unless they are critically examined by another person. Most of us fail to notice, for example, that the proverbial statements we teach our children are inconsistent: 'He who hesitates is lost' is contrary to 'Haste makes waste,' for example. The reason for this, as we shall see later, is that the language of commonsense is designed to regulate action as a means of social control, not as an expression of 'truth.' Thus a mother may say to a child who fell down, hurting himself: 'That will teach you to do what your mother says.' Similarly, proverbs are not just truths, but admonitions to act in a certain way: 'Haste makes waste' means 'Slow down.'

Fourth, commonsense thinking operates by illustration and example, not by formal rules and definitions. Its language is that of metaphor and proverb.

Fifth, commonsense is value-laden. Any aspect of knowledge is marked for significance such that, forced to choose, the man of commonsense knows to put 'First things first.'

Sixth, commonsense arguments are won, not by the person having the best reasons but by the one who 'has the last word.'

In sum, commonsense knowledge is coded for action and marked for value. Cognition, conation, and affect are undifferentiated. Although commonsense is primarily a set of procedures for achieving practical goals and for judging the relevance of any information to those achievements, it also offers a picture of reality, a world view. But not all humans live in the same world. Social experiences differ; the oppressed live in a different world than the oppressors; children live in a different world than adults, and so on. To this extent commonsense knowledge differentiates social groups, as Max Weber, Durkheim, Mannheim, and others pointed out. These differences provide the basis for community as well as for social conflict.

Scientific or theoretical knowledge negates many of the features of commonsense knowledge. Scientific knowledge is coded for reflection, not for action. It seeks universal laws; it seeks to eliminate contradiction; it is value-free in the sense that it is the consequence of the 'disinterested search for truth.' It is coded in premises from which true implications can be drawn. The model of explanation is formal, deductive, and mathematical. A proof is a proof by virtue of its compelling arguments, not by its utility or the authority of the one who speaks it. Science and philosophy take as a criterion for solution the reducibility of the problem to a small set of highly abstract general statements, *not* the achievement of a practical effect.

Scientific knowledge, then, is a specialized form of knowledge which, by suspending its concern with practical usefulness and with values or significance, results in the production of general theories which are conceptually sound and empirically supportable. But that very freedom from considerations of action and values often makes the theory useless. (Of course, action and value also have their forms of specialization as 'technology or design' and 'myth.')

The difference in orientation between practical commonsense knowledge and scientific conceptual knowledge is critical, both in regard to our understanding of cognitive development, and to our understanding of the consequences of schooling. Children come to school with a practical conception of reality only to encounter a theoretical conception of reality. Not only have they difficulty in understanding the nature and aspiration of the school but the knowledge they already have is in a form inappropriate to the demands of the school.

An interesting description of the discontinuity between common-sense knowledge and the conceptual models of literate man comes from Wallace Stegner's (1962) autobiographic essay on the effects of growing up on the Canadian prairies.

> The accident of being brought up on a belated, almost symbolic frontier has put me through processes of deculturation, isola-tion and intellectual schizophrenia that until recently have been

a most common American experience. The lateness of my frontier and the fact that it lay in Canada intensified the discrepancy between the part of me which reflects the folk culture and that part which reflects an education imported and often irrelevant. I am a product of the American earth, and in nothing quite so much as in the contrast between what I knew through the pores and what I was officially taught.

Education tried, inadequately and hopelessly, to make a European of me . . . almost everything I got from books was either at odds with what I knew from experience or irrelevant to it or remote from it. Books didn't enlarge me; they dispersed me. (1962, pp. 22-6)

It is the language structures and language functions of these two orientations, the commonsense and the schooled that shall concern us next. I shall contrast oral conversational language, the language of everyday speech, with the language of written prose. The former is embodied in the mother tongue which is a universal possession of all human beings in that it is primarily adapted to commonsense reality and to the regulation of social action; the latter, the language of written prose, is culturally specific, almost always tied to schooling, and primarily appropriate to a conceptual or theoretical usage. The first we call *utterance*, the second we call *text*. Commonsense knowledge is related to theoretical knowledge in the same way as utterances are related to text.[1]

Now, why should literacy have such
a dramatic effect on the development
of a form of knowledge?

Several lines of evidence converge to support the hypothesis that oral language or speech is substantially different in both structure and function from written language or text. Vico (1961) with his *New Science* was in 1744 among the first to indicate the importance of the distinction and to put his faith in the former. A more substantial case has recently been made by McLuhan (1962), Havelock (1973), Frye (1971), and Goody and Watt (1968). The evidence is of a cultural-historical, anthropological, and literary critical form. I will attempt to add some linguistic, psychological, and developmental evidence. All these lines of evidence converge to show that a 'mother tongue' is not the same as the language of prose text.

It may be worth noting that it is only recently that the language of schools became the vernacular. Latin was the 'schooled' language all over Europe until well into this century (1974) and only in 1976 did Greece abandon classical Greek (Katharevusa) for the vernacular (Demotiki) as the language of instruction in schools (*Globe & Mail*, 1976). In our schools the difference between the mother tongue and the schooled language is much less obvious. But, as I shall show, it is there.

In examining these relations between oral and written language, my primary purpose is to suggest that human intelligence is pluralistic and that oral and written language provide two quite different structures of knowledge and two ways of being intelligent. They are 'languages of experience.'

First, consider the cultural-historical evidence. Eric Havelock (1973) in his *Prologue to Greek Literacy* showed that the sudden blossoming of classical Greek thought could be attributed to the invention of the alphabet. The phonetic alphabet was invented much later than had been previously thought, so the Greeks of Plato's time were among the first to have access to it. Second, the much older Homeric epics were shown to be of strict oral composition — composed by authors who could not write for audiences who could not read (Parry, 1971). These poems constituted an oral or 'tribal' encyclopedia, including procedures for regulating all the major social events of the culture — the problems of orderly succession of authority, settling disputes, and the like. Two consequences of a reliance upon orally coded information are particularly significant: first, it put a severe demand on memory — memory, we may say, would be the dominant cognitive function; second, to make information memorable, the statements had to be biased in the direction of 'poetized' speech — speech dependent on rhyme and rhythm, 'sayings' of all sorts, aphorisms, and proverbial lore. The language code, as Havelock says, 'a panorama of happenings not a program of principles.'

All of this changed with the invention of the alphabet. First, the presence of an available record made it unnecessary to carry all that information in memory, enabling cognitive processes to be deployed differently. It is analogous to doing long division in the head compared to doing it on paper. Second, writing produced an enduring artifact that could be repeatedly scanned at the reader's leisure to see what was in fact said. Writing permits the criticism of statements in terms of what they *said* as opposed to what they *meant* or were intended to mean. In oral language, of course, it is almost impossible to differentiate what is said from what is meant. Third, and most important, because the alphabet was highly explicit, it did not rely to the same extent on the prior expectancies of the reader. An unvocalized syllabary text, for example, could not differentiate *bell, ball, bull*, and the appropriate rendering would have to come from the reader's expectancies. With an alphabet, one could write things that ran counter to expectancies. Text, therefore, became an *instrument for the exploration of new ideas*. While syllabic text could serve to retrieve what was previously known, alphabetic text could explore the unknown and still be read by another person.

The point I wish to draw from this argument is that
an oral tradition provides a model for ordinary spoken
language, language that is context-dependent and relies for
its meaning heavily upon the expectancies of the listeners.

Written language breaks this tie to context and expectancies in a significant way. It is this attention to the statements *per se* and their logical entailments which written language permitted that, according to Havelock, made possible the rise of Greek philosophy and Greek science.

The specialization of ordinary language in the form of written prose permits the growth of theoretical knowledge in science and philosophy. Written language becomes the means not only for explicitly formulating what is known but also for the discovery of new knowledge. The attempt to formulate extended logical prose, what I have called the essayist technique (Olson, 1977), contributed greatly to the development of powerful general theories and the mastery of this technique became an important educational goal. The essayist technique operates on two principles: first, making all the information explicit in the text so that it relies neither on context nor on personal knowledge, such that we may say 'the meaning is in the text'; and second, generalizing the explicit statements in such a way that true implications follow from them.

One step in this development is shown with remarkable clarity in one of the teachings of Luther. Prior to Luther it was widely assumed that statements could only suggest what they meant —

that they required 'interpretation' by means of scholar, context, or dogma. Luther, perhaps sustained by the rise of print and the translation of the Bible into the vernacular, insisted that 'the meaning of scripture depends not upon the dogma of the Church, but upon a deeper reading of the text.' For Luther, the scriptures said what they meant, the meaning was in the text *per se*; it did not require 'interpretation' for its meaning.

Havelock has concluded that the differences in explicitness of written language and the break of its tie to the limits of oral memory is sufficient to account for the effect of literacy on the evolution of science and philosophy. I shall suggest a second factor, namely that literacy has dramatically affected the uses to which language was put. It both realigned the functions of language and altered the linguistic structures to better serve these altered functions.

The functions of language have been classified in several ways (Austin, 1976; Buhler, 1934; Halliday, 1970; Searle, 1969). Two are of primary concern here: the function of specifying the logical relations within the sentence and between sentences and the function of maintaining social relations between the participants. These two correspond to J. L. Austin's distinction between locutionary and illocutionary acts (1976, pp. 144-5). On the first of these we may make judgments of truth or falsity of the utterance and on the second we may make judgments as to whether the utterance is in order or not in order. If one claims with Henny Penny that 'The sky is falling!' the utterance may be judged against at least two considerations. First, is it *true* that the sky is falling, that is, does the sentence correspond to the state of affairs? This aspect of meaning is the set of truth conditions specified by the sentence. Second, whether or not it is true, does one have the right, that is, *is it in order*, for the speaker to declare that the sky is falling? This aspect of meaning depends upon the social relations assumed by the participants, and these in turn depend on the speaker's authority, status in the field, reliability as an observer, and so on.

Any 'real' utterance meets both sets of conditions and the meanings of ordinary language would normally include both social and logical components. The first of these sets of considerations normally is that of the allowances made for the relations that exist between the speaker and listener — considerations that may roughly be called *rhetorical*. The second is the *logical* or truth value considerations. Speech is always directed to a particular individual with whom one has some particular social status or lack of status and who may or may not be influenced by the cold hard facts. Hence the rhetorical function is predominant over the logical function. If you fail to maintain appropriate social relations with the listener, the conversation simply terminates.

The primacy of the rhetorical or interpersonal over the logical functions of language is interestingly illustrated in Esther Goody's recent study (1975) of the use of questions among the Gonja of Ghana. The striking observation was that children rarely asked questions. Rather, questions tended to be asked by higher status individuals, usually adults, and they tended to be used not as requests for information, but rather as a means of control, of holding another person accountable. That questions are used for a similar purpose in our culture is shown by such mother's questions as 'Did you spill your milk?' or teacher's questions 'What is the capital of France?' In both cases it is clear that the speaker is not soliciting information, she already knows the answers, but rather is holding the child accountable for some action or some knowledge. The social controlling functions are also apparent if one denies the speaker the right to ask the question as when one answers a question with a question or more directly by saying 'Who wants to know?'

My primary hypothesis is that the invention of writing, and particularly the attempt to create autonomous text, resulted in the realignment and specialization of these functions, the rhetorical and the logical.

The language was specialized to better serve one of these functions, the one pertaining to the truth conditions, at the expense of the other, the one pertaining to social or authority conditions. More precisely, the authority or rhetorical conditions were collapsed onto the truth conditions so that, if the statement was true to the facts or to the text itself, that was a sufficient condition for its being 'in order.'

This realignment is, in fact, a major innovation of the British empiricists who made this altered conception of language a major part of their canons of language in their insistence that all statements correspond to the observations — 'so many things with an equal number of words.' The authority was passed from

ecclesiastical and political authorities or from 'dogma' to 'nature.'
Statements became the specialized instruments for description and
explanation by subordinating or negating their traditional function
of maintaining social and authority relations. And this specialized
tool of science and philosophy the members of the Royal Society
of 1662 took to be a 'natural, naked way of speaking' (Sprat,
1667).

To better serve this specialized function, language has to be
brought up to a much higher level of formal and explicit
conventionalization. Meaning has to be formulated in a set of
explicit definitions, operational definitions if necessary; grammatical structure has to be shaped up to better indicate logical structure
(Ryle, 1968); and the logical apparatus for specifying implications
and conclusions has to be rigorously conventionalized and observed.
This specialized use of language — formal written explicit prose —
is, of course, the language of science and philosophy *and* the
language of formal schooling. But it is not a language of doing and
saying, a mother tongue, or part of the 'oral tradition' generally; it
is the specialized tool of analytic thinking and explicit argument
and it is the tool that has been adopted as the predominant form of
school instruction.

Now let us consider how this literate language, because it is
assumed, wrongly, to be an 'ordinary language,' yields misleading
conclusions in psychological and educational circles. First, it yields
a biased picture of language as presented by the formal syntactic
theory of Chomsky (1965). My conjecture is that Chomsky's
theory applies to a particular use of language, namely, the explicit
written prose that serves as the primary tool of science and
philosophy. One basic feature of Chomsky's syntax is that it
consists of a set of transformation rules which have the property of
preserving meaning. But the meaning that is preserved is of a
narrow sort, excluding, for example, that of the interpersonal
relations specified in the sentence, but including the preservation
of logical meaning. The meaning of a sentence, from Chomsky, is
independent of the context in which it is uttered or the interaction
that lies behind it. A transformation rule is defined in such a way
as to not introduce meaning bearing elements or to delete lexical
items unrecoverably (1965, p. 132). Transformation rules of the
type specified by Chomsky are rules for translating deep structures
into surface structures *without altering the meaning*. But that
meaning, for Chomsky, consists of those aspects of meaning that

bear on truth valuability not those aspects of meaning that bear upon the interpersonal, authority functions served by the sentence. That is not to deny that Chomsky's theory is valid; it is completely appropriate for the analysis of logical prose. But it is not, I would suggest, a model of a 'mother tongue.'

Second, literate language permits the differentiation of what was said from what was meant. Prose is devoted to an analysis of what was *said*; oral speech is devoted to what was *meant*. The assumption that the meaning is in the text is not made in ordinary speech; rather the meaning is in the apprehension of what was intended 'if you get my meaning.' Let me give two or three examples of the subservience in ordinary speech of what was said to what was meant.

Bransford, Barclay, and Franks (1972) and their colleagues in a series of studies have shown that subjects understand connected sentences not by assigning semantic representations to a well-formed deep structure, but by assimilating what was heard to what they know or expect. In their example, subjects are given the sentence: 'The notes were sour because the seams are split.' This is a perfectly grammatically well-formed sentence but not only does the sentence appear strange, it does not even have a meaning until you know that it is a sentence about *bagpipes*. Then suddenly it has a rhetorical meaning; it makes sense.

In ordinary oral language then, I would suggest the meaning is not explicitly represented in the text, rather the meaning is in the assimilability to a commonsense reality or set of expectancies.

It may be argued that for logical analysis to occur the statements themselves must become the reality; what was in fact said becomes the critical aspect of the statement.

For ordinary speech, on one hand, what was *said* is less important than what was *meant* — that is the assimilability to the commonsense picture of reality held by the listener. For written text, on the other hand, what was said is more important than what may have been intended.

Grice (1975) has recently developed a general theory of the relation between what one *says* and what one *meant*. He compares the following two sentences.

Miss X sang 'Home Sweet Home'.

Miss X produced a series of sounds which corresponded closely with the score of 'Home Sweet Home'.

Suppose the reviewer said the latter. Why has he selected that complicated expression when he could have just said 'sang?' Presumably to indicate some striking differences between what Miss X did and what singing usually involves, that is, to indicate that Miss X's singing suffered from some hideous defect. That is presumably what the reviewer *meant* but that is not what the reviewer *said*. In logical prose, on the other hand, what we say and what we mean are expected to be the same; meaning is fully conventionalized.

As a result, oral language tends to be modified so as to play down the expectancies of the listeners. But speech which is biased to meet the needs of the listener becomes rhetorical rather than logical. It is only with the development and exploitation of writing that this rhetorical emphasis may disappear.

The rhetorical function is the bias of oral language while the logical function is the bias of written prose text.

And if we step further and ask how writing sustains the use of language specialized for its logical function we come back to the point that, while speech is an ephemeral and transparent code that maps onto a picture of reality that we called commonsense knowledge, writing changes speech into a permanent visible artifact, and becomes a reality in its own right.

The fact that it is a visible artifact means that the reader can go over the statements for his own purposes and at his leisure and in virtually any order. And the reader, presumably exploiting the resources of this medium, is led to the progressive visualization of knowledge, to translate the temporally organized knowledge of oral speech into the spatially organized knowledge of written prose, as Ivins (1953) and McLuhan (1962) have suggested. Havelock (1963, p. 51) illustrates this transformation. In Homer's oral culture, the concept of courage is described in the temporally ordered narrative accounts of the deeds of Ulysses, whereas for the literate classical Greeks, beginning with Plato, it is defined in the nontemporal, logical principle: 'Courage consists in a rational understanding of what is to be feared and not feared. . .'

All children encounter the discontinuity between oral and written language in the course of schooling — for some it is more serious than for others.

Let me illustrate this point by reference to some experiments carried out in our laboratory at the Ontario Institute for Studies in Education. We have known for some time that if you tell a child of, say, 5 years of age that 'John has more than Mary,' he is unable to answer the question 'Does Mary have less than John?' Similarly, if you tell him 'John hit Mary' he is unable to answer the question 'Was Mary hit by John?' We interpret this finding as a demonstration that young children fail to see the implications of statements. We were disturbed by the finding, however, that if you showed children a picture of the event portrayed by the first sentence they were able to answer the question. It seemed odd to claim that children could not draw implications from sentences if on some occasions they did appear to draw such implications.

We recently conducted three more experiments that cast a new light on this particular competence (Hildyard and Olson, n.d.; Olson and Nickerson, 1977; Pike and Olson, 1977). In one of these experiments (Olson and Nickerson) we simply varied the degree to which the characters of the sentence were known to the children. In the pilot studies we used names of siblings and classmates. In the experiment we used the familiar Peanuts comic-strip characters, Snoopy, Lucy, and Charlie Brown. There were four conditions. In the first, we used the arbitrary names John and Mary that we had used in earlier studies, in the second, we used the familiar Peanuts names, in the third, we used the Peanuts names embedded in a meaningful story, and in the fourth, we used our pictures.

Two findings emerged. The more well-known the characters the better able were children to draw the correct implications. In terms of the theory I have been developing here, the more readily sentences could be assimilated to the child's commonsense knowledge of the world, the more successful was his performance.

The second finding is more surprising. By performing an analysis on the number of correct responses to the sentence-question pairs we were able to show that children, when successful, proceed in a manner different from that of adults: for adults True Passives are most difficult; for children False Passives are most difficult. To account for these differences, we have postulated different processing models for children and adults. Adults, in these experiments, operate directly on the logical implications of the statements: If *x* hit *y*, then *y* was hit by *x*. Adults simply compare sequentially the constituents of the representations of the sentences keeping track of the mismatched by means of some truth index. Their reaction times reflect the number of these operations. For adults, we may say that the meaning operated on is in the text.

Children, on the other hand, cannot calculate the logical implications of the statements *per se*. Rather, they can compare a sentence *with what they know* to see if it agrees directly; if it does not, they can give a new description of what they know and see if this new description now agrees with the test sentence. This new description is identical in form to that generated logically by adults — hence, they often get the question correct, *but* they get it by assimilation and re-description of *known events*, as in a paraphrase, and not as the necessary logical implication of propositions. And that, of course, is the reason children can only answer the question when asked in a meaningful context.

Writing turns utterances as descriptions into propositions with implications.

Sentences may be treated in either way; and while our children treat them as descriptions of known events, our adults treat them as logical propositions. This jump is fundamental to cognitive development in a literate culture but it is achieved, I suggest, primarily through the reflection on statements made possible by writing systems. And the children here are doing what we literate adults frequently do in ordinary conversational language.

But if this is true, namely that children do not calculate the logical implications of texts directly, but rather, assimilate sentences to what they know and expect, we can make some further predictions. When the logic of the statements runs counter to the structure of known events, children will tend to follow the structure of these events, not the logical structure of the statements.[2] And if the analysis of implications of statements is tied to literacy rather than stage of development, we may expect to find that this achievement is related to passage through the school system in our culture and does not occur at all for adults in traditional, non-literate cultures. This is precisely what Cole, Gay,

Glick, and Sharp (1971) report in their studies of the cognitive processes of the adult Kpelle of Liberia. Here is one of their problems:

Experimenter: Flumo and Yakpalo always drink cane juice [rum] together. Flumo is drinking cane juice. Is Yakpalo drinking cane juice?

Subject: The day Flumo was drinking the cane juice, Yakpalo was not there on that day.

Experimenter: What is the reason?

Subject: The reason is that Yakpalo went to his farm on that day and Flumo remained in town on that day. (1971, pp. 187-8).

Notice that the subject's answer was both conjectural and plausible. It suffered only in that it did not logically follow from the explicit premise.

In our laboratory, Angela Hildyard (1976) recently required children who had had three, five, or six years of schooling (roughly 9-, 11-, and 12-year-olds) to draw logical inferences from presented premises involving spatial and temporal relations. Statements were of the form $A > B$, $B > C$. The questions involved inferences of the form $A > C$. The independent variable was the nature of the material in which these logical relations were embedded: Formal statements, Counter Factual statements and Meaningful texts and some other conditions I cannot detail here. As in the Nickerson study, Hildyard found that children had little or no difficulty drawing logical inferences when they were compatible with what the child knew or believed but had great difficulty when the same relations were given formally but without a supporting knowledge base. To illustrate, if children hear that 'The elephant is ahead of the giraffe and the camel is behind the giraffe' and they are subsequently asked if the camel is ahead of the elephant, they perform poorly in early grades and performance improves significantly with grade level.

If, however, they are told that 'The elephant is ahead of the giraffe because his long neck kept getting tangled in the thick tree branches' and 'The camel is behind the giraffe because he frequently stopped to eat,' the young children do very well in drawing the correct inference and, moreover, on such items there is little improvement with age. Hildyard concludes that children can indeed draw logical implications from stated relations if those relations can be represented in terms of the child's prior knowledge base. What grows with development, or with schooling, is the ability to draw logical inferences whose sole distinguishing quality is that they follow necessarily from the explicitly presented statements.

Our tentative conclusion is that the form of human competence involved in constructing a practical picture of reality, in making predictions intelligently on the basis of that model, and in assimilating oral statements to that picture of reality, what we have here called commonsense, is the general and largely universal possession of mankind, young and old, literate and illiterate. But the form of human competence involved in the ability to confine interpretation to the information explicitly stated in the text is tied largely to the development of literacy.

> *When we turn to the concept of intelligence, it becomes clear that what we call 'intelligence' in our culture is little more than a mastery of the forms of literate uses of language.*

What is called abstraction, for example, reflects largely the mastery of the genus/species structures implicit in all language but made explicit by the literate Greeks. Take as a simple example the IQ test question: 'How are an apple and a peach alike?' If a child responds in terms of the universal and oral coding of experience by saying 'They are both to eat,' he gets only one point; if, on the other hand, he gives the literate genus/species answer, namely, 'They are both fruit,' he gets 2 points by the test norms. A high IQ then reflects, I suggest, a high literate orientation. Being in power, we literates were in a position to define 'rational' and 'intelligent' as we saw fit and we defined them to reflect our special literate competencies. Competence with oral uses of language, that aspect of language that is universal, is not only not measured but reliance upon it would often tend to put one at a severe disadvantage in some tests.

Now consider the child when he is in testing situations. A student of mine, Bill Ford (1976), has shown that in a natural language the disjunctive *or* is used to link mutually exclusive events. We say 'chicken or beef?' 'tea or coffee?' Logical textual statements are quite different; the logical disjunctive is independent of the events being related. Now consider Piaget's famous test for operational thought. Children are shown, let us say, three rabbits and two ducks. Then they are asked 'Are there more rabbits or more animals?' Here the *or* does not relate mutually exclusive events but overlapping events. The child operating on his expectancies says 'More rabbits.' When asked why, he says 'Because there are only two ducks.' He assumes the question to have been about rabbits and ducks partly because *or* is ordinarily used for mutually exclusive events, not overlapping or inclusive ones. Schools provide the occasions for treating statements that violate these presuppositions and which, therefore, require a new way of understanding reality.

This is not to deny that it is worth mastering the skills associated with a literate use of language. It is merely to show that what we naively take to be a reflection of an underlying quality of mind, intelligence, is in fact the mastery of a particular, and biased, set of symbols for representing experience, primarily written language.

Our culture has tended to put great emphasis upon the language of explicit, logically connected prose text, so much so that we often equate literacy with the ability to use language and we make that literate language serve as the primary instrument of schooling.

Explicit written prose, the language of schooling
then, differs in two primary ways from the
language of the mother tongue.

First, the authority or rhetorical functions are subordinate to the logical functions. And second, the requirement for logical, descriptive, autonomous statements requires that the language be much more explicit and conventionalized than the mother tongue. For text to serve its functions, the meanings of the expressions and the ways they will be used are conventionalized or fixed across occasions of their use so that the reader will retrieve the appropriate meaning. The reader cannot ask the text what it means. Children's encounters with text or their preparations for those encounters constitute the one distinguishing feature of schooling.

I have sought to show that human cognition must be represented pluralistically, just as William James and John Dewey insisted in the early years of this century. There are as many ways to be intelligent as there are languages in which we can represent our experience. We then use these representations to 'go over our past experiences to see what we can make of them,' as Dewey (1916) said. I have discussed only oral and written language but a similar analysis could have been made of numbers, spatial representations, and the like. They are various languages for representing one's experience. They permit us to interrogate nature in different ways, and they provide what Goody (1973) calls the technologies of the intellect (Olson, ed., 1974; Olson, 1974).

Literacy is but one, albeit a most important one, of the types of human competence. Intellectual power is manifest in the development of a range of competencies some of which are the direct consequence of practical and social experience and some of which are primarily the consequences of the formal school activities of translating experience into the conventionalized symbolic forms of written logical prose and mathematics.

Written language, the language of schooling, is an instrument of great power for building an abstract and coherent theory of reality. It is the development of this explicit formal system which accounts for the predominant features of Western culture and for the distinctive properties of the cognitive processes of educated adults.

Yet the general theories of science and philosophy provide a poor fit to daily, ordinary, practical, and personally significant experience. Ordinary language, with its depths of resources, while an instrument of limited power for exploring abstract ideas, is a universal means for sharing our understanding of concrete situations and guiding practical actions. And it *is* the language which the child brings to school.

Notes

1. The theory to be presented here overlaps at several points Bernstein's (1971) theory of the relation between elaborated and restricted codes or between particularistic meanings and universalistic meanings. However, while Bernstein attributes the qualities of these codes to underlying social structures in the family and in the culture as a whole, the theory advanced here attributes them to the structure of the media of communication — the potentials and limitations of the oral as opposed to the written means of expression and communication.

2. Margaret Donaldson and Peter Lloyd (1974) and Eve Clark (1973) have provided evidence for the powerful effect of expectancies that the child forms on the basis of his scanning the perceptual environment (rather than the remembered or known environment that I have discussed) on children's comprehension of sentences. In Donaldson's study children are shown three cars inserted into four garages, leaving one garage empty. If asked 'Are all the cars in the garages?' he replies 'No, cause each of them got cars and that one's not.' That is, their perception of the situation induces a set of expectancies in terms of which they interpret the incoming sentence.

References

Austin, J. L. (1962) *How to do Things with Words*, J. O. Urmson (ed.), Oxford University Press, New York

Bernstein, B. (1971) *Class, Codes and Control*, Routledge & Kegan Paul, London

Bransford, J. D., Barclay, J. R. and Franks J. J. (1972) 'Sentence Memory: A Constructive Versus Interpretive Approach', *Cognitive Psychology, 3*, 193-209

Buhler, K. (1934) *Sprachtheorie*, Verlag, Jana

Chomsky, N. (1965) *Aspects of a Theory of Syntax*, MIT Press, Cambridge, Mass.

Clark, E. (1973) 'Non-linguistic Strategies and the Acquisition of Word Meanings', *Cognition, 2*, pp. 161-82

Cole, M., Gray, J., Glick, J. and Sharp, D. (1971) *The Cultural Context of Learning and Thinking*, Basic Books, New York

Dewey, J. (1916) *Democracy and Education*, Macmillan, New York

Dewey, J. (1938) *Logic: The Theory of Inquiry*, Basic Books, New York

Donaldson, M. and Lloyd, P. (1974) 'Sentences and Situations: Children's Judgments of Match and Mismatch', *Current Problems in Psycholinguistics*, Editions du Centre National de la Recherche Scientifique, Paris, pp. 73-86

Ford, W. G. (1976) 'The Language of Disjunction', unpublished doctoral dissertation, University of Toronto

Frye, N. (1971) *The Critical Path*, Indiana University Press, Bloomington, Ind.

Globe & Mail, 'Reform of Greek Language Defuses Emotional Political Issue', 30 Sept. 1976

Goody, E. (1975) 'Towards a Theory of Questions', draft of Malinowski Lecture, London School of Economics (Aug. 1975)

Goody, J. (1973) 'Evolution and Communication: The Domestication of the Savage Mind', *The British Journal of Sociology, 24*, 1-12

Goody, J. and Watt, J. (1968) 'The Consequences of Literacy' in J. Goody (ed.), *Literacy in Traditional Societies*, Cambridge University Press, Cambridge

Grice, H. P. (1975) 'Logic and Conversation' in P. Cole and J. Morgan (eds.), *Syntax and Semantics: Speech Acts*, Academic Press, New York

Halliday, M. A .K. (1970) *New Horizons in Linguistics*, Penguin, Harmondsworth

Havelock, E. (1963) *Preface to Plato*, Harvard University Press, Cambridge, Mass.

Havelock, E. (1973) *Prologue to Greek Literacy. Lectures in Memory of Louise Taft Semple* (second series), 1966-1971, University of Oklahoma Press for the University of Cincinatti Press, Cincinatti

Hildyard, A. (1976) 'Children's Abilities to Produce Inferences from Written and Oral Material', unpublished doctoral dissertation, University of Toronto

Hildyard, A., and Olson, D. R., 'On the Mental Representation and Matching Operations of Active and Passive Sentences by Children and Adults', unpublished manuscript (n.d.)

Ivins, W. M. (1953) *Prints and Visual Communication*, MIT Press, Cambridge, Mass.

James, W. (1907) *Pragmatism*, Longmans, London

Kneale, W. and Kneale, M. (1962) *The Development of Logic*, Clarendon Press, Oxford

Lonergan, B. J. F. (1957) *Insight: A Study of Human Understanding*, Philosophical Library, New York

McLuhan, M. (1962) *The Gutenberg Galaxy*, University of Toronto Press, Toronto

Ong, W. J. (1974) 'Agonistic Structures in Academia: Past to Present', *Interchange, 5(4)*, 1-12

Olson, D. R. (ed.) (1974) *Media and Symbols: The Forms of Expression, Communication and Education*, 73rd Yearbook of the NSSE, University of·

Chicago Press, Chicago

Olson, D. R. (1977) 'From Utterance to Text: The Bias of Language in Speech and Writing', *Harvard Educational Review*, *47*, 257-81

Olson, D. R. and Nickerson, N. (1977) 'The Contexts of Comprehension: Children's Inability to Draw Implications from Active and Passive Sentences', *Journal of Experimental Child Psychology*, *23*, 402-14

Parry, M. (1971) *The Making of Homeric Verse: The Collected Papers of Milman Parry*, Clarendon Press, Oxford

Pike, R. and Olson, D. R. (1977) 'A Question of "More" and "Less" ', *Child Development*, *48*, 579-88

Ryle, G. (1968) 'Systematically Misleading Expressions' in A. G. N. Flew (ed.), *Logic and Language* (first series), Blackwell, Oxford

Schutz, A. and Luckman, T. (1973) *The Structures of the Life World*, translated by R. Zaner and H. Engelhardt, Northwestern University Press, Evanston, Ill.

Searle, J. R. (1969) *Speech Acts: An Essay in the Philosophy of Language*, Cambridge University Press, Cambridge

Sprat, T. (1667) *History of The Royal Society of London for the Improving of Natural Knowledge*, London

Stegner, W. (1962) *Wolf Willow*, Viking Press, New York

Vico, G. (1961) *The New Science of Giambattista Vico*, translated from the third edition (1744) by T. G. Bergin and M. H. Fisch, Doubleday, Garden City, New York

16 THE LINGUISTIC SHAPING OF THOUGHT: A STUDY OF THE IMPACT OF LANGUAGE ON THINKING IN CHINA AND THE WEST

Alfred H. Bloom

Source: Bloom, A. H., *The Linguistic Shaping of Thought: A Study in the Impact of Language on Thinking in China and the West* (Lawrence Erlbaum Assoc., Hillsdale, NJ, 1981), pp. 34-60.

The Generic Concept

A child who learns English as a first language first learns to use the English article 'the' to signal a particularly determined object or objects rather than just any one of a kind.[1] Then, somewhat later, the child learns to use 'the' to refer to a particularly determined object only if the particularly determined object is either one of a kind (e.g., the President of the Senegal; the highest sand dune in Abu Dhabi; the first person to ski on Jupiter, etc.) or if there is some reason for the child to presuppose that his listener has some familiarity with the object referred to, either because it is actually present in the speech context, or because it has been previously mentioned or just because the child knows that his listener is already familiar with it. Even though, for example, the child may want to tell a friend about a particular dog he saw yesterday, he must start by stating, 'I met *a* (rather than 'the') dog yesterday' and then, only once his friend has gained through the child's comments some acquaintance with that dog, can the child begin to talk about 'the' dog. But mastery of these complex conditions governing the use of 'the' still does not constitute full mastery of the use of that English article. The child has still to learn that using 'the' with singular, concrete, count nouns that do not refer to one of a kind or to any previously familiar object, in other words, using it under precisely those conditions where its use should be ungrammatical, may not be ungrammatical at all, but rather the signal of another meaning altogether. In such a case, 'the' acts not to direct attention to a particular object but acts instead to direct attention to a generic concept conceptually extracted from the realm of actual or even imaginary objects. If an English speaker speaks of 'the kangaroo' while standing next to a large marsupial or after just having discussed his friend's pet kangaroo, his use of 'the' will be interpreted as entailing reference to the particular relevant kangaroo. But if the same speaker talks of 'the kangaroo' in the absence of any actual kangaroo or previous mutual familiarity with one, 'the' will no longer be interpreted as entailing reference to any particular kangaroo, but will rather be interpreted as a signal of the generic kangaroo — as a signal to the listener to direct his attention to a theoretical entity extracted from the world of actual kangaroos. With a herd of buffalo off in the distance, a comment like 'The buffalos are disappearing' will be interpreted as entailing reference to particular vanishing beasts. But in the same context, if the speaker shifts to the singular to say 'The buffalo is disappearing,' since there is no vanishing buffalo that is likely to constitute the object of his reference, his use of 'the' will act as a pointer, not to an actual or actual buffalos, but to the generic buffalo and to a descriptive model of the world built in terms of such theoretical entities.[2] Similarly, when the English speaker shifts from talking about 'his success' or the 'success of that venture' to talking about 'success,' or shifts from talking about 'his thoughts' or 'the thought that . . .' to talking about 'thought,' he likewise shifts from discussion of a particular instance or particular instances to discussion of a generic concept conceptually extracted from those instances. (With abstract rather than concrete nouns — the shift is signaled by the dropping of the article altogether, rather than by its use in circumstances that do not readily yield a referential interpretation.)

In Chinese, the situation is quite different. Specific demonstrative adjectives and specific quantifiers are used to denote distinctly the English 'this kangaroo;' 'that kangaroo;' 'these kangaroos;' 'one single definite or indefinite kangaroo;' 'the average kangaroo;' 'several kangaroos;' and 'all kangaroos.' The unmodified word 'kangaroo' is used generally to cover the range of cases in which English would use 'a kangaroo,' 'the kangaroo,' 'kangaroos' and 'the kangaroo/s arrived' (taishu lai le), with 'kangaroo' placed before the verb, carries the meaning that the particular, definite kangaroo or kangaroos expected have arrived; while 'arrived kangaroo/s' (lai le taishu), with 'kangaroo' placed after the verb carries the meaning that some unexpected, hence indefinite, kangaroo or kangaroos has/have arrived. The distinction between plural and singular usually remains unstated, to be inferred if needed from context, although it can be made clear by use of the demonstratives or quantifiers mentioned above. But Chinese does not have any direct means to specify that one is talking about a theoretical kangaroo, by contrast to a particular kangaroo or to all particular kangaroos.

One evening while I was talking in general about my work with a Chinese professor of comparative Chinese/English linguistics from Taiwan National University, he suddenly commented, 'You know, English has a whole complex of ways of talking, and hence thinking, on an abstract, theoretical level, which Chinese doesn't have. We speak and think more directly' — a comment, by the way, I have heard again and again from others equally well qualified to judge. He then continued in a more specific vein — 'For my students of English, besides the use of the counterfactual, the hardest thing to master is the use of articles — in fact, even most very good Chinese bilingual speakers cannot use articles correctly.' He went on about this for a moment more, then suggested that we ask his wife, who has a very modest command of English, how she understands the Chinese phrase 'kangaroo' (taishu). He gave her the Chinese sentence, '(The) kangaroo/s is/are eat turnip/s of animal/s' (Taishu shih ch'ih lopo ti tungwu) and asked her whether she understood it as talking about a singular kangaroo or plural kangaroos. From the generality of the content of the statement and the lack of any kangaroos in the vicinity or previous mention of any, she inferred that the sentence must be referring to plural kangaroos; in fact, to all kangaroos (soyu ti taishu). He then asked if it could alternatively be talking about a conceptual kangaroo (kuannien shang ti taishu), something other than an actual or all actual kangaroos; and she replied, 'What do you mean by "conceptual" kangaroo? Either you are talking about a single kangaroo or about all kangaroos. What else is there?'

One hundred and ten Taiwanese subjects, with varying levels of English ability, were later asked whether the same sentence 'Taishu shih ch'ih lopo ti tungwu,' in addition to referring to an actual kangaroo, to some actual kangaroos or even to all actual kangaroos, might have an additional interpretation, for example, as a conceptual kangaroo. Despite the suggestive wording of the question, only 41, or 37 per cent of the subjects, answered yes and most of those subjects had had extensive exposure to English. Perhaps the fact that English has a distinct way of marking the generic concept plays an important role in leading English speakers, by contrast to their Chinese counterparts, to develop schemas specifically designed for creating extracted theoretical entities, such as the theoretical buffalo, and hence for coming to view and use such entities as supplementary elements of their cognitive worlds.[3] Further research is certainly needed on this point, but the suggestion gains greater strength when viewed in the context of additional differences between English and Chinese relating to the relative inducements each offers its speakers for shunting aside their baseline models of reality in favor of assuming an extracted, detached theoretical perspective on them.

Entification of Properties and Actions

For English speakers, the shift from 'sincere' to 'sincerity,' from 'hard' to 'hardness,' from 'red' to 'redness,' from 'important' to 'importance,' from 'abstract' to 'abstraction,' and from 'counter-factual' to 'counterfactuality' as well as from 'to further' to 'the furtherance of,' from 'to accept' to 'the acceptance of,' from 'to proliferate' to 'the proliferation of' and from 'to generalize' to 'the generalization of' on one level is simply a shift from adjective to noun or from verb to noun. But on a deeper semantic level, this shift parallels the shift from 'the kangaroo over there' to 'the kangaroo' and from 'the success of that venture' to 'success,' in that it signals movement from description of the world as it is primarily understood in terms of actions, properties and things, to description of the world in terms of theoretical entities that have been conceptually extracted from the speaker's baseline model of reality and granted, psychologically speaking, a measure of reality of their own. In that baseline model, things are red, hard, important or imaginary; people are sincere and arguments, abstract. People accept, discover, proliferate and generalize. But when an English speaker adds '-ity,' '-ness,' '-ance,' '-tion,' '-ment,' '-age,' to talk of 'sincerity,' 'redness,' 'importance' and 'abstraction,' of 'the committee's "acceptance" of that proposal,' of 'John's "discovery" of that ancient theory,' of 'the "prolifera-tion" of nuclear arms,' or of 'Joan's "generalization" of the argument from one context to another,' he talks of properties and actions as if they were things; he converts in effect what are in his baseline model of reality characteristics of things and acts things perform into things in themselves — and by means of such entification, ascends to a more conceptually detached way of dividing up the world.

This is not to say that all English nouns constructed out of verbs or adjectives by the addition of nominalizing suffixes have, psychologically speaking, the status of entifications of actions or properties. 'Transportation,' for instance, does not represent to English speakers an entification of the act of transporting, but has rather evolved into an ordinary noun that denotes the means by which the act of transporting is carried out. Likewise, when English speakers talk of 'generalization' or 'discoveries,' they can mean the things that have been generalized or discovered rather than the acts of discovery or generalization. 'Hindrance' is usually used to refer to the result of hindering rather than to entify the act involved.[4] But English speakers frequently do make use of nominalizing endings, as well as of the related gerundive form (e.g., 'his furthering of,' 'his generalizing in that way') to convert acts into things, and they do often use nominalizing endings to convert properties into things as well and, as such, take advantage of another mechanism their language provides for moving in speech and thought from reliance on the categories of their baseline model of the actual world to reliance on theoretical categories extracted from and superimposed atop that model.

In Chinese, there are innumerable examples of distinct noun forms that have evolved to capture what are in effect the means or results of actions — forms parallel, in other words, to the English terms 'transportation,' 'generalization' in the non-entified sense and 'hindrance.' Since Chinese did not traditionally permit the affixation of derivational endings (e.g., '-ity,' etc.), these noun forms are not constructed out of verbal forms, but constitute separate lexical items that do not necessarily resemble in sound or written form the verbs with which they are semantically related. But just as the Chinese language does not have any mechanism with which to signal the counterfactual or any mechanism with which to signal the generic concept, nor has it had at least until recent data, any mechanism with which to entify properties or actions — any mechanism by which to shift to the more theoretically extracted categorization of the world that entification entails.

Some very significant changes have been occurring in both spoken and written Chinese as a response to the pressure of Western influence. Suffixes corresponding to the English '-ize,'

'-ism,' '-ology,' '-ist' and '-itis' have emerged in the Chinese language within the relatively recent past with which Chinese speakers can now convert, for instance, 'soft,' 'modern,' and 'normal' into 'soften,' 'modernize' and 'normalize'; 'capital' and 'Marx' into 'capitalism' and 'Marxism'; 'society' and 'language' into 'sociology' and 'linguistics'; 'science' into 'scientist' and 'appendix' into 'appendicitis.'[5] And, as part of this influx of suffixes, forms have also emerged for converting certain adjectives into nominal counterparts. With them, Chinese speakers can now transform the adjective 'possible' into a distinct form for 'possibility,' the adjective 'serious' into a distinct form for 'seriousness,' the adjective 'efficient' into a distinct form for 'efficiency' and the adjective 'important' into a distinct form for 'importance.' But the use of these nominalizing devices does not yet constitute a natural, freely productive aspect of Chinese grammar. Sentences employing such devices are still perceived as markedly foreign in flavor by a very large segment of the present-day Taiwanese and Hong Kong populations and, as such, are considered to be less aesthetic if, at times, unavoidable, alternatives to 'purely' Chinese adjectival forms. The use of these imported nominalizing devices does not as yet generalize, as it does in Western languages, from the nominalization of adjectives to the nominalization of verbs and even within the adjectival realm itself remains tightly restricted. Certain specific forms such as those exemplified above, do have currency; but as soon as one attempts to extend the accepted set on one's own, the limits of acceptability are quickly violated. In present-day Taiwan, for example, one can shift from talking about 'something being possible' to 'the possibility of something' and from 'something being important' to 'the importance of something,' but no acceptable means has yet emerged for converting 'white' to 'whiteness,' 'probable' to 'probability,' 'subtle' to 'subtlety,' or 'abstract' to 'abstraction,' much less for transforming 'accept' to 'acceptance,' 'preserve' to 'preservation,' 'elucidate' to 'elucidation' or 'generalize' to 'generalization.'

The linguistic traditions of the past are then still far from erased; but the evidence of penetration of Western forms is itself very revealing. It both points to probable future directions of language change in Chinese and brings further confirmation to the suggestion that traditional Chinese linguistic structures did not capture the cognitive implications of entified Indo-European forms, since it is surely for this reason that the new Chinese forms are evolving.[6]

In the Kung-sun Lung-tzu, a Fourth Century BC Chinese philosophical work, discussion focuses centrally on the distinction between property and entified property (e.g., white vs. whiteness; horse vs. horseness), in spite of the linguistic obstacles in its path. But as Wing-tsit Chan (1963) observes in his introduction to selections from the Kung-sun Lung-tzu:

> The school of logicians which produced the Kung-sun Lung-tzu was . . . (of all major ancient Chinese philosophical schools) . . . the only school that was primarily devoted to logical considerations . . . one of the smallest schools . . . (and, moreover, one which) . . . exercised no influence whatsoever after their own time. (p. 232)

In other words, what seems most remarkable in this regard is not the appearance of discussion of this distinction in the work of a Chinese philosophical school, but rather its virtual absence from the subsequent tradition of Chinese philosophy despite the fact that it played a central role in an important classical work.[7]

Entification of Conditions and Events

Moreover the English psycholinguistic processes of entification do not apply only to properties and actions, but to entire conditions and events as well; and it is in application to these latter, more complex structures that the processes of entification seem to make their most dramatic and unique contributions to the shaping of thought.

When, by adjoining nominalizing suffixes and concurrently making use of a nominalizing word-order transformation, the English speaker shifts from 'His attitude is sincere' to the 'Sincerity of his attitude,' from 'this rock is hard' to the 'Hardness of this rock,' from 'It is important to be earnest' to the 'Importance of being earnest,' and from 'China has been persistently reluctant to invade Swat' to 'China's persistent reluctance to invade Swat,' he is not only converting a completed sentence into a noun phrase, but, at the same time, on a cognitive level, moving from the description of a condition that is the case, may be the case, or is not the case, to an extraction of the idea of the condition as a purely theoretical entity. The speaker can go on to state that 'The sincerity of Jill's attitude is beyond question' just as easily as he can go on to state that 'The sincerity of Jill's attitude is to be seriously questioned' for the mere utterance of the nominalized expression 'The sincerity of Jill's attitude' does not commit him to any condition that is or is not the case, but only to the idea of the conditions, the notion of it, extracted from the world of actual, imaginary, or potential happenings.

Similarly, in discussing events rather than conditions, when the English speaker shifts from 'Interest rates rose' to 'The rise of interest rates,' and from 'That measure will be approved by Congress' to 'The approval of that measure by Congress,' he not only converts a completed sentence into a noun phrase, but on a semantic level moves from the description of an event that has happened, is happening or will happen to an extraction of the idea of the event as a purely theoretical notion. Starting a sentence with 'The approval of this measure by Congress . . .' the speaker can just as easily go on to complete the thought by saying, 'The approval of this measure by Congress was faster than expected' — implying that the approval has already occurred — as saying, 'The approval of this measure by Congress will depend on the subcommittee's report' — implying that approval may or may not occur in the future, for 'The approval of this measure by Congress . . .' acts only as a signal to transform the event described into a notion in preparation for further processing, rather than as a signal to accept the event as fact.

The English language then, through the structures it affords its speakers, facilitates movement both in speech and in thought, not only from 'The kangaroo over there' to the generic kangaroo, from 'white' to 'whiteness' and from 'accept' to 'acceptance,' but also from 'His attitude is sincere' to 'The sincerity of his attitude' and from 'Interests rates rose' to 'The rise of interest rates' — from descriptions of conditions and events to the projection of those conditions and events as theoretical notions, free of truth commitments in the actual world. And a comparison with the Chinese language again reveals that just as that language has not provided its speakers, at least until recent date, with the specific structural means and thus the motivation to create generic entities, or to entify properties or entify actions, neither has it provided them with the specific structural means and thus the motivation to entify conditions and events into truth-commitment-free ideas.

As in the case of the counterfactual, there are various ways by which speakers of Chinese can capture in traditionally Chinese forms roughly the same ideas as those carried by English entified forms. Rather than say 'If Bier had been able to speak Chinese, he would have done *X, Y,* and *Z,* the Chinese speaker can always make use of the straightforward descriptive statement, 'Bier couldn't speak Chinese and therefore he did not do *X, Y,* and *Z.*' Rather than talk about 'Mary's sincerity,' the Chinese speaker can always say that 'Mary is sincere.' Rather than state that 'Mary's sincerity cannot be doubted,' he can state that 'Mary is so sincere, (you) cannot doubt (her).' Rather than say, 'Sincerity is a virtue,' he can say, 'Sincere (i.e., being sincere or acting sincerely, since adjectives in this case are inseparable from verbs) is a virtue.' The notion, 'John's discovery of that restaurant makes me happy' can be translated into the statement, 'John discovered that restaurant, makes me happy,' and the statement, 'The acceptance of that measure depends on the approval of the subcommittee's report' into the statement 'Whether or not that measure is accepted depends on whether or not the subcommittee's report is approved.' But these substitute forms, though closely approximating the content of the corresponding English expressions, do not carry the same cognitive implications. Talking of Mary being sincere, of acting sincerely, of John discovering a restaurant, of a measure being accepted or not being accepted, of a report being approved or not being approved, involved talking in terms of a model of the world in which things (or people) have characteristics, and in which things (or people) act, rather than in terms of a model of the world in which these characteristics and happenings have been explicitly transformed into things in themselves, have gained a degree of ontological status independent of the things or people who possess them or the actors who perform them.[8]

Just as contact with Western languages has brought about changes in modern Chinese with respect to the entification of properties, so has it brought about changes with respect to the entification of conditions and events. Modern Chinese uses what is called the 'de' construction (ti) to express equivalents of the English possessive and the English descriptive subordinate clause. The noun to be modified is placed after the particle 'de' and the name of the possessor or the subordinated descriptive clause which modifies that noun is placed before the 'de.' For example, the English phrase 'John's book' would translate as 'John "de" book';

the sentence, 'The man I met on the street yesterday is the manager of Taipei's largest bank' as 'I yesterday met on the street "de" man is Taipei largest bank "de" manager'; and the sentence, 'Congress just passed a law which imposes a tax on private cars and encourages the use of public transportation' as 'Congress just passed an impose tax on private cars and encourage (people) use public transportation "de" law.' The very fact that, in contrast to English, Chinese descriptive clauses precede rather than follow the nouns they modify, itself gives rise to some interesting psycholinguistic consequences. As a result of such 'left embedding,' the Chinese hearer/reader, by contrast to his English counterpart, must hold in memory the content of the descriptive clause before he/she gains knowledge of what it is that is being described — must code a description, in other words, before constructing the mental representation to which to subordinate that description; and this processing burden seems in turn to place severe constraints on how complex subordinated descriptive clauses can become. The constraints do not relate to length, *per se*, but rather to the number of internal levels of subordination that a clause can incorporate. One can, for example, freely talk about an 'impose tax on private cars, encourage people to use public transportation, discourage the use of gasoline and, at the same time, promote coal, etc., etc., "de" law', but as soon as a speaker attempts to introduce an additional layer of subordination, for example, by further modifying the term 'private cars' with the restrictive clause 'used in large cities' to talk about 'a law which imposes a tax on the use of private cars in large cities and encourages . . .' (in Chinese — 'an impose a tax on in large cities use "de" private cars and encourage . . . "de" law') then the sentence begins to strain the boundaries of acceptability. As more layers of internal subordination are embedded and more 'de' 's are employed to express them, the sentence quickly becomes not only utterly objectionable, but extremely difficult to interpret unambiguously. English speakers have no trouble comprehending what, specifically, is to be discussed when they hear the sentence 'We will put off to next week discussion of the further implications of the new method for calculating the relationship between the rate of economic development and individual standard of living.' But the direct Chinese translation equivalent, which, by the use of multiple 'de' constructions, leaves the levels of internal subordination of the English sentence intact — 'We will put off discussing until next week calculate economic development "de" rate and individual standard of living "de" relationship "de" new method "de" further implications' — not only direly offends the aesthetic sensitivities of Chinese speakers, but left 58 per cent (70 out of 120) of the Taiwanese subjects queried unsure as to what exactly will be discussed — further implications, and/or a new method and/or a relationship between economic development and individual standard of living and/or all three, etc. Fluent Chinese might present the relationship first, then in a second sentence talk of the new method of calculating it, and then in perhaps a third sentence state that next week we will talk specifically about the further implications of that method.

Interest in the 'de' construction in this context is only indirectly related, however, to the highly interesting limitations it appears to impose in spoken Chinese on the compact expression of internally subordinated speech/thoughts. The principal reason for introducing it stems from the fact that it is the 'de' construction which in response to pressures from Western languages has more recently been conscripted by the Chinese language, to serve as its means of entifying conditions and events into truth-commitment-free ideas. The core adjective (in its nominalized form if it has acquired one) or the verb of the condition or event is placed after the 'de' in the traditional slot of the noun to be modified, and the remaining components of the description of the condition or event are placed before the 'de' in the traditional slot of the possessor or the subordinated descriptive clause. Hence in Hong Kong and Taiwan today, one runs across such constructions as 'That matter "de" importance' equivalent to the English, 'The importance of that matter'; 'That measure "de" effectiveness' equivalent to the English, 'The effectiveness of that measure'; 'His "de" sincere,' equivalent to the English 'His sincerity'; 'His at school "de" succeed' equivalent to the English 'His success at school'; and 'Taiwan "de" develop' equivalent to the English 'The development of Taiwan,' in contrast to the traditional Chinese, 'That matter is important,' 'That measure is effective,' 'He is sincere,' 'He succeeded at school' and 'Taiwan is developing or has developed.'

These constructions, although in use, are still considered by many Chinese as corruptive influences that should be eliminated from the language altogether; by a majority of the subjects interviewed as aesthetically less attractive alternatives to the traditional non-entified forms; and by just about everyone, whether they oppose them, favor them, or remain indifferent to them, as prime examples of what is called in Chinese 'Westernized Chinese speech.' Observations of subject use of them, combined with subject reactions to them and subject ratings of sentences employing them, suggest, moreover, that as soon as a speaker goes beyond the relatively small set of widely used entified structures and attempts to coin new ones, acceptability declines; that as soon as a speaker tries to move from entification of events such as 'The rise of interest rates' — in which the interest rates are doing the rising — to the entification of events such as 'The approval of this measure' — in which the measure itself is not doing the approving — acceptability tends to decline even more sharply; and that as soon as a speaker attempts to embed internally subordinated information into an entified construction or to embed one entified construction into another, he not only quickly violates the boundaries of acceptability but the boundaries of comprehensibility as well. Thus, in Taiwan today, one can get away with talking about 'His theft' and 'other people's property' but not with 'His theft of other people's property' (He other people 'de' property 'de' 'thieve'). Hearers will listen to 'The sincerity of his attitude' and 'His attitude towards democracy' but will not tolerate 'The sincerity of his attitude towards democracy' (He towards democracy 'de' attitude 'de' sincere). 'The rise of interest rates' and 'The importance of interest rates' are both acceptable, but not 'The importance of the rise of interest rates'; and it is totally impossible to talk sensibly in this form about 'The importance of the acceleration of the rise of interest rates' much less about 'The contribution of the rise of overall prices to a decline in the importance of the acceleration of the rise of interest rates,' etc. In sum then, the case of entification of conditions and events parallels that of entification of properties. Novel linguistic structures have recently emerged in Chinese in response to Western pressure in order to close a translation gap between Chinese and Western languages. A certain number of such structures have gained currency; but their use still remains far from freely productive.

In an effort to gain some insight into the cognitive underpinnings of these linguistic facts, Chinese and American subjects were presented with the following sample transformations in their native languages:

Paul and Priscilla got married ⟶ The marriage of Paul and Priscilla

This thing is important ⟶ The importance of this thing.

Subjects were then asked to transform, again in their native languages, the following sentences according to the principle exemplified in the above examples:

A. It is possible that he already arrived ⟶
B. Jeremy succeeded ⟶
C. His attitude towards that issue is sincere ⟶

As one might expect, English-speaking subjects exhibited little difficulty in extracting the principle exemplified, and in generalizing it across the three sentences presented — in transforming 'It is possible that he already arrived' into 'The possibility that he already arrived,' 'Jeremy succeeded' into 'Jeremy's success' or 'The success of Jeremy' and 'His attitude is sincere towards that issue' to 'The sincerity of his attitude towards that issue.' One-hundred and one out of 116 or 87 per cent of the subjects tested transformed all three sentences correctly, and 115 out of 116 or 99 per cent got two out of three correct. By contrast, only 34 out of 321 or 11 per cent of the Chinese-speaking subjects consistently and accurately generalized the principle of 'entification' across the three novel contexts presented, although 197 out of the 321 or 61 per cent got at least one sentence correct. Certainly continued exposure to and use of entified forms can be expected to lead Chinese speakers to develop 'entification schemas' and so, for better or worse, to come to think in these Western ways. But one might interpret these data as suggesting that in the meantime there exists a situation in the English-Chinese cross-linguistic arena which closely resembles one often observed in first-language learning, in second-language learning, or even in the mastering of a new discipline. The child or the student begins to make use of a newly acquired linguistic form before he gains command of its full meaning potential, before he has, as it were, consolidated the cognitive schema required for its freely productive use. Then he is led on the basis of the feed-back he receives for his use of that form and his observations of others' use of it to construct a cognitive schema for it of the parameters required. Similarly, we might imagine that at some point a small set of 'entificational' constructions were introduced into Chinese in order perhaps to translate specific Western thoughts. Monolingual Chinese speakers more recently have begun to assimilate these forms into their own speech without, however, necessarily developing at first the cognitive underpinnings required for their freely productive use.

Then as these speakers continue to make use of the forms and to be exposed to their use, they are gradually led by the linguistic experience itself to develop cognitive schemas of the parameters required, schemas which provide the cognitive bases for free generalization of these forms across novel contexts. The fact that language may in this case provide direction to the development of thought rather than the other way around, should, moreover, not be surprising, for as in the case of the counterfactual, the generic concept and the entification of properties and actions, we are dealing with a cognitive schema whose development does not merely involve further differentiation of the perceptual world but rather a special kind of abstraction from it — in other words, with the sort of schema that is most likely to be dependent for its development on the directives that language provides.

Entification and the Construction and Manipulation of Theoretical Frameworks

Furthermore, one reason, if not the principal reason, why English speakers entify conditions and events is that by so doing the conditions and events can be transformed into individual conceptual units, which can then be fitted, as individual components, into more general theoretical/explanatory frameworks. Contrast, for example, the typical Chinese sentences 'He is so industrious, he will certainly succeed' and 'Interest rates decline, makes the housing industry grow more rapidly' with their entified English equivalents 'His industriousness insures his success' and 'The decline of interest rates accelerates the growth of the housing industry.' The Chinese sentences call attention to two conditions or two events and then, in addition, stipulate relationships holding between those conditions or events, so that the hearer or reader comes to consider the individual conditions or events on their own terms as well as the intercondition or interevent relationships that link them to one another. By contrast, the entified English sentences convert the subject/predicate descriptions of conditions or events into individual noun phrases and then insert those noun phrases into single subject/predicate frameworks, thereby in effect subordinating the conditions or events to the relationships that link them to one another. The hearer or reader is no longer led to consider the conditions or events on their own terms, but to consider them only as a function of the role they play in the relationships under discussion. The relationships themselves take on a reality of their own, a law-like quality, which derives from the fact that they are understood, not merely as descriptions of observable or imaginable real-world phenomena, but as examples of a different domain of discourse altogether, as theoretical explanatory frameworks designed to provide a clarifying perspective on the world of actual conditions and events and their interrelationships, while at the same time maintaining a certain cognitive distance from the speaker's or hearer's baseline model of that world.

In English the constructions 'The fact that . . .' and simply 'That . . .' as in '(The fact) that foreign troops line its borders leads that nation to behave conservatively' act in similar manner to signal to the listener or reader that the information being conveyed in the subordinate clause is not to be coded on its own terms, but rather in terms of its contribution to an explanatory model being projected. And just as Chinese traditionally has had no structures equivalent to the English processes of entification of conditions and events, neither has it had structures equivalent to 'The fact that . . .' or 'That . . . .' So a typical Chinese formulation of the above sentence would take the general form, 'Foreign troops line its borders, makes that nation behave conservatively' in which the focus of attention falls on the description of two discrete facts as well as on their inter-relationship rather than on the fact that one fact is being used to explain the other in a projected theoretical model of explanation.

By embedding entified conditions and events within one another, moreover, English speakers can expand their theoretical, explanatory structures into entities of considerable complexity. Whole series of events or conditions can be woven into single theoretical structures with consequent shifts of focus from the component conditions or events to the roles they play in those projected explanatory frameworks. The sequencing of events in the theoretical structures becomes a function of the perspectives the structures are designed to emphasize, rather than of the logical, causal or temporal order in which the component conditions or events have or would have actually occurred. And this further break with actuality serves to further reinforce the psychological impact of the movement away from the world of actual happenings carried by the underlying processes of entification themselves. An English speaker can, for example, take a series of events like:

1. European imperialism in Asia began to wane.
2. At the same time, American presence in Asia began to grow.
3. The two met in conflict.
4. As the conflict accelerated, Japanese leaders became increasingly concerned over protecting sources of raw materials.
5. This increasing concern contributed significantly to their decision to attack Pearl Harbor.

Then, by entifying these events and embedding the entified units into a theoretical, explanatory structure, the speaker can weave them into whatever sequence best befits the needs of his argument. He can state that:

The uncertainties arising from the accelerating conflict between European imperialism and the growth of American presence in Asia, in increasing concern among Japanese leaders over protecting sources of raw materials, contributed significantly to their decision to attack Pearl Harbor;

or, alternatively, that:

Increasing concern among Japanese leaders for protecting sources of raw materials, brought on by the uncertainties arising from the accelerating conflict between the waning of European imperialism and the growth of American presence in Asia, contributed significantly to their decision to attack Pearl Harbor;

or, alternatively, that:

The decision by Japanese leaders to attack Pearl Harbor was significantly influenced by their increasing concern for protecting sources of raw materials brought about in turn by the uncertainties arising from the accelerating conflict between waning European imperialism and the growth of American presence in Asia.

Chinese speakers often characterize such Western recountings of events as insufferably abstract and as 'proceeding in circles,' for in Chinese, where each event is expressed individually in subject/predicate form, even in complex recountings of interevent relationships, the individual component events seem to retain their individual identities and as such to force the author to remain more closely tied to the logical, temporal, or causal sequence in which they actually fall. A typical Chinese equivalent of all three of the above highly entified examples of English explanatory, theoretical talk might, for example, take the following much more accessible and straightforward form:

While European imperialism began to wane in Asia, American presence began to grow; these two phenomena met in conflict; as the conflict accelerated, Japanese leaders became increasingly concerned how to protect sources of raw materials; strongly influenced them to decide to attack Pearl Harbor.

Furthermore, from a cognitive point of view, we might imagine that repeated exposure of talk of entified conditions and events and to theoretical accountings constructed out of them would over time tend to lead English speakers to develop cognitive schemas that would enable and in fact predispose them not only to move freely in speech from talking about conditions and events as actual or potential occurrences to talking about them as if they were conceptual units of abstracted, theoretical structures, but to move freely in thought as well, from operating with conditions and events and their interrelationships *qua* actual or potential occurrences to operating with them as a function of the roles they play or might be made to play in abstracted, theoretical structures.

Consider the following paragraph and the questions based upon it:

A recent report on pollution stated: Living in a polluted environment can cause lung disease; but living in a polluted, comparatively high altitude location increases the danger and, conversely, living in a polluted, low altitude location decreases it. Oddly enough, however, living in a polluted high altitude location and eating a lot of fatty foods turns out to be just like living in a polluted, low altitude location.

According to the above report, which of the circumstances below would be likely to be the most harmful to your health?

A.	A polluted,	low altitude location	and eating a lot of fatty foods.
B.	A polluted,	relatively high altitude location	and eating a lot of fatty foods.
C.	A polluted,	relatively high altitude location	and eating very little fatty foods
D.	Crazy question		

A subject might attempt to solve this task by one of two principal strategies. The subject might proceed by focusing systematically on particular conditions, considering in turn people in polluted environments at varying altitudes who do and do not eat lots of fatty foods, and then inferring from the data presented how great a risk of lung disease each group is likely to incur. People who live in polluted, high altitude environments have a greater risk of getting lung disease, while people who live in polluted, low altitude environments have a lesser risk of getting such a disease. But those living in high altitude environments who, in addition, eat lots of fatty foods incur a risk similar to those living in low altitude environments, i.e., a lesser risk. So living in a high polluted environment and eating little fatty food (i.e., alternative C) is the condition most harmful to health.

Or the subject might approach the task in a very different manner. Rather than proceed to imagine in turn a set of potential real world conditions, he/she might attempt to build, on the basis of the data presented, a theoretical model of the relationships involved. The subject might begin, for example, by interpreting 'living in a polluted environment' and 'getting lung disease' as two entified notions; fit them as such into the abstracted relationship — the relationship between living in a polluted environment and getting lung disease —; endow that relationship with a reality of its own, so that it, rather than its component conditions, can serve as a basis for the next operation; then proceed to interpret 'high altitude' as a factor that strengthens the extracted relationship, 'low altitude' as a factor that weakens it, and the entified condition, 'the eating of lots of fatty foods' as a factor that acts within the model of theoretical relationships being constructed to negate the effects of 'high altitude.' The effect of 'high altitude,' in the absence of the negating factor 'the eating of lots of fatty foods,' is then the most damaging to health.

Now consider this second version of the above task:

> A recent report on pollution stated: There exists a relationship between living in a polluted environment and getting lung disease; at comparatively high altitudes the relationship is stronger and at comparatively low altitudes it is weaker. Oddly enough, moreover, at comparatively high altitudes, eating more fatty foods renders the relationship between living in a polluted environment and getting lung disease equivalent to that existing in low altitude locations.

According to the above report, which of the circumstances below would be likely to be the most harmful to your health?

A.	A polluted,	low altitude location	and eating a lot of fatty foods.
B.	A polluted,	relatively high altitude location	and eating a lot of fatty foods.
C.	A polluted,	relatively high altitude location	and eating very little fatty foods.
D.	Crazy question		

This second version is identical in content to the one above and is followed by the same response alternatives; but it is written expressly in terms of relationships rather than conditions, so as to be readily interpretable by the subject who approaches the task by attempting to formulate a theoretical model of the relationships involved and yet to be more difficult to interpret for the subject who approaches the task by attempting to enumerate systematically the conditions involved. If, then, Chinese-speaking subjects are unlikely, as a result of their linguistic enviroment, to have developed schemas specifically suited to transforming conditions and events into the entified component elements of theoretical frameworks and to operating with them as a function of the roles they play in such frameworks, then they should find the second version of the task appreciably more difficult than the first. And if, by contrast, English-speaking subjects are, as a result of their own particular linguistic environment, likely to have developed schemas specifically suited to transforming conditions and events into the entified component elements of theoretical frameworks and to operating with them as a function of the roles they play in such frameworks, then they (1) should not find the second version of the task appreciably more difficult than the first; (2) should do about as well on the first version of the task as Chinese-speaking subjects of equivalent experience, education and intelligence; but (3) should outperform their Chinese-speaking counterparts on the second version of the task.

Direct groups of 59 students from Taiwan National University and Hong Kong University (the finest universities in Taiwan and Hong Kong respectively) and 48 students from Swarthmore College responded in their native language to each version of the task — a comparative sample that should offer roughly equivalent levels of experience, education, and intelligence. As summarized in Table 1, the results strongly confirm each of the above expectations:

Table 1

	Correct Reponses	
	Chinese Speakers	*English Speakers*
Version 1	46/59 or 79%	38/48 or 81%
Version 2	31/59 or 59%	38/48 or 79%

Chinese responses to the first version of the task are significantly more accurate than responses to the second version ($X^2_{df = 1} = 8.41$, $p<.01$); while English responses remain essentially unaffected by movement from Version One to Version Two. The level of accuracy for Chinese and English speakers is roughly equivalent on Version One; yet on Version Two, English speakers significantly outperform their Chinese counterparts ($X^2_{df = 1} = 8.19$, $p<.01$).

The English text of a third, considerably more complex version of the task follows — see appendix for the Chinese text:

John Donahue has the following peculiar characteristics: When the humidity in the atmosphere is relatively low, the hotter the temperature and the less fish he eats, the more comfortable he feels. However, when the humidity is very high, these relationships reverse.

According to the paragraph above, which two of the following conditions make John Donahue least comfortable:

1. high temperature doesn't eat much fish   relatively low humidity
2. high temperature doesn't eat much fish   very high humidity
3. high temperature eats a lot of fish   relatively low humidity
4. high temperature eats a lot of fish   very high humidity
5. low temperature eats a lot of fish   relatively low humidity

This version differs from the first two in several respects: (1) The correct solution requires the choice of two rather than a single alternative; (2) the paragraph centers on two simultaneous relationships (temperature to comfort; and eating fish to comfort), which are affected by one additional variable (humidity) rather than on one relationship (living in a polluted environment to lung disease), which is affected by two additional variables (altitude and eating fatty foods); and (3) and most significantly, because of the way the paragraph is expressed, there is no way to arrive at an accurate solution to this version of the task unless one attempts to deal with it by constructing a theoretical model of the data presented. The final line of the paragraph instructs the subject to reverse a set of relationships that are not labeled as relationships in the preceding text. If then the subject does not spontaneously project a theoretical model that casts the data as a set of relationships, affected by the additional variable 'humidity,' he/she has no way to figure out what relationships are to be reversed and hence cannot arrive at an accurate solution. If however, in reaction to the sentence 'The hotter the temperature and the less fish he eats, the more comfortable he feels,' the subject turns away from the attempt to imagine John Donahue in a set of distinct situations and projects instead a model of the data in which, under low humidity, hotter temperatures and less fish are each linked in a theoretical relationship to more comfort, then it is easy for the subject to understand that a reversal of these relationships for high humidity would imply that there, low temperature and more fish entail greater comfort — making John most uncomfortable, under low humidity, when the temperature is low and he eats a lot of fish and, under high humidity, when the temperature is high and he eats less fish (i.e., choices #2 and #5.)

Only eight out of 109 or 3 per cent of the Chinese university subjects who responded to this question constructed the theoretical model necessary to arrive at both correct alternatives, as compared to 33 out of 94 or 35 per cent English-speaking Swarthmore College subjects ($X^2_{df=1} = 24.11, p<.0001$). In later interviewing, Chinese subjects consistently reacted that the question was overly complex, overly abstract and blatantly 'unChinese.' When I attempted to explain what was required, they responded in effect that they are used to talking and thinking about relationships between people, situations or occurrences, but not about relationships between such things as 'eating more fish' and 'feeling more comfortable;' in other words, that they are used to talking and thinking about relationships between things that exist or take place within their baseline models of reality but not about relationships between entified things, between reified theoretical entities that have been extracted from those baseline models. English-speaking subjects also found the question very complex and often ambiguous, but they did not perceive it as foreign to their way of speaking and thinking about the world.

When one considers then the English process of entification — of properties, actions, conditions, and events — and the theoretical accountings to which these processes lead, alongside the generic use of 'the' and the English signals of entry into the counterfactual realm, one begins to get a clearer picture of the range of incentives the English language offers for developing cognitive schemas that enable and incline its speakers to shift not only in speech but also in thought from involvement with the world of actual or imagined things, actions, properties, events, or conditions, to the assumption of a detached theoretical perspective on that world — incentives that at least until recent date, have had few if any analogues in Chinese.

Even the English lexical term 'theoretical' leads the thoughts of English speakers in directions quite distinct from those to which its Chinese counterpart (lilunshang) points. The Chinese term literally means within or from the perspective of a theory or theory in general. It is currently used in Taiwan to talk about the contents of a specific theory, to contrast what a given theory says with what is actually the case and, by extension, to characterize any argument that smacks of a theory in being abstract, difficult to conceive, complex. 'Theoretically speaking' means speaking from the perspective of a given theory or the world of theory. A 'theoretical example' is an example of fact taken from the actual world to prove a theory; and the notion 'theoretical possibility,' to my informants, made no sense at all. But when English speakers say that they are speaking 'theoretically,' they do not necessarily mean that they are speaking in terms of any given theory or theories, nor that they are necessarily speaking complexly, but rather that they are shifting from description of actual events or even from a description of a given explanation of events incorporated in a given theory to speak as if such were the case, to speak of a consciously hypothesized possible world. For English speakers 'a theoretical example' is not a fact taken from the actual world that demonstrates a theory, but a hypothesized example that fits the constraints of a theoretical world being projected. 'A theoretical possibility' is one that could occur within the constraints of that projected world. What differentiates the Chinese term for 'theoretical' from its English counterpart, then, is that the meaning of the Chinese term derives principally from its link to the noun 'theory'; while the English term, although related to the noun 'theory' derives its meaning principally from its link to a separate schema that places emphasis, not on the existing set of abstract explanations of phenomena or extensions of that set, but rather on the deliberate severing of truth commitments to the actual world the formulation and projection of theories presuppose. For the Chinese speaker, 'speaking and thinking "theoretically" ' remain pretty much confined to the domain of the scientist but, for the English speaker, since they are not equivalent to theory-building, they can become a part of the speaker's everyday linguistic and cognitive activity.

One hundred and fifty-nine Taiwanese subjects, 68 Hong Kong subjects and 112 American subjects of varied backgrounds, age and occupation responded to the following question in their native language:

> Everyone has his or her own method for teaching children to respect morality. Some people punish the child for immoral behavior, thereby leading him to fear the consequences of such behavior. Others reward the child for moral behavior, thereby leading him to want to behave morally. Even though both of these methods lead the child to respect morality, the first method can lead to some negative psychological consequences — it may lower the child's self-esteem.

According to the above paragraph, what do the two methods have in common? Please select only one answer.

A.   Both methods are useless.
B.   They have nothing in common, because the first leads to negative psychological consequences.
C.   Both can reach the goal of leading the child to respect morality.
D.   It is better to use the second.
E.   None of the above answers makes sense. (If you choose this answer, please explain.)

109 or 97 per cent of the American subjects chose alternative C, for that is in fact exactly what the paragraph says, but only 88 or 55 per cent of the Taiwanese subjects and only 44 or 65 per cent of the Hong Kong subjects made that choice. (The Chinese-English differences are significant at $p<.001$ ($\chi^2{}_{df=1} = 58.32$) and $p<.0001$ ($\chi^2{}_{df=1} = 35.30$) respectively.) Most of the remaining Chinese-speaking subjects chose D or E and then went on to explain, based on their own experience and often at great length and evidently after much reflection, why, for instance, the second method might be better, or why neither method works, or why both methods have to be used in conjunction with each other, or, perhaps, why some other specified means is preferable. For the majority of these subjects, as was evident from later interviewing, it was not that they did not see the paragraph as stating that both methods lead the child to respect morality, but they felt that choosing that alternative and leaving it at that would be misleading since in their experience that response was untrue. As they saw it, what was expected, desired, must be at a minimum an answer reflecting their personal considered opinion, if not, a more elaborated explanation of their own experiences relevant to the matter at hand. Why else would anyone ask the question? American subjects, by contrast, readily accepted the question as a purely 'theoretical' exercise to be responded to according to the assumptions of the world it creates rather than in terms of their own experiences with the actual world. Not a single American subject made reference to his or her own experience. The few American subjects who were unsure about alternative C were concerned with such logical issues as whether 'both methods lead . . .' as stated, entails 'that each method leads

individually . . .' But no American subject appeared to have any difficulty, either of a cognitive or ethical nature, in leaving the actual world aside to work within the constraints of the theoretical world provided, no matter how simplistic or even inaccurate they might hold the content of that world to be.[9]

The contrasting cognitive proclivities of English and Chinese speakers reflected in these data are, moreover, certainly not limited in their influence to the domain of cognitive tasks. The scientific and more broadly philosophical thought of any culture derives ultimately from the cognitive activities of its individual participants and must, therefore, reflect proclivities inherent in that activity. And the present case is certainly no exception. Needham (1956) in his major work on the history of science in China, presents an impressive array of evidence in support of the claim that traditional China developed both a very rich tradition of empirical observation and an active skeptical orientation, but did not develop a scientific tradition as we know it, for it lacked the third necessary ingredient to such a tradition — namely a theoretical orientation, an inclination to leave the world of practical application behind in an effort to construct and test purely theoretical explanatory frameworks. A disinclination towards the theoretical in this context should not be understood as implying a disinclination towards framing explanations of reality in terms of highly abstract notions, such as 'yin,' 'yang,' 'li,' and 'chi'i,' but rather as involving a disinclination towards entertaining such abstract notions as truth commitment-free hypotheses that retain purely theoretical status until confirmed by empirical evidence. According to Needham, the one area of mathematics that was least developed in China before the arrival of Western influence was geometry — the area Needham views as most particularly dependent on theoretical rather than practical thoughts. Upon hearing about the research reported in this chapter, a professor of Physics at Swarthmore wondered 'whether Chinese mathematics ever developed imaginary numbers, for imaginary numbers much more than negative numbers or even variables, would seem to reflect counterfactual/theoretical thoughts?' Needham (1959) observes that, despite the fact that Chinese mathematics had developed both negative numbers and variables at a very early date, imaginary numbers did not enter Chinese mathematical thought until their introduction from the West; and he then sums up the state of mathematics in traditional

China with the following comment: 'In the flight from practice into the realm of the pure intellect, Chinese mathematics did not participate' (p. 15).

Joseph Levenson, in *Confucian China and its Modern Fate* (1965), argues that the orientation of even the most empirical branch of Ch'ing Confucianism should be compared to the pre-scientific nominalism of Abelard rather than the inductive science of Bacon. According to Levenson, Bacon and the scientific orientation he spawned, unlike Abelard or the empiricists of the Ch'ing:

> . . . went beyond simply ascribing ultimate reality to the world of phenomena instead of to a hypothetical realm of pure Being. He meant not merely to define the real world but to encroach upon it. It was not enough for him to banish abstractions, which can only be contemplated, in favor of tangibles, which can be observed, for observation was not enough. One had to observe with a method and purpose. Bacon's method was induction from experimentally verified 'irreducible and stubborn facts,' his purpose the eliciting of general laws for the organization of facts into science . . . [Although according to Levenson the Ch'ing empiricists] . . . might pride themselves . . . on looking around them and 'testing books with facts,' they rarely asked questions systematically which might make them see the essential relevance of some orders of facts to others, they never aspired, as Bacon did, 'to establish forever a true and legitimate union between the experimental and rational faculty.' Though he might go as far as the Renaissance scientist in deprecating search for the universal, eternal form of particular things, the empirically-minded Ch'ing Confucianist had a temper predominantly nominalist, unembarrassing to scientific spirit, but by no means its equivalent nor its guaranteed precursor. (Part I, pp. 8-9)

Neither formal logic, nor religious philosophy, nor moral philosophy, nor political philosophy, nor economics, nor sociology, nor psychology, as theoretical systems independent of each other, bearing their own internal systemic constraints and entailments, divorced from the factual content they seek to explain, emerged in China other than as a consequence of importation from the West.[10] The theoretical component of

Buddhism tended to be discarded as that religion was assimilated by the Chinese. Confucianism and Taoism both reject the theoretical system-building characteristics of Western religions; the former, in favor of providing precepts for ethical and social conduct, the latter in favor of providing a path by which the individual might bring himself into harmony with the rhythm of nature, rather than distance himself intellectually from it. Maoism, in response to Marx, stresses the integration of theory with practice.

Needham (1956) likewise suggests, however, that Western proclivity for theoretical modeling, while prerequisite to certain stages of scientific advance, was inhibitive to others. Such modeling, he argues, involves the extraction of single patterns of causal explanation from factual data that are in reality characterized by a multiplicity of internal interassociations and interrelationships and hence necessarily gives rise to overly simplistic and constrictive assumptions about the nature of the phenomena it seeks to describe. As Needham sees it, for Western science to have moved beyond classical mechanics to the notion of relativity, it had, in fact, to overcome the narrowing influence of its own purely theoretical perspective; and that was possible only as a result of its confrontation with Chinese philosophical awareness of the infinite interdependence and interrelatedness of natural phenomena, first transmitted to the West, according to Needham, in the work of Liebnitz.

And as the Chinese are quick to observe, it is not only in the realm of science that theoretical thoughts have their inherent shortcomings. In choosing to view the world through one theoretical perspective rather than another, to adopt an exclusively political, social, psychological, behavioral, or cognitive view, one easily forgets that one has adopted that perspective for the sake of analysis only and begins to perceive the world and our knowledge of it as inherently compartmentalized in those ways. When analyzing theoretically, moreover, as the Chinese see it, it is particularly easy to separate what is seen as morally right from what is seen as economically, politically, or socially effective; particularly easy to allow a set of abstract justifications and considerations to obscure the concrete effects that a decision or policy may have on individual human beings; and particularly easy to rearrange (i.e., rationalize) one's interpretation of those effects, just as one rearranges events or conditions once entified to fit the needs of a theoretical structure being created. When one projects an abstract, theoretical structure as the explanatory and justifying framework for social or political action — e.g., 'saving the world for democracy' or upholding the right of diplomatic immunity — it is particularly easy to allow that structure to take on a moral imperative quality of its own, making it much more difficult to remain flexible to the need for a continuing reexamination of its appropriateness to the changing situation at hand and a continuing reassessment of the moral weight it should carry amongst the conflicting claims involved.[11] And more generally, in moving away from involvement with the real world to the assumption of a theoretical perspective on it, it is particularly easy to delegitimate the dictates of one's own emotional and intuitive life and thereby to undercut the source of one's own sense of personal confidence and autonomy and restrict unnaturally the potential dimensions of one's own experience. From the Chinese point of view, then, the kind of thinking that leads one to accept, if only for the sake of argument, that a triangle is a circle, or that two given methods of moral training are effective even when you know they are not, is a kind of thinking that can often lead not only to an overly simplistic, but also to an alienating, a personally debilitating, and, in fact, an amoral perspective on the world.[12]

F. S. C. Northrop (1946) in *Meeting of East and West* contrasts the Orient's propensity for analyzing things with respect to their perceptual, aesthetic component with the Occident's propensity for analyzing things with respect to their theoretic component. André Malraux (1961) in *Temptation of the West*, writes from the perspective of a young Chinese who is reacting to the impact of Western thought on his society:

But we *experience* this existence: it dominates and shapes us without our being able to grasp it. We are filled with it, since we are men, while you are geometers, even of divinity . . . [p. 22] . . . Confronted with a chaotic universe, what is the first requirement of the mind? To comprehend the universe. But we are unable to do this with the images it offers us, since we immediately realize how transitory they are; thus we try to assimilate its rhythm. Experiencing the universe is not the same as systematizing it, no more than experiencing love is the same as analyzing it. Only an intense awareness achieves understanding. Our thinking . . . is not as is yours, the result of a body of knowledge, but it is the equipment, the preparation for knowledge. You analyze what you have already felt; we think in order to feel. [p. 87]

Marcel Granet (1934) observes in *La pensée chinoise*:

> Themes evocative of free meditation, that is, what the Chinese demand of their Sages, and not ideas — no less dogmas . . . The Chinese have no taste for abstract symbols. They see within Time and Space only a collection of occasions and locations. It is the interdependencies, the solidarities which constitute the order of the Universe. The Chinese doesn't believe that man can form a reign in nature or that the mind can disengage itself from the material . . . Law, the abstract, and the unconditional are excluded — the Universe is one — as much with respect to its societal as with respect to its natural aspect . . . Hence the despise of all that involves uniformity, of all that would permit induction, deduction or any form of constraining reasoning or calculation . . . (pp. 473-9, translation mine)

And the Third Century BC Confucian philosopher, Hsun-tzu, in reacting to the work of the Kung-sun Lung-tzu, makes the following comment (Needham, 1956):

> There is no reason why problems of 'hardness and whiteness,' 'likeness and unlikeness,' 'thickness or no thickness' should not be investigated, but the superior man does not discuss them; he stops at the limit of profitable discourse (p. 202). (The use of '-ness' is a function of translation)

Historically-speaking, it is certainly not the case that structural differences between Chinese and English bear primary responsibility for creating the culturally-specific modes of thinking reflected in the above quotations and in the findings of this chapter as a whole. From a historical point of view, languages are much more the products of their cultures than determiners of them. What one can and cannot express distinctly in any particular language at any particular point in its development is the aggregate result of the totality of social, political, environmental, and intellectual influences that have, from generation to generation, affected its speakers' lives. A new insight, a new experience, a new discovery, a new invention, a new institution, or new contacts with another language-world lead to the development of new linguistic forms. The disappearance of old ways of thinking, of out-worn conventions, and of objects, which have no use in the present scene, lead to the disappearance of the linguistic forms that had been used to speak about them. Historically-speaking, the fact that Chinese has not offered its speakers incentives for thinking about the world in counterfactual and entificational ways is likely to have contributed substantially to sustaining an intellectual climate in which these modes of thinking were less likely to arise;[13] but if Chinese speakers at some point in the past had felt a sufficient need to venture into the realm of the counterfactual or the theoretical, the Chinse language would have evolved to accommodate that need, as it is doing today. And so, to explain historically why counterfactual and entificational thinking did not develop on a general scale, one would have to look not only to the characteristics of the language but to the social and intellectual determinants of why a perceived need for such thinking did not arise. Similarly, the proliferation of new Western modes of speech in present-day Hong Kong and Taiwan society is certainly contributing significantly to the proliferation in turn of Westernized modes of thought, but to understand why more recently Chinese speakers have begun to construct forms to match those of Western language, and to explain why, once these forms emerge, they are assimilated rather than rejected, as they may very well have been in the past — on the grounds that they lead speakers 'beyond the limit of profitable discourse' — one has to look beyond the characteristics of the language to the social, political, and intellectual pressures that have in effect guided the language's development during the past fifty years.

But the argument of this book is not about the role languages play in shaping their own historical development — in contributing to the creation or maintenance of intellectual climates in which specific linguistic forms are more or less likely to emerge. Nor is it about, in more general terms, how languages come to have the specific forms that they have; but it is rather about how languages, through the forms they do and do not have, lead their speakers within each generation to come to be participants in and bearers of distinctive cognitive worlds. It is not about why the Chinese language did not traditionally develop forms for counterfactual and entificational ways of speech or why Western languages did, but rather about the effects such linguistic facts have within each generation on their speakers' cognitive lives.

Notes

1. See Maratsos, 1976.
2. See Plotkin, 1977.
3. Extracting theoretical entities from one's baseline model is quite different from creating an imaginary entity such as a spirit, a ghost or a dragon and placing it within one's baseline model.
4. It seems reasonable to support that entified forms are created by the speaker as he needs them from their underlying adjectival or verbal forms, while nominalized forms that have come to represent things on their own are coded separately from any corresponding adjectival or verbal forms. In other words, to make use of the concept 'furtherance,' the speaker may call upon the schema for 'to further' as well as the schema for 'entification' and to make use of the concept 'opacity,' call upon the schema 'opaque' plus the schema for 'entification'; while, by contrast, to utilize the concept 'transportation' or 'discovery' in the ordinary nominal sense, the speaker may make use of individual nominal schemas specifically designed to those concepts, which may or may not have corresponding verbal counterparts (cf. Chomsky, 1972; Fromkin, 1973).
5. For further discussion, see Chao, 1968, pp. 225-8.
6. See Weinreich, 1968.
7. For further discussion of this point, see Fung (1952), Needham (1956), pp. 201-2, Hu Shih (1963).
8. In fact, the independent ontological status of entifications of events is so complete in English that they can be quantified just as any ordinary object — one naturally speaks of 'rises of interest rates,' 'declines in SAT scores,' or 'frequent discoveries of new bacteria . . .' etc. (I am indebted for this observation to Hugh Lacey.)
9. For parallel results among different populations, see Luria, 1976, and Scribner, 1977.
10. For discussion of a typical early Chinese intellectual response to imported Western scientific ideas, see Sivin, 1970.
11. See Kelman, 1973 and Sanford and Comstock, 1971.
12. Within Kohlberg's theory of moral development (see Kohlberg 1969, 1971; Lickona, 1976) a theoretical approach to morality, or more specifically the construction of a personal, theoretical moral framework based on consciously derived and deliberately formalized universal principles, is seen as prerequisite to the attainment of the highest stage of moral thought. Hence it is not surprising that Kohlberg found so few subjects in his Chinese sample who he interprets as having reached that stage. One can, however, ask whether the core of that stage should be considered the construction of such a formalized theoretical value framework, or whether it should be seen rather as the development of an autonomous moral orientation that may or may not take such a formalized form. Under this latter assumption, movement from a feeling of responsibility to accept unanalytically the demands of the state and/or society to a feeling of responsibility to become one's own moral arbiter, to weigh and resolve personally the moral claims present in any given conflict situation, would become the mark of post-conventional reasoning, and the resolution of such claims based on considered intuition would count as

highly as an approach based on logical deduction from a formalized theory of right and wrong, as long as in each case the resolution is autonomously performed. Confucius, Mencius, and Lao-tzu as well as Aristotle, Montaigne, and Camus would then be admitted along with Plato and Rawls into the pantheon of higher stage post-conventional thinkers, and the post-conventional thinkers in Chinese samples would emerge classified as such, as they did in a questionnaire survey relating to this point conducted in Hong Kong in 1973 (see Bloom, 1977a, 1977b).
13. See Hu Shih, 1963.

References

Bloom, A. H. (1977a) 'Two Dimensions of Moral Reasoning: Social Principledness and Social Humanism in Cross-cultural Perspective', *Journal of Social Psychology*, *101*, 29-44(a)

Bloom, A. H. (1977b) A cognitive dimension of social control: The Hong Kong Chinese in cross-cultural perspective. In A. A. Wilson, S. L. Greenblatt, & R. W. Wilson (eds.), *Deviance and social control in Chinese society*. New York: Praeger Publishers

Chan, W. T. (1963) *A Source Book in Chinese Philosophy*, Princeton University Press, Princeton, NJ

Chao, Y. R. (1968) *A Grammar of Spoken Chinese*, University of California Press, Berkeley

Chomsky, N. (1972) 'Remarks on Nominalization' in N. Chomsky, *Studies on Semantics in Generative Grammar*, Mouton, The Hague

Fromkin, V. A. (1973) 'Slips of the Tongue', *Scientific American*, *229*, 110-16

Fung, Y. L. (1952) *A History of Chinese Philosophy*, Princeton University Press, Princeton, NJ

Granet, M. (1934) *La pensée chinoise*, Renaissance du Livre, Paris

Hu Shih (1963) *Development of the Logical Method in Ancient China*, Paragon Books, New York

Kelman, H. C. (1973) 'Violence Without Moral Restraint: Reflections on the Dehumanization of Victims and Victimizers', *Journal of Social Issues*, *29(4)*, 25-61

Kohlberg, L. (1969) 'Stage and Sequence: The Cognitive Developmental Approach to Socialization' in D. A. Goslin (ed.), *Handbook of Socialization Theory and Research*, Rand McNally, Chicago

Kohlberg, L. (1971) 'From is to Ought: How to Commit the Naturalistic Fallacy and Get Away With it in the Study of Moral Development' in T. Mischel (ed.), *Cognitive Development and Epistemology*, Academic Press, New York

Levenson, J. R. (1965) *Confucian China and its Modern Fate*, University of California Press, Berkeley

Lickona. T. (ed.) (1976) *Moral Development and Behavior: Theory, Research and Social Issues*, Holt, Rinehart & Winston, New York

Luria, A. R. (1976) *Cognitive Development: Its Cultural and Social Foundations*, Harvard University Press, Cambridge, Mass.

Malraux, A. (1926) *The Temptation of the West*, Random House, New York (Original French edition, 1926)

Maratsos, M. P. (1976) *The Use of Definite and Indefinite Reference in Young Children: An Experimental Study in Semantic Acquisition*, Cambridge University Press, Cambridge

Needham, J. (1956) *Science and Civilization in China, Vol. 2: History of Scientific Thought*, Cambridge University Press, Cambridge

Needham, J. (1959) *Science and Civilization in China, Vol. 3: Mathematics and the Sciences of the Heavens and the Earth*, Cambridge University Press, Cambridge

Northrop, F. S. C. (1946) *East Meets West*, Macmillan, New York

Plotkin, H. (1977) *Noun Usage in Chinese and English: A Comparative Study in Language and Thought*, unpublished senior paper, Swarthmore College

Sanford, N., Comstock, C., *et al.* (1971) *Sanctions for Evil*, Jossey-Bass, San Francisco

Scribner, S. (1977) 'Modes of Thinking and Ways of Speaking: Culture and Logic Reconsidered' in P. N. Johnson-Laird and P. C. Wason (eds.), *Thinking: Readings in Cognitive Science*, Cambridge University Press, Cambridge

Sivin, N. Wang Hsi-shan (1970) in *Dictionary of Scientific Biography*, Scribner, New York, *14*, 159-68

Weinreich, U. (1968) *Languages in Contact*, Mouton, Paris

GLOSSARY

Act/action. In *case grammar*, that part of a sentence traditioally identified as the verb phrase, which involves a change of state, e.g. 'John *kicked* the ball'; 'His hands *got* dirty'. (See *Agent*, *case-grammar*, *instrument*, *patient*.)

Agent. The animate perceived instigator of the action identified by the verb. (See *action*, *case grammar*, *instrument*.)

Allophone. Variant forms of the same phonological unit or phoneme, e.g. the way 'p' is sounded in 'pan' differs from the way it is sounded in 'span'. Both are allophones of the phoneme.

Aspirate. Pronounce by audible breathing, i.e. with the sound of *h* (as in *hat*, *hot*, *hammer*).

Association. A connection between two or more stimuli, e.g. a particular sound with a particular object, that is held by some psychologists to be the basis of all learning, including the learning of language.

Anthropoid. Family of anatomically 'human-like' apes: the gorilla, orang-utan and chimpanzee.

Australopithecine. Putative ancestor of modern humans living 1.5-4 million years ago and known by abundant fossil remains.

Avoidance learning. A term used in behaviourist psychology to denote a conditioned response to avoid an unpleasant (often painful) stimulus.

Canonical form. The fundamental or standard version.

Case. A term originating from the Greeks which serves to distinguish between the true form of the noun (now known as the *nominative case*) and the deviations from the true form (such as the *accusative* or *genitive cases*).

Case-grammar. A grammatical theory which represents sentences as a verb and one or more noun-phrases, each noun-phrase being associated with the verb in a particular case-relationship, such as subjective, objective, agentive, instrumental, locative.

Communicative intent. The deliberate use of communication to have a specific effect on another person and through that person to bring about a specific consequence.

Conation. Striving; used either as a general term inclusive of all experienced mental activity or as itself the experience of activity as an ultimate type of experience.

Conditioning. The process by which an association is formed through a sequence of experience. (See also *association*).

Conjoin. To combine. In linguistics the term refers to the combination of two clauses or sentences so that *both* retain their sentential status. The simplest form is the linking of two co-ordinate clauses by a conjunction, e.g. 'The boy rang the bell *and* the dog barked'. (See also *Embedding*.)

Copula. A grammatical term referring to a linking verb such as 'to be', e.g. 'John *is* naughty'; 'John *is* a boy'.

Correlation. A statistical relationship between two variables. If it is found that as one variable changes the other also changes in a related way, the two variables are said to be correlated. The standard measure of correlation, r, indicates the strength of the relationship, and takes a value between 1 and -1. A value of 1 for r shows a *perfect positive correlation* where variations in one variable are associated with exactly parallel variations in the other. A value of 0 indicates no correlation, i.e. the variables change quite independently. A value of -1 indicates a *perfect negative correlation*: i.e., as one variable increases in value so the other decreases in an exactly parallel manner.

Covariance analysis. A statistical technique used to assess the simultaneous effects of more than one factor or covariate, and where the variables are of both metric and non-metric types.

Cranial. Pertaining to the cranium or roof of the skull.

Deixis. The use of spatial, temporal and interpersonal features of linguistic and non-linguistic context to provide joint reference, e.g. pointing to an object.

Dialogue. Communication involving exchange between two or more persons (not limited to *oral* communication).

Dyad. Involving two persons, e.g. parent and infant.

Embedding. A term used in phrase-structure grammars (such as that of Chomsky) to denote the inclusion of a sentence or clause *within* another sentence, e.g. 'The boy *who lost his kite* has gone home'. (See also *Conjoin.*)

Epistemic. Relating to knowledge; epistemology being the study of knowledge, its structure, logic, etc.

Hominids. Family (*Hominidae*) of species which includes only modern humans and ancestors.

Instrument(al). A grammatical function from *case*-grammar, thus in the sentence *John hit Mary with a stick*, 'a stick' has the instrumental function. (See also *act, agent, case grammar.*)

Intersubjective. Relating to understandings, knowledge, attention, etc., shared between individuals.

Lexicon. A store of words, e.g. in a specific language or in an individual's memory.

Mandibular. Pertaining to the lower jaw-bone.

Mastoid. Bony process directly behind the ear in humans.

Maxillary. Pertaining to the upper jaw-bone.

Metalinguistic/metalanguage. Metalanguage is a term derived from formal logic; the language used to speak about language or a formal system. Metalinguistic is used in psychology to refer to a degree of awareness of linguistic rules, or the ability to reflect on linguistic form and function.

Midline. Imaginary line drawn vertically down the centre of an individual's body.

Morphology. A branch of linguistics concerned with the form of words, including inflexions and historical change. Traditionally, morphology is the study of word structure and is distinguished from syntax, the study of word order.

Multiple correlation. A statistical technique for measuring the relationship between more than two variables, based on an extension of those techniques used to assess correlation between two variables. (See *Correlation*.)

Occipital. Pertaining to the occipitum or rounded projection at the back of the skull.

Ontogenesis. The evolution and development of the individual (as opposed to *phylogenesis*, the origin and development of the species).

Over-extension. A term applied to the child's wider range of meanings for a lexical item, e.g. *dog* for all four-legged animals.

p (e.g. p<0.05). Shorthand for *probability*: indicates the probability that the result obtained occurred by chance variations, as assessed by a statistical test applied to the data. In the example given, the probability of the result obtained having occurred by chance is less than (<) 5 in 100.

Paleolithic. Stone-age period from two million to about 12,000 years before present.

Patient. A term used in *grammar* to denote the entity affected by the action of the verb, e.g. 'She hit *the ball*'.

Phoneme. Generally regarded as the minimal significant unit of sound in a language. The phonemic distinctions in a language can be established by setting up series of words which are distinguished by one contrast, e.g. pin, bin, tin, din, gin, chin, kin, gin, thin, sin, shin, win. This process can be continued until all the significant distinctions made in the sound system of a language have been discovered (there are 44 in received pronunciation). A variety of different letters can be used to represent a single phoneme and a variety of phonemes can be represented by a single letter or combination of letters.

Phonemic symbols. Any set of symbols used to represent phonemes. By convention these are placed between oblique strokes, i.e. /d/.

Phonetics. The part of linguistics that deals with speech sounds. It is concerned with how these sounds are made in the human vocal tract and transmitted to the hearer.

Prelinguistic. Pertaining to the period of a child's life prior to the emergence of language ability (usually productive ability).

Pre-Neanderthal. A period before the emergence of the distinct group of hominids known as Neanderthals about 100,000 years ago.

Pre-speech. Sounds and movements of the mouth made by infants prior to the onset of true speech.

Proform. A grammatical term used to denote a substitute form (as, for example, a pronoun is a substitute for a noun).

Protocol. A transcribed record of a sample of speech.

Reference. The use of communication to identify a specific object or event.

Reify. To give materialistic status to an abstract concept.

Reinforcement. The facilitation of conditioning through the contiguous occurrence of some (usually satisfying) consequence.

Representation. The manner in which information is transformed, stored or displayed. In cognitive psychology, the term refers to the mode of storage in the brain (e.g. imagistic).

Semantic feature theories. Suggest that when a child first begins to use identifiable words, she does not know their full (adult) meaning, but relies on partial lexical entries based on salient features (which would also be present in the adult lexicon). Thus the child would begin by identifying the meaning of a word based on only a few of the combination of meaning components used criterially by an adult.

Semantics. The science of meaning; usually refers to the meaning of words.

Sign. Something which is intended to convey meaning, through a medium other than words.

Supraorbital. Above the orbits (sockets) of the eyes.

Syllabary (syllabic). List of characters representing whole syllables. Some languages are written in syllabic form (as opposed to our own system, which is alphabetic).

Tabula Rasa. Literally, blank slate. Used to convey the idea that a child is born with the complete absence of knowledge: all is learned.

Voiced. A sound produced with vibration of the vocal chords (rather than with breath alone). The presence or absence of voice is one of the distinctive features of speech sounds, e.g. between /d/ (voiced) and /t/ (unvoiced), /z/ (voiced) and /s/ (unvoiced).

INDEX

abstraction: Romanes and 26; writing and 223
accent 74
actions: and event, child's understanding 94; comparisons 98; event sequences 94; on objects 94
adjective: Chinese forms 248; in early syntax 154
alphabet 228
analysis-by-synthesis 62
anticipation 41
apes, language abilities 50
attenuation: biological cycle 13; names 62; withdrawal 13
auditory techniques 71
awareness: levels 178; linguistic 171

babbling 6
baby: development as a person 4
behaviorism: counter position 5; mechanisms 5
Bernstein: Bernstein 189; public and formal languages 189; theoretical framework and social class 192
bilingual entity-locative relations 162
brain: filing analogy 55; phonemes and filing 56; size and language capacity 50
Brown: the original word game 46

caregiver: child interaction 13-19; facilitating effects 14; research 113; turn taking 112
caretaker and deaf child 145
caretaker-child interaction: joint action and 14
cerebral hemispheres 52
child: actions 94; acuity 71; adult response to 11; alternate actions 97; cognitive structure 16; deafness 141; development periods 6-8; hearing 70; institutionalised 103; language experience 141; manipulation and 95; nominalisation 64; prepositions 89; pronunciation 78; self-consciousness 35; sound variation and 74
chimpanzee: gestural behaviour 51;

language discovery by 39-40; language learning by 39
China: Needham 267-9
Chinese: article use 244-5; cognition 266-77; comparative linguistics 245; 'de' construction 251; entification 247, 255, 259, 261; forms 247-8; grammar 248; possessive 205; reasoning 270-1; science 267; thinking 270; Western influence 247
Chomsky: abstract principles 5; children, language testing by 6; deep and surface structures 232; language reinvention 40; sensorimotor to linguistic transition 108; syntax 232; transformation rules 232
classical cognitive view of early language 100
cloze procedure 200
clustering of phonemes 80
cognition: alphabet 228; classical view 100; languages of experience 222
cognitive development: Chinese and English compared 267; common sense and science 226; early, in semantic development 161
cognitive processes: children's knowledge, and 222; literacy and 219
cognitive psychology: phonology and 70
colour 166
common sense and science 223-6
communication: between generations 18; deafness 141; framework 107; functions 2, 10, 11; gestures and deafness 142; infant initiation prerequisite 136; intention 110; mother and child 17; sensorimotor to linguistic 107; speech-act 167-9
comparisons: child by 98
complex constructions 7
comprehension 174
concepts 28
conceptual prerequisites 95
Confucianism 268
consciousness 27
consonants: child's first distinction 8;